MONEY AND CAPACITY GROWTH

Money
AND
Capacity
Growth

JEROME L. STEIN

Columbia University Press

New York and London

1971

Copyright © 1971 *Columbia University Press*
ISBN: 231–03372–9
Library of Congress Catalog Card Number: 73–160844
Printed in the United States of America

Jerome L. Stein
is Eastman Professor of Political Economy
at Brown Univeristy.

To Hadassah

PREFACE

RESEARCH leading to this book began in 1965 when I spent a year at the Hebrew University in Jerusalem, supported by a Social Science Research Council Faculty Research Grant. My aim was to develop a growth model which would be a generalization of post-Keynesian economics to a growing economy, where the input of capital is endogenously determined and growing over time. If the inputs of labor and capital were arbitrarily fixed, it would look like a dynamic version of Don Patinkin's short-run aggregative model. The result of that research, bearing the title of this book, appeared in 1966 in the *Journal of Political Economy*.

Rapid progress occurred in this field as a result of a conference on money and economic growth held at Brown University in June, 1968. Financial support was provided by the National Science Foundation, and organizational assistance was given by James Blackman, program director for economics. At this conference most of the researchers in the field of money and economic growth participated as authors or discussants. The concentrated critique of different points of view enabled the participants to understand the relative strengths and weaknesses of the various approaches. The rivalry of scholars increased wisdom, and the resulting papers appeared in a special issue of the *Journal of Money, Credit and Banking* in 1969.

After the conference I was anxious to write a book which would relate the topics of growth, stabilization policy, and optimality in the framework of a monetary economy. The success of this effort will be measured in terms of the research and criticism it stimulates. No sooner was an idea formulated and a chapter written than I discovered that there was a better way to present the material. My wife suggested that I impose a time limit upon myself to complete this book and put an end to the endless revisions. Present the ideas and take the consequences. As usual, I benefited from her advice, and I dedicate this book to her.

I have learned much from my students and colleagues, who criticized drafts of chapters or of articles upon which this book is based. John Black, George Borts, Karl Brunner, Phillip Cagan, Milton Friedman, Jürg Niehans, Alvin Marty, Harl Ryder, Ryuzo Sato, and S. C. Tsiang contributed valuable ideas. Chapter 5 was inspired by a suggestion from Jürg Niehans. My former students, Polly Allen, Gerald Miller, and Keizo Nagatani, criticized earlier drafts of this book. From them I have gained a better understanding of what I was doing. Miss Marion Anthony and Mrs. Marie Roderick typed this book at their usual standard of excellence. The National Science Foundation provided financial assistance during the period in which this book was written. I want to thank them for their advice, assistance, and patience.

Providence, Rhode Island   Jerome L. Stein
August, 1970

CONTENTS

MONEY AND CAPACITY GROWTH

CHAPTER ONE

𝕍𝕍𝕍𝕍

Monetary Theory and Policy in a Growing Economy

MONETARY GROWTH THEORY is concerned with the role of money in a growing economy. Money is a medium of exchange and a store of value which may, or may not, be costless to produce; and it is a liability of either the government or of a privately owned banking system. Monetary policy is concerned with the management of these types of money. Several questions immediately arise. To what extent can financial policies and institutional arrangements affect the time profiles of the capital-labor ratio, the real wage, and the rent per unit of capital? It is clear that the growth of a commodity money (for example, gold) will affect the real variables in the system, because resources (labor, capital) are required for the production of gold. Can variations in the rate of growth of a type of money which is costless to produce affect the time profiles and steady state solutions of these real variables in a fully employed economy which is growing over time? Is there an optimum growth of the various types of money? What are the most desirable stabilization policies in a growing economy when there is qualitative, but not quantitative, knowledge of the parameters of the economic system? Under what conditions will competitive markets lead to optimal growth? If there is a deviation between the market-generated growth path and the optimal growth path, how can this deviation be corrected, when we do not have detailed quantitative

This chapter is based upon my article "Monetary Growth Theory in Perspective," *American Economic Review*, LX (March, 1970), 85–106.

knowledge of the economy? The object of this book is to discuss and answer these fundamental questions.

There are several different ways of analyzing the effects of monetary policy in a growing economy. The analysis need not be restricted to a money which is costless to produce. Jürg Niehans (1969, pp. 228–51) considered the case where some fraction of the stock of money consists of monetary gold. The opportunity cost of producing gold (or exports to purchase gold) is output which is no longer available for consumption and investment. The realism of this assumption is unquestionable and paves the way for a discussion of growth in an open economy which uses money.

The Neoclassical approach[1] assumes that: (a) the rate of capital formation is identically equal to planned savings and (b) markets are always in equilibrium regardless of the rate of price change. This approach attempts to introduce monetary variables into the growth model developed by R. M. Solow (1956, pp. 65–94).

On the other hand, the Keynes-Wicksell approach[2] assumes that: (a) there are independent savings and investment functions and (b) price changes are related to an excess demand for or an excess supply of goods. During inflationary periods, when all demands cannot be satisfied, capital formation may differ from planned savings. The object of this approach is to formulate a general macro-economic model which contains money in an essential way regardless of whether it is a liability of the government or of a privately owned banking system. If the inputs of labor and capital were arbitrarily fixed, then it would look like a dynamic version of Don Patinkin's short-run aggregate model. Alternatively, this growth model would be the generalization of post-Keynesian macro-economics to a growing economy where the input of capital is endogenously determined and growing over time. Long-run equilibrium is nothing other than the steady state solution of the short-run dynamic model with endogenous capital.

How useful are these approaches in answering the basic problems of monetary growth theory posed above? Chapters 1 and 2 are devoted to the Neoclassical model: its method of analysis, conclusions, and consistency with rational behavior. Chapters 3 and 4 develop the pure

[1] See the references cited in section I of this chapter.
[2] See Chapter 3, footnote 1.

Keynes-Wicksell model where prices are changing if, and only if, there is an excess demand for or an excess supply of goods. A model which synthesizes the Neoclassical and the pure Keynes-Wicksell model, called the Synthesis model, is the subject of Chapter 5. It is Keynes-Wicksell outside the steady state, but becomes the Neoclassical model in the steady state. Stabilization policy is discussed in Chapter 6. Feedback control laws are developed which will stabilize an economy and drive it to a desired point, even though we only have qualitative (but not quantitative) knowledge of the structural parameters. Optimality is discussed in Chapters 7 and 8. Two models are discussed in these chapters: an economy consisting of immortal families and an intergeneration model of economic growth. It is proved that, if the economy is competitive with no externalities, then the model consisting of immortal families will grow in the optimal way. On the other hand, in the intergeneration model, competitive growth cannot be expected to be efficient, let alone optimal. There are, however, social institutions which do not entail government foresight or direct controls whose existence will guarantee that the economy converge to the optimal steady state. Chapter 8 examines Milton Friedman's proposal that anticipated deflation should be used as an instrument to achieve optimal growth. It is shown that this proposal should be rejected on theoretical grounds: (a) he cannot infer the optimal rate of monetary expansion per worker from historical data, and (b) this policy will tend to destabilize the economy.

I

THE NEOCLASSICAL MONETARY

GROWTH MODEL

Neoclassical models are characterized by the assumption that markets are always in equilibrium. In particular, planned investment is identically equal to planned savings. There are, however, many different types of Neoclassical models, depending upon the author's view of the role of money in an economy. The aim of this chapter is to discuss the following aspects of Neoclassical models. What are the relations among the different approaches? What are the relative strengths and weaknesses of the various models? What are the substantive differences among models; and which differences are inconsequential? To what extent is the distinction between outside and inside money crucial to the analysis? My main conclusion is that equally plausible models yield fundamentally different results.

Underlying the various approaches is a very simple framework for the analysis of economic growth in a single sector economy. Assume that full employment always prevails and the labor force $N(t)$ grows exponentially at rate n. If technological change is of the Harrod neutral type, then n may be interpreted as the growth of "effective" labor: the natural rate of growth plus the rate of Harrod neutral technical change. Then output $Y(t)$ depends upon the inputs of capital services, which are assumed to be positively related to the stock $K(t)$, and of effective labor services $N(t) = N(O)e^{nt}$. Output per unit of effective labor $y(t) \equiv Y(t)/N(t)$ is assumed to depend upon the ratio of capital per effective worker $k(t) \equiv K(t)/N(t)$, equation 1.[3]

(1) $$y(t) = f[k(t)].$$

Investment per worker can be considered as the sum of two parts: the investment per worker required to maintain the current capital-labor ratio nk plus the time rate of change of the capital-labor ratio Dk (where $D \equiv d/dt$). Only if investment per worker exceeds the amount required to provide the new workers with the same capital per worker as is used by the existing labor force will the amount of capital per worker rise. From the definition of $k \equiv K/N$ we derive:

(2) $$DK/N = nk + Dk.$$

Output per worker is divided between consumption per worker c and investment per worker DK/N. Therefore:

(3) $$y = c + nk + Dk$$
or
(4) $$Dk = (y - nk) - c.$$

---

[3] Not only is this production function assumed to be smooth and concave, but capital and labor are assumed to be essential for the production of output. Output per unit of capital y/k would fall to zero, if the capital intensity grew infinitely large. Assume also that the marginal product of capital is larger than the growth rate when the capital-labor ratio is zero.

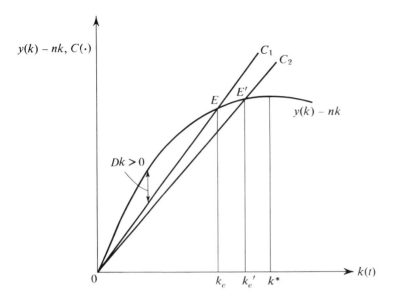

FIGURE 1. The Neoclassical growth model. A rise in the rate of monetary expansion shifts the equilibrium from E to E'. $Dk = y(k) - nk - C[k + \theta L(k, \mu - n)]$.

Figure 1 graphs equation 4. The curve $y - nk$ represents the amount of output per worker available for consumption per worker plus the change in the ratio of capital to labor. The previous assumptions imply the shape of $y - nk$.

Assume that consumption per worker C_1 is positively related to the capital intensity k. This assumption seems safe since a rise in k raises both output per worker and wealth per worker. At present, disregard the consumption function C_2.

When the capital intensity $k(t)$ is below k_e, then $y - nk$ exceeds c. Some output per worker is available to raise the capital intensity; and $k(t)$ rises. If $k(t)$ exceeded k_e, then the capital intensity would decline since c exceeds $y - nk$. Equilibrium capital intensity k_e is stable in Figure 1. At k^*, the output per worker available for consumption per worker and for a rise in the capital intensity is maximal. Obviously $y'(k^*) = n$ at this "Golden Rule" value.

In this exposition it is assumed that there is no commodity money: that is, all money is costless to produce.[4] Moreover, for the sake of simplicity, we shall focus upon aggregative variables.

Monetary policy can affect the time profile of the capital intensity, as well as its steady state solution k_e, if it can shift either the consumption function or the net production function (defined as) $y - nk$. The Neoclassical monetary growth model considers how these shifts can occur within a fully employed economy.

Accordingly, a dichotomy is made concerning the role of real balances in the Neoclassical model. First, under what conditions will variations in the rate of monetary expansion (and hence in real balances per worker) shift the consumption function? Second, under what conditions will the net production function $y - nk$ be affected by variations in the rate of monetary expansion? The first question is usually subsumed under the heading "real balances as a consumer good" and is discussed in part C of this section. The second question is usually subsumed under the heading "real balances as a producer's good" and is discussed in part B of this section. Although the dichotomy is analytically convenient, it is difficult to keep these roles of money separate from each other.

A. THE LOGICAL STRUCTURE OF NEOCLASSICAL MODELS

The Neoclassical monetary growth model was first presented by James Tobin (1965) and was a development made possible by the pioneering work of Robert Solow (1956) and T. Swan (1956). It assumes that the rate of capital formation is identically equal to planned savings and all markets are always in equilibrium, regardless of the rate of price change.

Monetary policy affects the consumption function in this model, even in the steady state.[5] In this manner monetary policy could affect the equilibrium capital intensity. Tobin assumed that consumption of goods per worker is a constant fraction of "disposable income" per worker.

---

[4] See Niehans' study (1969) for the case where there is a commodity money.

[5] Sidrauski (1967) derived a long-run consumption function which is independent of monetary influences. His conclusion was based upon two assumptions: (a) the economic unit is an immortal family maximizing utility over an infinite horizon, and (b) the marginal rate of time preference is constant. The relaxation of any one of these assumptions could change his results drastically. See Chapter 2 for a discussion of consumption functions based upon rational behavior.

The latter is the sum of output per worker $y(k)$ and the increment of real balances per worker[6] $D(M/p)/N$. The stock of money consists of the claims of the private sector upon the public sector, which varies as a result of net transfer payments to or from the public. There is no other type of public debt or type of money. Assume that M grows exponentially and exogenously at rate μ; and define the proportionate rate of change of the price level $\pi = D \ln p$, where p is the absolute price level. Then his consumption function is (5).

(5) $$C/N = C[y(k) + D(M/p)/N]$$

(5a) $$C/N = C[y(k) + (\mu - \pi)m],$$

where $m = M/pN$ is real balances per worker.

It would have been simpler, more general, and more amenable to a dynamic analysis had Tobin used consumption function (6), which he suggested in an earlier paper.[7] Let consumption (of goods) per worker depend upon wealth per worker where wealth consists of real capital per worker k plus the real public debt per worker. It is not necessary to assume that the real public debt per worker is M/p. We could assume that it is $\theta M/p$, where θ represents the ratio of the nominal public debt to the stock of money M. Variable θ would be equal to unity if there were neither government bonds nor inside money. We may simply assume that θ is a positive constant. Then:

(6) $$c = C/N = C[k + \theta m]$$

is the consumption function.[8]

Monetary policy will be able to shift the consumption function if it can vary real balances per worker m held, given the capital intensity.

It is assumed in all the Neoclassical monetary growth models that

[6] Tobin assumed that total consumption C depended upon total real disposable income Y'. The latter is the sum of (a) total real output Y and (b) the change in the real value of the claims of the private sector upon the public sector $D(M/p)$, where M is outside money and there are no government bonds. Deflate by the size of the labor force N to obtain the measure of real disposable income per worker: $y(k) + D(M/p)/N$.

[7] See Tobin (1955).

[8] If the equilibrium $\mu - \pi = n$ is always positive, then it really does not matter in the steady state solution whether (5) or (6) is used. I shall use (6) rather than (5) in describing the Neoclassical approach, since it is analytically more appealing and much simpler to use in a dynamic analysis. Tobin's 1965 paper was concerned with steady state solutions rather than a dynamic analysis.

the supply of, and demand for, real balances per worker are always equal, regardless of the rate of price change. On the other hand, the Keynes-Wicksell monetary growth models assume that prices are changing if, and only if, there is an excess demand for (or supply of) goods.

The demand for real balances per worker is a function of (a) transactions demand per worker reflected by y, (b) the stock of the complementary asset per worker k, and (c) the opportunity cost of holding real balances. Capital yields an expected return equal to its expected rent; and real balances yield an expected return equal to the negative of the expected rate of price change π^*. It is generally assumed that the expected rent is equal to the current level $r(k)$. The demand for real balances per worker can be written as equation 7.

(7) $m = L(k, \pi^*).$

Clearly, $L_2 < 0$ since a rise in the expected rate of price change decreases the quantity of real balances demanded per worker at any given capital intensity. The sign of L_1 is positive since a rise in k raises the transactions demand for real balances and also reduces the opportunity cost (the yield on real capital) of holding real balances.

The stability of the system is profoundly affected by the price expectations function. In the steady state, real balances per worker $m = M/pN$ are constant. Therefore, the price level eventually grows at a rate π_e equal to the growth of the money supply per worker. Let μ be the growth of the money supply. Then the steady state rate of price change π_e is equal to:

(8) $\pi_e = D \ln (M/N) = \mu - n.$

A simple[9] price expectations function, which is both a stabilizing influence and is consistent with the steady state solution, is:

(9) $\pi^* = \mu - n.$

[9] Alternatively, adaptive expectations function $D\pi^* = b(\pi - \pi^*)$ could be used. This function is not simple insofar as it adds a differential equation to the model. Moreover, the system will explode for a sufficiently high value of b, the adaptive expectations coefficient. If we assume that π^* is always equal to π, for all $D\pi^*$, then $D\pi^*/b = \pi - \pi^* = 0$ implies that b would be infinite. Such a model would not be stable.

Therefore, the consumption function is:

(10) $$C/N = C[k + \theta L(k, \mu - n)];$$

and the time rate of change of the capital intensity is:

(11) $$Dk = y(k) - nk - C[k + \theta L(k, \mu - n)].$$

Figure 1 graphs this fundamental differential equation of Neoclassical monetary growth theory.

A rise in the rate of monetary expansion shifts consumption function C downward. Why? The rise in $\mu - n$ raises the expected rate of price change $\pi^* = \mu - n$. Thereby, there is a decline in the quantity of real balances demanded $L_2(k, \pi^*) < 0$ at any capital intensity $k > 0$. Since wealth per worker is $k + m$ (when $\theta = 1$ in most models), the decline in $L(k, \pi^*) = m$ reduces real wealth per worker.

Consumption per worker is positively related to wealth per worker. Consequently, the rise in μ lowers the consumption function from C_1 to C_2. The dynamics of this situation raises[10] the equilibrium capital intensity from k_e to k_e'. Monetary policy is able to affect the time profile of the capital intensity and its steady state solution, even if money is costless to produce.

B. REAL BALANCES AS A PRODUCER'S GOOD IN A NEOCLASSICAL ECONOMY

Two conclusions which have been questioned recently seem to emerge from the previous model. First, it would appear that inflation is conducive to economic development. A rise in the rate of growth of the money supply lowers the consumption function and raises the capital intensity. The average productivity of labor and the real wage are positively related to the capital intensity. Therefore, should developing countries, which want to raise real per capita income, be advised to inflate the growth of the money supply? Second, monetary policy was able to affect the time profile of the capital intensity because there was a real balance effect in the consumption function. If, however, all money were "inside" money, that is, liabilities of a regulated but privately owned banking system, would there be a real balance effect in the consumption function? In that

[10] Stability requires that, at the equilibrium, the C function be steeper than the $y - nk$ function. At this stage of the argument, the $C(\cdot)$ function could cut the $y - nk$ function above or below the Golden Rule level of k.

case, would monetary policy be able to affect the time profile of the capital intensity[11] in this model?

Whether or not money is of the "inside" or the "outside" type, real balances may be viewed as generating a productive service, complementary with labor and capital. If there were no medium of exchange, then the inefficiencies of a barter economy would result. Labor and capital would have to be diverted from the production of goods to their distribution in order to achieve the double coincidence of wants. Firms would be established to act as brokers between potential buyers and sellers of goods and services; and the open book credit of those broker firms would undoubtedly develop as an inefficient money supply. What makes such a situation inefficient is that these firms use labor and capital to distribute goods and services which would otherwise be available for the production of goods and services. An explicit medium of exchange which is costless to produce increases the productivity of the economy by permitting a more efficient means of distribution, and hence a greater rate of production of goods and services with given aggregate inputs of capital and labor.

There may be a real loss to society resulting from a reduction in real balances below a certain level. Either there must be more frequent payments, involving additional bookkeeping and other administrative expenses, or part of one's wage will be paid in kind entailing the use of some barter. For these reasons, aggregate output may be a monotonic nondecreasing function of real balances, regardless of whether money is of the inside or the outside type. We continue to assume that fiat money is used, which is costless to produce.

If real balances are productive services, then the Neoclassical model should be revised.[12] Output per worker should depend upon[13] both capital

[11] If the banking system uses a commodity money as reserves, then we must use something similar to Niehans' (1969) model.

[12] This aspect of the role of money has been stressed by Marty (1969) and Levhari and Patinkin (1968). J. Niehans commented on this approach as follows: "While treating money as a 'productive service' may be better than neglecting it, it is still in the tradition of 'solving' problems of monetary theory by metaphor instead of analysis. In fact, money is quite unlike the usual factors of production." We shall confine our attention to the aggregative level, and not try to answer Niehans' profound comment.

[13] It is an oversimplification to assume that the production function $Y = Y[K, N]$, where N is effective labor, is unchanged during the process of economic development. For example, the allocation of resources between sectors has been improved during the process of economic development. See Borts and Stein (1964).

per worker k and real balances per worker m as described in equation 12.

(12) $y = y(k, m); \quad y_k > 0, \quad y_m \geqq 0.$

A limiting case that may occur with fully developed financial institutions is $y_m = 0$, that is, an increment of real balances does not liberate any perceptible amount of resources.

The private sector is assumed to allocate its wealth between the two assets: capital and real balances. In equilibrium, the net expected yields from each type of wealth will be equal. The anticipated return on capital is its expected rent, which is assumed to be equal to its current marginal product $y_k(k, m)$. The anticipated return on real balances has three components. First, there is the anticipated marginal product of real balances, which is assumed to be equal to its current level $y_m(k, m)$. Second, there is the anticipated appreciation $-\pi^*$ in terms of its command over goods. Third, there is the "liquidity" yield of money $Z(k, m)$, which reflects the feeling that usually real balances are safer to hold than real capital. Real balances are not treated here as a consumer good which yields utility directly. The liquidity yield reflects the price that asset holders are willing to pay, in terms of yield sacrificed, to hold an asset which may fluctuate less in real value. Assume that the "liquidity" yield is positively related to k and negatively related to m, that is, $Z_k > 0$ and $Z_m < 0$. It is, of course, possible that $Z(k, m)$, the relative liquidity of money compared to real capital, is negative, but that would be unusual. In any case $Z(k, m)$ reflects the relative variances of the expected returns on capital and real balances.

Equilibrium requires that equation 13 be satisfied: the net yields of the two assets must be equal when the risk factor is taken into account.

(13) $y_k(k, m) = y_m(k, m) - \pi^* + Z(k, m).$

Differentiate equation 13 and solve for dm in terms of dk and $d\pi^*$. Equation 14a is derived; and equation 14b is a more compact version of the same thing. If there are diminishing returns to substitution ($y_{ii} < 0$) and if the two inputs are complementary or independent ($y_{km} \geqq 0$), then the denominator in equation 14a is positive.

(14a) $dm = \dfrac{(y_{mk} - y_{kk} + Z_k)}{(y_{km} - y_{mm} - Z_m)} \, dk - \dfrac{1}{(y_{km} - y_{mm} - Z_m)} \, d\pi^*.$

(14b) $dm = L_1 \, dk + L_2 \, d\pi^*.$

Solving explicitly for the desired quantity of real balances per unit of effective labor, equation 14c is derived. This is just the familiar portfolio balance equation.

(14c) $m = L(k, \pi^*)$; $L_1 > 0$, $L_2 < 0$.

Equation 14c can be derived regardless of whether money is a liability of the public sector or of the private sector. The significant features of money, insofar as (14c) was concerned, are that it is a medium of exchange and a store of value.

An interesting and important question arises concerning the role of real balances as an argument in the consumption function. Assume that the quantity of real balances is an argument in the production function. Defer considering the role of real balances as a consumer good until part C of this section. Continue to assume that consumption depends upon wealth. Should real balances be considered part of wealth if money is a liability of the public sector, but excluded from a definition of wealth if money is a liability of the private sector? The question takes on added significance in the present context where real balances affect the productive capacity of the economy, regardless of who issues the money.

This question has been discussed by Pesek and Saving (1967), Friedman and Schwartz (1969, pp. 1–15), and Patinkin (1969, pp. 1140–60). My point of view is that wealth is the capitalized value of the flow of goods and services produced by the economy. Real balances (viewed as productive services) are wealth if and only if their existence contributes to an increase in the production of goods with given quantities of the other productive services.[14] It makes absolutely no difference whether or not the money is a liability of a nationalized or a denationalized institution, or whether or not interest is paid on money, in determining if it is part of wealth.

For example, suppose that a single bank were granted the monopoly privilege of issuing a given quantity of money. The value of this charter is the capitalized value of the real net returns that the bank stockholders will be able to earn as a result of this monopoly privilege. They will be able to

---

[14] In the general case, where the quantity of real balances is both a producer's good (i.e., an argument in the production function) and a consumer's good, wealth is the capitalized flow of the output of goods and services. Included in the flow of services are the value of the services of real balances held by consumers. See part C of this section.

earn a return because nonbank firms regard real balances as productive services. To obtain these services, they are prepared to give up output to the producers of the medium of exchange. Real balances are to be viewed as a form of capital goods which are relatively costless to produce. It is part of wealth only because it has an imputed rent: that is, it has a positive marginal product.

Suppose that the institutional structure were changed such that (a) the bank were nationalized. The only change that has occurred is that the rents are transferred from the stockholders to the people as a whole. The source of the payments is the marginal productivity of the real balances; and that is not directly affected by the change in ownership. Why then should the identity of the issuer of money be relevant in determining whether a given quantity of real balances is part of national wealth? The distinction between inside and outside money (viewed as a productive service) does not seem important for our purpose. Only the marginal product of the real balances should be considered in determining whether it is part of wealth.

Suppose that (b) horizontal disintegration occurred and the competitive rate of interest were paid on bank deposits. If the quantity of real balances were unchanged, then the rents attributable to the real balances are constant. However, they are redistributed from the stockholders to the depositors. Whether or not real balances are productive is independent of the distribution of their marginal product. The act, per se, of paying interest on real balances at the competitive rate does not determine whether or not they have positive marginal products and hence are part of wealth. What happens is that the payment of the competitive rate of interest on money reduces its opportunity cost to zero. Consequently, if the users of real balances maximize profits, these inputs will be used until their marginal products are driven down to zero. When that occurs, real balances will no longer be part of wealth because they will no longer be able to increase the flow of output. They become free goods. It is the end result concerning the marginal product of real balances that determines whether or not they are part of wealth.

Wealth per worker, both human and nonhuman, is just capitalized output: that is, national income per worker divided by the marginal product of capital. Such a measure of wealth is independent of how the returns to the productive services are distributed or the forms of the rent producers. Insofar as real balances are productive services, that is, they are not consumer goods, then consumption per worker should depend upon capitalized output per worker. Let us examine the implications for Neoclassical growth theory of several different consumption functions when real balances are productive services.

1. Wealth Consists of Capitalized Output. For simplicity, assume that (i) current output per worker $y(k, m)$ is expected to remain constant, and (ii) the discount factor is the marginal product of capital $y_k(k, m)$. Then wealth per worker a is capitalized output per worker.

(15a) $$a = y(k, m)/y_k(k, m);$$

and consumption per worker c depends upon wealth per worker a.

With competitive pricing the share of output earned by capital is β, where:

(15b) $$\beta = y_k(k, m) \cdot k/y(k, m) = \beta(k, m).$$

Therefore, wealth per worker is simply:

(15c) $$a = k/\beta(k, m).$$

Empirically, the elasticity of substitution is equal to or less than unity: that is, empirical studies suggest that $\beta_1 \leqq 0$. Therefore, the consumption function becomes:

(15d) $$c = C[k/\beta(k, m)],$$

and c is positively related to k as before.

The remaining question is whether the share of capital β is affected by the quantity of real balances. Suppose that the share β were not affected by m. Under these assumptions the growth model is described by equations 15, 14c, and 9.

(15) $Dk = y(k, m) - nk - C[k/\beta(k)];$ $\beta' \leqq 0.$
(14c) $m = L(k, \pi^*).$
(9) $\pi^* = \mu - n.$

No distinction whatsoever is made between inside and outside money if they are indistinguishable as media of exchange and as productive services. There is no real balance effect in the consumption function if the share of output earned by capital is independent of the quantity of real balances. On the other hand, there is a real balance effect in the net production function.

No ambiguity exists in this model concerning the effect of a rise in the rate of monetary expansion upon the steady state capital intensity: it must decline.

A rise in the rate of monetary expansion lowers the quantity of real balances demanded at any given capital intensity: $L_2 < 0$. Real balances are productive services and therefore output per unit of effective labor changes by $y_m L_2 < 0$. The net production function declines from $(y - nk)_1$ to $(y - nk)_2$ in Figure 2. Consumption per effective worker is unaffected by a change in the quantity of real balances per worker if capital's share of output is independent of the quantity of real balances per worker. As a result of the rise in the rate of monetary expansion, the steady state capital intensity declines from k_1 to k_4.

No ambiguity exists here. A rise in the rate of inflation lowers the

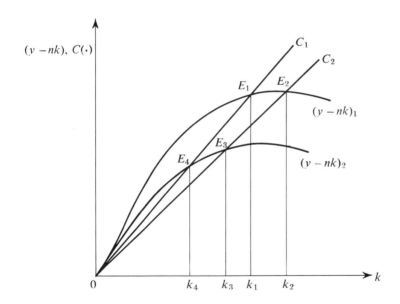

FIGURE 2. Real balances are productive services. A rise in the rate of inflation affects both the production function and the consumption function.

steady state capital intensity when wealth is measured as capitalized output. Inflation (in Figure 2) lowers the steady state output, and consumption, per unit of effective labor.

2. Wealth Consists of Capital and Real Balances. Suppose that consumers, in the aggregate, do not view wealth as capitalized output but consider a dollar of outside money to be a larger increment to private wealth than a dollar of inside money, because there is a private liability associated with the latter but not with the former. What are the implications of this assumption for growth theory? Let M' represent outside money and M'' inside money. Nominal private wealth may be considered to be equal to $pK + \theta_1 M' + \theta_2 M''$, where $1 > \theta_1 > \theta_2 > 0$ represents the fraction of each type of money which the public considers to be private wealth. One assumption is that inside money is not part of private wealth ($\theta_2 = 0$). But it is quite unnecessary for purposes of analysis. Let $M' = \xi M$ and $M'' = (1 - \xi)M$ be the division of the total money supply between outside and inside money, respectively. Private nominal wealth is: $pK + [\theta_1 \xi + \theta_2(1 - \xi)]M$. If the weight θ_1 and the division of the money supply ξ are constant, then $\theta = [\theta_1 \xi + \theta_2(1 - \xi)]$ will be constant. Real private wealth (per effective worker) would be $k + \theta m$. If all money were inside money, then real wealth per worker would be $k + \theta_2 m$; if all money were outside money, then real wealth per worker would be $k + \theta_1 m$. Using consumption function (6), price expectations function (9), and production function (12), the basic differential equation for the time path of k can now be derived: equation 16. It is graphed in Figure 2.

(16) $Dk = y[k, L(k, \mu - n)] - nk - C[k + \theta L(k, \mu - n)]$.

Equation 16 is more general than equation 11, for we allow for the possibility that $y_m > 0$, that is, that the loss of real balances will adversely affect the production of output with given total supplies of labor and capital.

Let the rate of monetary expansion rise from μ_1 to μ_2. When money is of the outside type, then a rise in μ entails a rise in the growth of the volume of net transfer payments. If money is of the inside type, then the liabilities of a privately owned banking system rise at a faster rate than before. There are now two effects. First, there may be an effect upon the demand for consumption per worker at any given capital intensity. A rise in μ raises the expected rate of price change π^* (equation 9) and reduces the quantity of real balances demanded per worker ($L_2 < 0$ in equation 14). If money is purely of the inside type, $\theta = \theta_2$, then wealth will be affected by $\theta_2 L_2$, and there will be an effect upon the consumption function equal to $C'(\cdot) \theta_2 L_2$. On the other hand, if money were of the outside type, then there will be a larger effect upon wealth equal to $\theta_1 L_2$, and the consumption function will shift by $C'(\cdot) \theta_1 L_2$. The magnitude of the downward shift of the consumption function, given k, is:

$$\partial C(\cdot)/\partial \mu = C'(\cdot)[\theta_1 \xi + \theta_2(1 - \xi)]L_2 = C'(\cdot) \theta L_2$$

and is described by the shift of the consumption function from C_1 to C_2 in Figure 2.

Second, the decline in the quantity of real balances demanded per worker may affect output per worker, that is, $y_m L_2$ may be substantial (especially in an economy whose financial institutions are not fully developed). This means that the function $y - nk$ declines at the same time that the consumption function declines from C_1 to C_2.

What will be the effect of a rise in the rate of monetary expansion upon the equilibrium capital intensity k? It depends upon which effect dominates. In the original Neoclassical model the decline in the quantity of real balances per worker at any capital intensity did not affect output. This means that, in effect, a fully developed financial economy was considered where $y_m(k, m)$ was approximately zero. Hence, the $y - nk$ function did not shift. However, the economy contained outside money: that is, real balances are considered part of wealth. The decline in m reduced wealth and thereby lowered the consumption function. The rise in the rate of monetary expansion in that case raised the steady state capital intensity from k_1 to k_2.

In the more general case analyzed here, it is not clear that inflation should be recommended as an aid to economic development. If real balances are highly productive (that is, y_m is large), the decline in $y - nk$ could exceed the decline in $C(\cdot)$. The magnitude of the decline in $C(\cdot)$ depends upon the division of the money stock between inside and outside money (ξ) and the different weights attached to each form of wealth. If (i) θ_2 is small, that is, there is a weak real balance effect in the consumption function derived from inside money, and (ii) most of the money consists of inside money, that is, ξ is close to zero, then there will be a small decline in the consumption function. Then a rise in the rate of inflation would lower the $y(k, m) - nk$ curve to $(y - nk)_2$ and lower the consumption function to C_2. As a result of the rise in the rate of inflation, the equilibrium capital intensity would be lowered from k_1 to k_3. In this formal, but general, case it was shown that inflation can lower output per capita and consumption per capita. A variety of results can be obtained from this model.

C. REAL BALANCES AS A CONSUMER GOOD

Real balances are part of wealth if, and only if, their existence contributes to an increase in the production of goods and services. Insofar as real balances are producers' goods, their contribution to the flow of consumer goods is indirect via the production function. On the other hand, real balances may also produce services of direct benefit to the consumer. One service is the increased leisure derived from having larger inventories of real balances. The consumer thereby saves "trips to the bank." Another service is the feeling that an asset held in the form of real balances is a relatively safer store of value than is an asset held in the form of capital. In each case the value of the service to the consumer is reflected by the product of the opportunity cost of real balances and the quantity of real balances held by consumers. Wealth is the capitalized flow of output produced by firms plus the capitalized flow of services of real balances of direct benefit to consumers. One could construct a consumption function based upon the assumption that consumption depends upon this general measure of wealth; and the implications of such an assumption for the growth process could be analyzed. This treatment of consumption would be a direct extension of the analysis in part B of this section. Let us critically examine, instead, some of the consumption functions used in models of money and growth which treat real balances exclusively as a consumer good.

Several authors (Johnson, 1967, and Levhari and Patinkin, 1968) focus exclusively upon the role of real balances as consumer goods. They view the services of real balances as similar to the services of owner-occupied homes: they are both part of national income and of consumption. Instead of assuming that consumption of goods depends upon wealth, these authors assume that total consumption of goods and services depends upon "disposable real income."

Disposable real income per worker in this framework is equal to output per worker $y(k)$, plus the real transfers per worker from the public sector $(\mu - \pi)\theta m$, plus the value of the services of real balances per worker. Most authors assume $\theta = 1$. How should the value of the services of real balances per worker be measured?

One approach (taken by Levhari and Patinkin, 1968) measures the value by the opportunity cost of holding real balances: the yield on capital less the yield on real balances. Assume that the expected yield on real capital is equal to its current rental r. What is the return derived from holding real balances? There may be a positive nominal interest rate paid on money i. Then, the expected yield on real balances is $i - \pi^*$, the nominal interest rate less the expected rate of price change. Therefore, the opportunity cost of holding real balances relative to capital is $r + \pi^* - i$, which is equal to the marginal utility of real balances as a consumer good. The value of the services of real balances is the quantity m multiplied by the opportunity cost $r + \pi^* - i$. Disposable real income, according to this approach, would be Y' (equation 17).

(17) $Y'/N = y(k) + (\mu - \pi)m + (r + \pi^* - i)m.$

Another approach (taken by Johnson, 1967) measures the value of the services of real balances, a component of disposable real income, as the integral under the demand curve for real balances per worker. Let $U(m)$ be the total utility per worker associated with the possession of real balances per worker of quantity m. Function U is monotonic nondecreasing. Then disposable real income per worker is (18).

(18) $Y''/N = y(k) + (\mu - \pi)m + U(m).$

There are serious criticisms which can be levied at each approach. First, the usual definitions of real national income accounting are violated. Real output y is presumably measured in constant prices. Each item in the bundle of outputs is valued at constant prices, and the total is summed. This was not done for the services of real balances. In equation 17, the "real" value of the services of real balances is measured in current prices since $r + \pi^* - i$ is not constant during the analysis. A paradox would arise if the demand for real balances had an inelastic section. A rise in the quantity m would be associated with a decline in $(r + \pi^* - i)m$, the total "real" value. The value of real output y is not measured this way. Why treat the value of the services of real balances in an asymmetrical way?

Equation 18 is not much better in this respect. The real value of the services of output consumed, a component of y, is not measured as an integral under a demand curve reflecting the total utility associated with the given quantity. Why measure the services of real balances as an integral under a demand curve ? There is no justification for the asymmetry of treatment between currently produced output and the services of real balances in a measure of disposable real income.

Second, there is a difficulty in interpreting the real balance effect in this approach. There are two components of consumption: the consumption of goods and the consumption of the services of real balances. These models generally assume that total real consumption of goods and real balances is a constant fraction $1 > c > 0$ of real disposable income. Therefore, the consumption of goods per worker C/N is derived from each definition of disposable real income.

Using the definition of disposable income in (17), the demand for consumption of goods per worker can be derived. Assume that $\theta = 1$ and there is no interest on money $i = 0$. Consider the steady state solution $\pi^* = \pi = \mu - n$. Then:

(19) $\qquad C/N = c\,Y'/N - (r + \mu - n)m.$

$\qquad\qquad C/N = cy(k) + cnm - (1 - c)(r + \mu - n)m.$

Suppose population were constant, $n = 0$. Then, the consumption function for goods is:

(19a) $\qquad C/N = cy(k) - (1 - c)(r + \mu)m.$

A negative relation exists between real balances held per worker m and the consumption of goods per worker. This is an unusual result.

Definition (18) yields the same paradox. This is described by equations 20 and 20a.

(20) $\qquad C/N = c\,Y''/N - U(m), \qquad U' > 0.$

$\qquad\qquad C/N = cy(k) + cnm - (1 - c)U(m).$

(20a) $\qquad C/N = cy(k) - (1 - c)U(m), \quad \text{when} \quad n = 0.$

Again, C/N and m are negatively related when population is constant.

When the services of real balances are regarded as a component of disposable income which yields utility directly, and total consumption is assumed to be proportional to disposable income, many paradoxes arise.

For this reason one attempts to construct consumption functions on the basis of a utility maximizing model. In the next chapter we assume that the services of real balances yield utility directly to the consumer who determines his saving and portfolio behavior on the basis of an optimizing procedure. The resulting consumption function is examined in terms of its implications for monetary policy in a growing economy.

D. HOW MONEY ENTERS THE ECONOMY

All of the Neoclassical models are very sensitive to the manner in which the money supply grows. It has hitherto been assumed in the outside money models that the money stock grows exclusively because of net transfer payments to or from the public. Therefore, wealth is affected by the rate of monetary expansion. Relax this assumption and suppose that the medium of exchange is a liability of the government which grows exclusively because it bears an interest rate i. Then, the growth of the money supply $D \ln M \equiv \mu$ is equal to i. Consider (for the sake of simplicity) the case where money is a producer's good, though similar results occur in the case where m yields utility directly. The steady state rate of price change is $\pi = \mu - n$. Therefore, the expected real rate of interest on money is $i - \pi^* = \mu - \pi^* = n$. The interest rate paid on money $i \equiv \mu$ offsets completely in the steady state the effects of changes in the rate of price change $\mu - n$.

When both k and m are held as producers' goods, their marginal returns must be equal. The yield on capital $y_k(k, m)$ must be equal to the real yield on money $y_m(k, m) + n + Z(k, m)$. The demand for real balances per worker in the steady state must satisfy:

(21) $$y_k(k, m) = y_m(k, m) + n + Z(k, m)$$

or

(22) $$m = L(k, n), \qquad L_2 > 0$$

for the reasons discussed earlier. Real balances demanded per worker will be independent of monetary influences.

As long as real balances have some productivity $y_m > 0$, or are considered to offer a convenience or liquidity yield $Z > 0$, the marginal product of capital $y_k(k, m)$ must exceed the growth rate. Otherwise, people would not wish to hold capital. If the yield on capital were less than the growth rate, capital decumulation would result; and the marginal product of capital would rise. There could occur no equilibrium with a positive capital stock if the marginal product of capital were less than the growth rate.

A simple institutional change, whereby the growth of the money supply results exclusively from the payment of interest on money, forces the steady state rent per unit of capital to be at least as great as the growth rate. Variations in the rate of monetary expansion cannot affect the steady state capital intensity.

E. THE INSTABILITY ELEMENTS IN THE NEOCLASSICAL MODEL

In the Neoclassical model the supply of and demand for real balances are always equal: that is, portfolio balance is always assumed to prevail. This assumption will lead to the instability of the model unless frictions are introduced.

Suppose that the expected rate of price change π^* were always equal to the rate currently experienced π. Or, we could assume that the expected rate of price change was positively related to the current rate, but $\pi^* = \pi$ in the steady state. Then, the equality of the supply of and demand for real balances per worker implies that:

(23) $m = L(k, \pi); \qquad L_1 > 0, \qquad L_2 < 0,$

based upon equation 7 and the assumption that π^* is positively related to π. To induce people to hold a larger quantity of real balances, given k, the rate of price change must decline.

From (23), we derive equation 24. Solving explicitly for π, equation 25 is derived.

(24) $dm = L_1\, dk + L_2\, d\pi$

(25) $\pi = \pi(k, m), \quad \text{where} \quad \pi_1 = L_1/(-L_2) > 0$

$$\pi_2 = 1/L_2 < 0.$$

Equation 25 is a condition for portfolio balance; but it does not explain what causes the price level to change.

The growth of real balances per worker $D \ln (M/pN)$ is the growth of the money supply per worker $\mu - n$ less the growth of the price level π. As usual, it is assumed that M grows as a result of unexpected transfer payments from the public to the private sector. Since portfolio balance is always assumed to prevail, the growth of the price level is given by equation 25. We therefore derive:

(26) $D \ln (M/pN) = Dm/m = \mu - n - \pi(k, m)$.

An aspect of instability is quite apparent. Say that k is given and m is displaced above its equilibrium value. Will m return to its equilibrium? The answer is no. Why? To induce people to hold a larger stock of real balances, the rate of price change must decline. Therefore, real balances per worker rise at a faster rate than before; and m deviates further away from equilibrium. Formally:

(27) $\partial(Dm/m)/\partial m = -\pi_2 > 0$,

which is instability in the m direction.

The question arises whether the variations of k will tend to stabilize such a model. To answer this question we must simultaneously consider the manner in which k varies. If consumption per worker is $C(k + m)$, then:

(28) $Dk = y(k) - nk - C(k + m)$.

We consider the case where real balances are not productive services. They are held as a store of value because it is less risky to hold money than it is to hold real capital. Differential equations 26 and 28 constitute the dynamic model, which we shall solve graphically.

If k were constant, then there would be a negative relation between m and k. Consider Figure 1. If m declined, then the consumption function C_1 would decline and the equilibrium would shift from E to E' such that the steady state value of the capital intensity would rise from k_e to k_e'.

Formally, on the basis of equation 28, find the set of k and m such that $Dk = 0$. This set would satisfy the equation:

(29) $Dk = 0 = y(k) - nk - C(k + m)$.

Solving for the slope of this curve, dm/dk, derive equation 30.

(30) $dm/dk = \dfrac{(y' - n - C')}{C'} < 0$.

We know from Figure 1 that C' exceeds $(y' - n)$ in the neighborhood of an equilibrium. That is, the slope of the consumption function exceeds

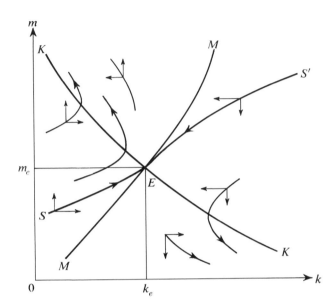

FIGURE 3. Saddle point instability occurs in the Neo-classical model if the expected rate of price change is equal to (or positively related to) the current rate of price change.

the slope of the net production function in the neighborhood of a stable equilibrium. Solving (30) explicitly for m as a function of k, we derive equation 30a.

(30a) $m = F(k),$ $F' < 0.$

This equation is graphed in Figure 3 below as the KK curve: it is the set of k and m such that k is constant.

It should be clear that, given m, deviations of k from the KK curve will tend to be eliminated. Again consider Figure 1. If m is given, then the consumption function is given. If $k(t)$ were displaced above the equilibrium k_e, then C would exceed $y - nk$; and $k(t)$ would revert to k_e. Similarly, if $k(t)$ were displaced below the equilibrium k_e, then $y - nk$ would exceed C; and $k(t)$ would return to k_e. Formally, in the neighborhood of an equilibrium, using equation 28:

(30b) $\partial(Dk)/\partial k\big|_{\substack{m \\ k=k_e}} = y'(k_e) - n - C'(k_e + m) < 0$

The horizontal arrows in Figure 3 have been drawn to describe this phenomenon. Given m, displacements of $k(t)$ from the curve $m = F(k)$ tend to be eliminated.

Define the MM curve as the set of k and m such that real balances per unit of capital (m) are constant. From equation 26 it is the set of k and m such that:

(31) $$\mu - n = \pi(k, m); \qquad \pi_1 > 0, \qquad \pi_2 < 0.$$

The slope of this function is:

(32) $$\frac{dm}{dk} = \frac{\pi_1}{-\pi_2} > 0$$

and is described in Figure 3.

On the basis of the previous discussion, summarized in equation 27, we know that deviations of m from the MM curve are cumulative. Given k, a rise in m leads to a further rise; and a decline in m leads to a further decline. The vertical arrows in Figure 3 describe equation 27.

Equilibrium is at point E, where both the capital intensity (k_e) and real balances per unit of capital (m_e) are constant. Deviations from the equilibrium are cumulative, except along branches SE and $S'E$. Point E is a saddle point. Only if the initial conditions are "just right," that is, lie along SE and $S'E$, will the system converge to equilibrium. Otherwise, the values of k and m will diverge. Several trajectories have been drawn in Figure 3 to illustrate these possibilities.[15]

This source of instability is the same as the Hahn paradox (1966). The trouble with this Neoclassical model is that ". . . the price of money was changing because this was required for asset equilibrium and not because any reason was adduced why, in fact, it should change." (Hahn, 1969).

Stability of the Neoclassical monetary growth model can be guaranteed[16] if a sufficiently sluggish price expectations function is introduced.

---

[15] An algebraic analysis of the dynamic system indicates that the product of the characteristic roots is negative.

[16] Assume that, in $y = f(k)$, $f'(0) = \infty$ and $f'(\infty) = 0$.

Price expectations function (9) was excellent for this purpose: it was constant at $\mu - n$, the steady state rate of price change. That is why we did not encounter any instability earlier. The adaptive expectation equation can also be stabilizing if the value of coefficient b in $D\pi^* = b(\pi - \pi^*)$ is sufficiently small.[17] When portfolio balance is always assumed to prevail, frictions in the formation of price expectations are necessary for stability.

[17] This assumption is made by Cagan (May, 1969) and Sidrauski (1967).

CHAPTER TWO

Rational Behavior
and the Utility Yield
of Real Balances

THE PRINCIPAL CONCLUSION of the Neoclassical monetary growth model developed by James Tobin (1965) is that a rise in the rate of monetary expansion will raise the steady state capital intensity (ratio of capital to labor). He assumed that: (a) output per worker depends upon capital per worker: real balances are not productive services (that is, are not arguments in the production function), and (b) the money supply grows exclusively as a result of unexpected transfer payments from the public to the private sector. In the previous chapter it was shown that if these assumptions are relaxed, for example, if real balances are productive services, then very different conclusions may be derived from a Neoclassical monetary growth model.

Harry G. Johnson (1967, 1969) has criticized the assumptions and conclusions of Tobin's model. Underlying his criticism is the fundamental question: What is the proper way to treat the utility yield of real balances?

For the sake of simplicity Tobin assumed that consumption per worker was a constant proportion of real disposable income per worker, where real disposable income is the sum of current output and the increment of real balances.[1] His critics claim that:

The assumption of a demand for real balances . . . implies that such balances yield a flow of "convenience" services or utility, which is at once a component

---

[1] Tobin's results would follow just as easily from the assumption that consumption of goods is positively related to wealth, i.e., capital plus real balances.

of real consumption and real income, and should be included in the definition of the income that determines savings behavior. (Johnson, 1967, p. 168.)

Controversy concerns the nature of the savings function: What are its arguments and what is its form? Johnson in 1969 continued the criticism that he raised in 1967 on this subject.

Contemporary growth models have for the most part been built on the assumption that savings is a constant proportion of income. This is an assumption of a naiveté amounting to deliberate stupidity, in sharp contrast to the sophistication of the theory of production in such models, which originated with Keynes' failure to reinforce the concept of the propensity to consume with any rational utility-maximizing rationale, and has been perpetuated by his followers' acceptance of Kuznets' empirical finding of constancy in the long-run savings ratio and their realization of the convenience of this assumption for mathematical analysis of the growth process.

On the basis of these criticisms by Johnson (1967, 1969), Levhari and Patinkin (1968), and others, it is not agreed that a rise in the rate of monetary expansion must raise the steady state capital intensity. When the utility yield of real balances is taken into account then, according to Johnson (1967, p. 170):

... the direction of the influence of monetary policy on the growth equilibrium of the economy is no longer unambiguous. A more inflationary policy may raise or lower the current growth rate of output and the long-run equilibrium level of output per head, depending on whether the growth stimulating (long-run equilibrium output-raising) effect of lower real balances outweighs the growth inhibiting (long-run output reducing) effect of a lower utility yield on real balances.

Johnson's views have been discussed in Chapter 1. In the present chapter we examine the implications of the assumption that real balances are arguments in the utility function. What type of Neoclassical model is implied by this assumption? Are Tobin's results consistent with a utility maximization model?

Ambiguity has characterized our previous analysis. By selecting one out of a number of plausible consumption functions, any result was shown to have been possible: a rise in the rate of monetary expansion could either raise or lower the steady state capital intensity. To resolve this unsatisfactory ambiguity, it is natural to construct a consistent model of rational behavior. Then we can investigate the nature of the consumption-savings function that is implied by a model of rational behavior. It can be shown, however, that ambiguity still prevails: the result depends upon the utility maximization model used. Two models of rational behavior will be described. The first model, which will just be sketched, is associated with the late Miguel Sidrauski (1967). It implies that monetary neutrality exists in the steady state. The equilibrium capital intensity depends exclusively upon the form of the production function and the subjective discount rate. Monetary policy cannot affect the steady state capital intensity. The second model is a development of the intergeneration models studied by Samuelson (1958), Diamond (1965), Cass and Yaari (1967), and Stein (*Economica*, 1969). It can be proved that the original Tobin Neoclassical results, presented in Chapter 1, are consistent with such a model of rational behavior: a rise in the rate of monetary expansion raises the steady state capital intensity. It is assumed that real balances are not productive services. Recourse to a consistent model of rational behavior does not resolve the controversy concerning the effect of a change in the rate of monetary expansion upon the steady state capital intensity.

The questions at issue are clear. Suppose that all functions were derived from a particular utility maximizing process in a monetary economy, where real balances produce utility directly.

1. Are the effects of a change in the rate of monetary expansion upon the capital intensity, both in the short-run and in the steady state, ambiguous?

2. What savings (or consumption) function is derived from a model where the consumer units attempt to maximize utility over their life spans? Will savings be proportional to disposable income?

3. What will be the relation between the demand for real balances and the savings function under these conditions?

To answer these questions we construct several Neoclassical monetary growth models based upon utility maximizing households.

I

AN INFINITE HORIZON MODEL

Consider Sidrauski's economy consisting of many identical families. Each one has the instantaneous utility function:

(1) $$u = u(c, m),$$

where c is per capita consumption and m is real balances per capita. It is assumed that the possession of real balances produces a flow of services which yield utility directly. Assume, for the sake of simplicity, that the size of each family is constant and that each family attempts to maximize the present value of utility, defined on c and m, over an infinite horizon. Formally, each family strives to maximize equation 2.

(2) $$\int_0^\infty u(c, m)e^{-\delta t}\,dt.$$

A justification for using $m(t)$, real balances per worker, as an argument in the utility function has been offered by Harry Johnson (1969):

... if people choose to forego the holding of capital equipment that yields a positive and observable flow of output, in order to hold noninterest bearing money, they are behaving as if they derived satisfaction from their money stocks equivalent at the margin to that derived from the goods and services produced by more conventional forms of capital equipment, whether they so conceive of themselves or not. (Alternatively, if the idea of money yielding direct utility does not appeal, the "utility yield" can be considered as the value of the additional leisure made possible by the replacement of barter by money.)

This argument is not entirely convincing. Why should m yield utility directly rather than indirectly via its effects upon the stream of consumption? Tobin (1958) derived a liquidity preference function from a model where consumption was the only argument in the utility function. The optimum quantity of m was such that the expected utility of consumption, derived from an investment in risky assets, is equal to the expected utility of consumption derived from an investment in safer assets.[2] In either case utility is derived from the resulting consumption and not from the ownership of real balances.

In subsequent chapters money will be considered exclusively as a store of value alternative to real capital and bonds. No direct utility yield will be attributed to the ownership of real balances. In the present chapter we shall simply accept the Johnson-Sidrauski assumption that u

---

[2] By sacrificing a unit of consumption in period t, the individual loses $u'(c_t)$, the marginal utility of present consumption. He may invest his funds in capital with an uncertain return r_t; or he may invest his funds in (say) money with a return of i_t. In the former case the expected marginal utility of consumption will be $E\{u'(c_{t+1})(1 + r_t)\}$; and in the latter case it will be $E\{u'(c_{t+1})(1 + i_t)\}$. On the margin when both assets are held, the two expected returns should be equal.

is a function of both $c(t)$ and $m(t)$. Our interest is in deriving the implications of this commonly used, but arbitrary, assumption.

The subjective discount rate $\delta > 0$ was assumed by Sidrauski to be constant. For some unexplained reason the family is not indifferent among permutations of a stream of consumption. It has a strictly positive rate of time preference.

This family has two sources of receipts: produced income and an increment of real balances. Produced income per family member is $y(k)$, where k is capital per family member. The increment of real balances is $D(M/p)/N = (\mu - \pi)m$, where μ is the proportionate rate of expansion of outside money, π is the rate of price change, and m is real balances per family member. Recall that N was assumed constant for simplicity of exposition. The government produces the change in the money supply by making unexpected transfer payments to the families. Each family is, by assumption, the economy in microcosm. Real receipts per family member, $y(k) + (\mu - \pi)m$, are disposed of in two ways. Part of the output is consumed and part of it is used to accumulate more real assets. Let c refer to real consumption per family member and Da refer to the time rate of change of real assets per family member denoted by a. Recall that family size was assumed to be constant. Therefore:

(3) $$y(k) + (\mu - \pi)m - c = Da$$

is the constraint on the change in real assets. Of course, k and c must be nonnegative.

Assets can be held either in the form of real balances m or in the form of real capital k per member of the family.

(4) $$a = k + m.$$

The optimal growth path is found by maximizing (2), subject to constraints (3) and (4). Thereby the optimum value of c, k, and m are derived at each moment of time for this representative family.

Only the steady state solution concerns us since we wish to know if the choice of μ by the monetary authorities can affect the steady state capital intensity. A simple method can be used to analyze the steady state solution. Suppose that we are at the stationary point (c_e, k_e, m_e) of the optimal growth path of the representative family, where c_e and k_e are strictly positive. No small change in c should be able to raise the steady state utility $u(c_e, m_e)$.

If the family sacrifices a unit from its flow of consumption, then utility declines by u_1, the marginal utility of consumption (per member of the family). This act of saving is used to acquire more capital. The latter allows consumption to rise by $1 + y'(k)$ units since both the additional capital and its marginal product can be consumed. Utility rises by $u_1 \cdot [1 + y'(k)]$ in the future. However, future utilities are discounted at rate $\delta > 0$. Therefore, the gain in utility is $\dfrac{u_1[1 + y'(k)]}{(1 + \delta)}$. At the stationary point on an optimal growth path, the loss of utility u_1 should exactly counterbalance the gain in utility derived from a higher rate of savings. Equations 5 and 6 should be satisfied.

$$(5) \qquad\qquad -u_1 + u_1 \frac{[1 + y'(k)]}{(1 + \delta)} = 0$$

or

$$(6) \qquad\qquad y'(k_e) = \delta.$$

The capital intensity $k = k_e$ must be such that the marginal product of capital $y'(k_e)$ must be equal to δ, the constant subjective rate of time preference. Obviously, monetary policy cannot affect the steady state capital intensity within the model of rational behavior. The assumption of a constant size of family can easily be relaxed without changing any fundamental conclusion.

Sidrauski's results followed from very restrictive assumptions. Monetary nonneutrality could easily be produced by relaxing some assumptions. Assume that (a) the marginal rate of time preference is a function of both k and m, or (b) the real balances are arguments in the production function. Then marginal condition (5) becomes marginal condition (7).

$$(7) \qquad\qquad -u_1 + u_1 \cdot \frac{[1 + y_k(k, m)]}{1 + \delta(k, m)} = 0.$$

From which it follows that:

$$(8) \qquad\qquad y_k(k, m) = \delta(k, m).$$

The steady state capital intensity will not be independent of the steady state level of real balances per worker. If the rate of monetary expansion can affect the steady state value of m, it can affect the steady state value of k. Recourse to an explicit utility maximization model fails to resolve the question: What will be the effect of a change in the rate of monetary expansion upon the steady state capital intensity?

II

AN INTERGENERATION MODEL
OF RATIONAL BEHAVIOR

Instead of assuming that all persons are identical and have infinite life spans, consider a variant of the Samuelson (1958) and Diamond (1965) intergeneration model. At any time two generations are alive: a younger generation which works to produce output and an older generation which is retired. Each generation lives for two periods of equal but arbitrary length, and then it disappears. Arbitrarily assume that the household derives utility from its consumption of goods and the services of its real balances. On the basis of a utility maximization procedure and the menu of assets available, the households determine their desired life cycle of consumption and their desired real balances. Aggregate savings and demand for real balances (liquidity preference) functions are thereby derived. Using these derived functions the dynamic course of the growing economy is generated. The resulting model is not amenable to the criticisms of Johnson and others, that the functions are not based upon rational behavior. Moreover, the "proper" way of taking the utility yield of real balances into account should follow directly from the utility maximizing procedure.

Not only is this a step in the direction of manageable disaggregation but also it is more realistic than the assumption that each family attempts to maximize utility over an infinite horizon. Samuelson and Diamond proved that if real capital is the only store of value, then dynamic inefficiencies can occur within the framework of this model, even if all markets are competitive and there are no externalities. If money is introduced as an additional store of value in the Samuelson model[3] (1958), then its mere existence will guarantee that the yield on capital will not be less than the growth rate of the economy, provided that the money supply changes solely because it bears a positive or negative interest rate. The manner whereby the money supply changes is crucial.

My purpose is to extend the Samuelson, Diamond, and Cass-Yaari model to an economy where (a) real balances produce a direct utility, and (b) the money supply grows as a result of transfers to the younger generation (which, obviously, are unexpected).[4] Are the Johnson and Sidrauski criticisms of the Neoclassical model convincing? Does the mere existence of money guarantee dynamic efficiency?

My major conclusions are:

1. The Tobin Neoclassical model is quite consistent with the utility maximization model presented here. A rise in the rate of monetary expansion must unambiguously raise the steady state capital intensity. Johnson's criticisms are not well taken.

2. The Cass-Yaari conclusion that the mere existence of money prevents dynamic inefficiency is not valid in this model. When the money supply grows as a result of (unexpected) transfers to the younger generation, the steady state rent per unit of capital could be below the growth rate. Dynamic efficiency (such that the marginal product of capital is not less than the growth rate) can be assured only if the money supply is not growing.

Recall that each person[5] lives for two periods of equal but arbitrary length. During his youth the person works to earn income, and he is retired during the second period of his life. Population grows exogenously at rate n, so there are $(1 + n)^t = L(t)$ workers and $(1 + n)^{t-1} = L(t - 1)$ retired people alive at time t.

The real wage per worker is $w(t)$. In the aggregate the workers receive $p(t)W(t)$ in wages, where $p(t)$ is the price level and $w(t)L(t) = W(t)$ constitute total real wages. Assume that the government transfers

[3] See also Cass and Yaari (1967).
[4] These two assumptions differ from those made by Cass and Yaari, and hence our conclusions differ.
[5] The basic unit is a household whose head is a worker in his youth and a retired person during the next period. The terms person and household will be used interchangeably.

TABLE 1. YOUNGER GENERATION, TOTALS

Receipts	Expenditures
1. Wages $p(t)W(t)$	3. Consumption $p(t)C_1(t)$
2. Transfers $M(t) - M(t - 1)$	4. Money balances $M(t)$
	5. Capital $p(t)K(t + 1)$

$M(t) - M(t - 1)$ of legal tender to the younger generation, and this transfer is the means whereby the money supply changes.[6]

The younger generation disposes of total money receipts $p(t)W(t) + M(t) - M(t - 1)$ in three ways. First, $p(t)C_1(t)$ is the money value of their total consumption where $c_1(t)$ is real consumption per worker and $c_1(t)L(t) = C_1(t)$. Second, they save by acquiring output which they do not consume. These goods are rented to firms and constitute the stock of capital $K(t + 1)$ to be used in the next period. Savings in the form of capital are $p(t)K(t + 1)$ in nominal terms. Third, they save by acquiring the stock of money in existence, $M(t)$.

Table 1 describes the sources of receipts and expenditures by the younger generation in the aggregate.

An older generation exists at time t, which consists of those who were workers in the previous period. Their total consumption is $p(t)C_2(t)$, where $c_2(t)$ is real consumption per retired person and $C_2(t) = c_2(t)L(t - 1)$. This consumption is financed by the rental incomes received from their ownership of the stock of capital, the consumption of their capital, and the exchange of their money balances for goods.

The value of the capital owned by this generation is $p(t)K(t)$. Total rents received are $p(t)r(t)K(t)$ and the older generation owns $M(t - 1)$ of the fiat money. The value of their consumption is precisely equal to the sum of these three elements since the older generation bequeaths nothing to the future. Table 2 describes the sources of receipts and expenditures of the retired generation in the aggregate.

Consolidate Tables 1 and 2 and derive equation 9. The stock of capital available in period $t + 1$, denoted by $K(t + 1)$, is:

$$(9) \qquad K(t + 1) = K(t) + W(t) + r(t)K(t) - C_1(t) - C_2(t).$$

[6] Negative transfers are taxes. If there are net taxes, then the money supply contracts: $M(t)$ is less than $M(t - 1)$ in Table 1. The means whereby the money supply changes is of great significance. See Chapter 1.

TABLE 2. OLDER GENERATION, TOTALS

Receipts	Expenditures
1. Rentals $p(t)r(t)K(t)$	4. Consumption $p(t)C_2(t)$
2. Capital $p(t)K(t)$	
3. Money $M(t-1)$	

Since current output $Y(t)$ is distributed between wages $W(t)$ and rentals $r(t)K(t)$, the stock of capital in period $t+1$ is equal to $K(t)$ plus output $W(t) + r(t)K(t)$ less total consumption $C_1(t) + C_2(t)$.

Examination of Table 2 will reveal that $C_2(t) - r(t)K(t) - K(t)$ is precisely equal to the real value of cash balances $M(t-1)/p(t)$ owned by the older generation. These real balances are acquired by the younger generation in return for output which is consumed by the older generation. The value of $M(t-1)/p(t)$ cannot exceed $W(t)$, the maximum output that the younger generation can transfer to the older generation.

From Table 1 equation 10 can be derived. It describes the determination of $K(t+1)$ in terms of the behavior of the younger generation. Since $K(t+1)$ is nonnegative, an upper bound on $M(t-1)/p(t)$ exists.

(10) $\qquad K(t+1) = W(t) - C_1(t) - M(t-1)/p(t).$

Output produced is $r(t)K(t) + W(t)$ and the existing stock of capital is $K(t)$. The older generation consumes $r(t)K(t)$ and $K(t)$, items 1 and 2 in Table 2, in addition to $M(t-1)/p(t)$. The younger generation has a claim on $W(t)$ of output and consumes $C_1(t)$. This generation transfers $M(t-1)/p(t)$ of output to the older generation, which is consumed in exchange for money. What is left for next period's stock of capital is $K(t+1)$ in equation 10.

Assume that the money supply grows (or declines) at rate μ such that $M(t) = M(t-1)(1+\mu)$. Denote real transfers per worker by:

$$g(t) = \frac{M(t) - M(t-1)}{p(t)L(t)},$$

and real balances per worker by:

$$m(t) = \frac{M(t)}{p(t)L(t)}.$$

Then Table 1 can be rewritten as Table 3, when the magnitudes are

TABLE 3. YOUNGER GENERATION, REAL MAGNITUDES PER WORKER

Receipts	Expenditures
1. Real wage $w(t)$	3. Real consumption $c_1(t)$
2. Real transfer $g(t) = \dfrac{\mu m(t)}{1 + \mu}$	4. Real balances $m(t)$
	5. Capital $(1 + n)k(t + 1)$

expressed in real per worker terms. Let $k(t) \equiv K(t)/L(t)$. Then, $\dfrac{K(t + 1)}{L(t)}$ is equal to $(1 + n)k(t + 1)$.

The capital intensity in period $t + 1$ can be expressed in terms of equation 11, based upon Table 3.

$$(11) \qquad (1 + n)k(t + 1) = w(t) - c_1(t) - \frac{m(t)}{1 + \mu} .$$

Within the framework described by Table 3, or equation 11, the real value of the acquired balances $m(t)/(1 + \mu)$ must be no greater than $w(t)$. The reason is that the real value of acquired balances represents output transferred from the young generation to the old. However, the maximum amount that can be transferred is $w(t)$. Therefore, $m(t)/(1 + \mu)$ cannot exceed $w(t)$ and certainly must be finite.

It is clear from equation 11 that the older generation has no control over the capital intensity prevailing in period $t + 1$. The difference between $C_2(t)$ and $K(t) + r(t)K(t)$ is determined exclusively by the real balances $M(t - 1)/p(t) = M(t)/(1 + \mu)p(t)$, which the younger generation chooses to hold.

Assume that the economy is competitive. The workers are paid the value of their marginal products; and the rent per unit of capital, paid by firms to the owners of capital, is equal to the value of the marginal product of capital. Moreover, assume that each firm has the same production function subject to constant returns to scale in labor and capital. Let $y(t) \equiv Y(t)/L(t)$ be output per worker, let $w(t)$ be the real wage, and let $r(t)$ be the rent per unit of capital. Then:

$$(12a) \qquad y(t) = y[k(t)]; \quad y' > 0, \quad y'' < 0, \quad y(0) = 0,$$
$$(y/k) \to 0 \quad \text{as} \quad k \to \infty.$$

$$(12b) \qquad w(t) = w[k(t)] = y - y'k; \quad w' > 0, \quad w'' < 0.$$

$$(12c) \qquad r(t) = r[k(t)] = y'[k(t)]; \quad r' < 0, \quad r \to 0 \quad \text{as} \quad k \to \infty,$$
$$r \to \infty \quad \text{as} \quad k \to 0.$$

These equations describe our assumptions concerning production and factor pricing. Both capital and labor are assumed to be essential for the production of output.

A. THE HOUSEHOLD OPTIMIZING PROCESS

Assume that the head of each household selects $c_1(t)$, $c_2(t + 1)$, and $m(t)$, which will maximize his lifetime utility, subject to the constraint that he not die owing any debts. As long as he derives positive marginal utility from $c_1(t)$ or $c_2(t + 1)$, he will not die leaving any estate. Therefore, he will plan to consume the entire value of his assets during his retirement period.

Let his utility function be described by equation 13; and, for the sake of simplicity, assume that everyone has the same utility function.

(13) $u = U[c_1(t), c_2(t + 1), m(t)]$.

Utility is derived from consumption during youth $c_1(t)$, consumption during the retirement period $c_2(t + 1)$, and (following Johnson and Sidrauski) from the possession of real balances $m(t)$.

It is desirable to use a specific form of the utility function in order to derive precise results. Assume the U has the form described by equations 13a and 13b.

(13a) $u = \beta_1 \ln c_1(t) + \beta_2 \ln c_2(t + 1) + \varphi[m(t)]$.

(13b) $\varphi[m(t)] = \beta_3 \ln m(t)$,   for $m(t) < \bar{m}$ (a constant)

               $= \beta_3 \ln \bar{m}$,   for $m(t) \geqq \bar{m}$,

where $\bar{m}$ is the satiety level. Therefore:

(13c) $\varphi'[m(t)] = \beta_3/m(t)$,   for $m(t) < \bar{m}$;

               $= 0$,   for $m(t) \geqq \bar{m}$.

There is diminishing marginal utility to $c_1(t)$ and $c_2(t + 1)$. There can be no satiation with respect to real consumption, and the marginal utility of a zero level of consumption is infinite. In this way we avoid periods of zero consumption.

There can be satiation with respect to real balances as Figure 1 indicates, based upon equation 13c. When the household obtains $m(t) \geqq \bar{m}$

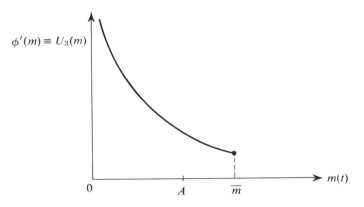

FIGURE 1. The marginal utility of real balances.
Satiation occurs at $m(t) \geqq \bar{m}$.

of real balances, its marginal utility falls directly to zero. No additional leisure or psychic satisfaction is produced by having more real balances.[7]

The ex-ante constraint facing the household is that $c_2(t + 1)$ be equal to the value of its assets during the retirement period. During his youth the head of the household receives $w(t) + g(t)$ of real receipts. He consumes $c_1(t)$ and acquires $m(t)$ of real balances. Part of these real balances comes from the transfer from the government, and the remainder is purchased from the older generation. Therefore:

$$w(t) + g(t) - c_1(t) - m(t) = K(t + 1)/L(t)$$

consists of savings in the form of real capital. During period $(t + 1)$ the person expects to consume this capital plus the expected rent $r^*(t + 1)K(t + 1)/L(t)$, where $r^*(t + 1)$ is the expected rent per unit of capital. He expects his real balances to be $M(t)/p^*(t + 1)$ in period

---

[7] I would think that satiety would not occur if the value of $m(t)$ were less than the real wage. The latter represents a certain level of transactions. As long as $m(t)$ is less than $w(t)$, real capital will have to be exchanged for consumer goods. Additional leisure could be gained if consumer goods were purchased directly for money, without the necessity of selling real capital. Therefore, I would expect $U_3(m) \equiv \varphi'(m)$ to be positive for $m \leqq w$. But this is not an important assumption for what follows.

The marginal utility cannot be negative since it is no more troublesome to hold a large bank balance (or bill) than a small one.

I have not examined the sensitivity of the model to the specific form of the utility function used.

$(t + 1)$. The expected price level in $t + 1$ is $p^*(t + 1)$, and $\pi^*(t + 1)$ is the expected rate of price change. Consequently, he expects his real balances during retirement to be $m(t)/(1 + \pi_{t+1}^*)$.

Equation 14 describes the ex-ante constraint faced by the head of the household.

(14) $[w(t) + g(t) - c_1(t) - m(t)]$

$$\times \ [1 + r^*(t + 1)] + \frac{m(t)}{1 + \pi^*(t + 1)} = c_2(t + 1).$$

Maximize Lagrangian expression (15) with respect to $c_1(t)$, $c_2(t + 1)$, and $m(t)$ to obtain equations 15a, 15b, and 15c. Unless it is absolutely necessary, the time subscripts will not be used.

(15) $H = \beta_1 \ln c_1(t) + \beta_2 \ln c_2(t + 1) + \varphi(m_t)$

$$+ \lambda \Big\{ [w(t) + g(t) - c_1(t) - m(t)](1 + r_{t+1}^*)$$

$$+ \frac{m(t)}{1 + \pi_{t+1}^*} - c_2(t + 1) \Big\}.$$

(15a) $U_1 = \beta_1/c_1 = \lambda(1 + r^*)$.

(15b) $U_2 = \beta_2/c_2 = \lambda$.

(15c) $U_3 = \beta_3/m = \lambda \left[(1 + r^*) - \dfrac{1}{(1+\pi^*)} \right]$, for $m(t) < \bar{m}$;

$U_3 = 0$, for $m(t) \geq \bar{m}$.

The economics of these equations is clear and important. By fore-going a unit of consumption $c_1(t)$, the individual loses the marginal utility $U_1 = \beta_1/c_1(t)$. If he saves in the form of real capital, he will obtain $1 + r^*(t + 1)$ of goods during his retirement. The marginal utility of consumption during retirement is $U_2 = \beta_2/c_2(t + 1)$. Therefore, he gains $U_2(1 + r_{t+1}^*)$ of utility against a loss of U_1. In equilibrium with a positive stock of capital, equation 16a must be satisfied. Given utility function (13), an interior maximum (with respect to consumption) will exist.

(16a) $-u_1 + (1 + r_{t+1}^*)u_2 = 0$.

Savings may be either in the form of real capital or in the form of real balances. With utility function (13), there will be consumption during both periods of life; and there must be savings to finance $c_2(t + 1)$. The question is: In what form will they be held?

The savings in the form of capital increase utility by $U_2(1 + r^*_{t+1})$, that is, the utility derived from the consumption of the capital and real rents during period $t + 1$. Savings in the form of real balances yield utility in both period t and period $t + 1$. During period t they yield a marginal utility U_3, which reflects (say) the leisure gained by having more real balances to finance transactions. Unless $m(t) \geq \bar{m}$, the value of U_3 is positive. In addition these balances are expected to command $1/(1 + \pi^*_{t+1})$ of goods during retirement. Therefore, the increment of utility expected to be derived during $t + 1$ from the consumption of these savings is $U_2/(1 + \pi^*_{t+1})$.

Both stores of value will be held only if equation 16b is satisfied. The left-hand side is the utility yield derived from real balances, and the right-hand side is the utility yield derived from real capital.

(16b) $$\frac{U_2}{1 + \pi^*_{t+1}} + U_3 = (1 + r^*_{t+1})U_2.$$

Define the nominal rate of interest $\rho(t)$ as the money yield to be derived from holding capital: the rent plus (minus) the expected capital gain (loss), equation 17.

(17) $$\rho(t) \equiv (1 + r^*_{t+1})(1 + \pi^*_{t+1}) - 1.$$

A dollar of capital in period t will allow the owner to purchase $1 + \rho(t)$ dollars of goods in period $t + 1$. For this reason $\rho(t)$ is called the nominal rate of interest. Using equation 17 in (16b) and rearranging terms, we can write the equilibrium condition 16b as equation 18 when both stores of value are held.

(18) $$U_3 = \frac{\rho(t)}{1 + \pi^*_{t+1}} U_2.$$

The denominator cannot be zero since it is just the ratio of the expected price $p^*(t + 1)$ to the current price $p(t)$, and a zero price level is excluded. Why? Let $M(t)$ be positive. At a zero price level $M(t)/p(t)$ would be infinite. However, the younger generation cannot purchase an infinite quantity of real balances from the older generation in exchange for a finite quantity of output. Therefore, only a positive price level need be considered.

From equation 18 we may conclude that, as long as $m(t) < \bar{m}$ such that $U_3 > 0$, capital will only be held if the nominal rate of interest ρ is positive. Otherwise, all savings will be held in the form of real balances.

If the nominal rate of interest were zero, then the workers would wish to hold the satiety level of real balances ($\bar{m}$) such that $U_3 = 0$. However, that may be impossible if $\bar{m}/(1 + \mu)$ exceeds the real wage $w(t)$. Therefore, it may be impossible for a zero nominal rate of interest to be established in the market.

Interesting conclusions emerge if we make specific assumptions concerning the formation of price expectations $\pi^*(t + 1)$. Many different reasonable expectation functions may be used. Some people assume that expectations are self-realizing such that $\pi^*(t + 1)$ is equal to the rate that actually prevails. Others use the adaptive expectations function:

$$\pi^*(t + 1) - \pi^*(t) = \gamma[\pi(t) - \pi^*(t)], \quad \gamma > 0,$$

where $\pi(t)$ is the actual proportionate rate of price change. Still another function is:

$$\pi^*(t + 1) = g[\pi(t)], \quad g' > 0,$$

which includes the myopic expectations function $\pi^*(t + 1) = \pi(t)$ as a special case. Each function has different properties, and some may imply that the economy is unstable.

I have selected a simple price expectations function which is consistent with the equilibrium solution of the model. It is based upon the assumption that people form their expectations on the basis of historical experience. The expected rate of price change is equal to the equilibrium rate of price change given the current values of the exogenous and policy variables.

In the steady state, real balances per worker $m(t)$ are constant. This means that the equilibrium rate of price change π_e is described by equation 19. It is equal to the growth of the money supply per worker.

(19) $1 + \pi_e = (1 + \mu)/(1 + n).$

Assume that the expected rate of price change $\pi^*(t + 1)$ is equal to the equilibrium rate of price change π_e, based upon the current values of μ and n. Equation 20 will be consistent with the actual rate of price change that prevails in the steady state.

(20) $1 + \pi^*(t + 1) = (1 + \mu)/(1 + n).$

Using price expectations function (20) in the equation for the nominal rate of interest, equation 21 is derived.

(21) $$\rho(t) = \frac{(1 + r^*_{t+1})(1 + \mu)}{(1 + n)} - 1.$$

From utility maximization equations 15, 15a, 15b, and 15c, equation 21, and budget constraint (14), the desired levels of $c_1(t)$, $c_2(t + 1)$, and $m(t) < \bar{m}$ can be determined. These demand functions of the household are stated in equations 22a, 22b, and 22c.

(22a) $$c_1(t) = b_1[w(t) + g(t)].$$

(22b) $$c_2(t + 1) = b_2(1 + r^*_{t+1})[w(t) + g(t)].$$

(22c) $$m(t) = b_3 \frac{(1 + \rho_t)}{\rho_t} [w(t) + g(t)],$$

where $b_i \equiv \beta_i/(\beta_1 + \beta_2 + \beta_3)$ is a positive fraction. If $m(t) \geqq \bar{m}$, then $U_3 = 0$, that is, satiety has been reached. Positive quantities will be held of real capital and real balances when $U_3 = 0$ only if the nominal rate of interest is nonnegative. If the interest rate turned negative, then no one would want to hold real capital. This is a well-known result (Samuelson, 1958).

It is reasonable to define $w(t) + g(t)$, the left-hand side of Table 3, as real disposable income per worker. Then equation 23a, based upon (22a), states that savings per worker $s_1(t)$ is a constant fraction $(1 - b_1)$ of real disposable income per worker.

(23a) $$s_1(t) \equiv w(t) + g(t) - c_1(t) = (1 - b_1)[w(t) + g(t)].$$

This savings function is not the same as real capital formation per worker since it includes savings in the form of real balances. Equation 23a was derived from a consistent utility maximization model and differs fundamentally from the view expressed by Johnson (1969) that a proportional saving function is inconsistent with utility maximization. The usual Neoclassical savings function can be derived from a consistent theory of rational behavior.

From equations 22c and 23a, a relation between savings per worker $s_1(t)$ and the quantity of real balances demanded per worker $m(t)$ can be derived.

(23b) $$m(t) = \frac{b_3}{1 - b_1}(1 + 1/\rho_t)s_1(t).$$

Given the nominal rate of interest $\rho(t)$, the quantity of real balances demanded per worker is proportional to savings per worker. However, given $s_1(t)$, the quantity of real balances demanded per worker is negatively related to the nominal rate of interest. Alternatively, from (22c), given real disposable income the quantity demanded of real balances per worker is negatively related to the nominal rate of interest. The conventional Neoclassical model (Tobin, 1965) did not make assumptions inconsistent with utility maximization.

Real transfers per worker $g(t)$ are seen (in Table 3) to be a multiple of real balances per worker $m(t)$ since the money supply has been assumed to change as a result of transfers to the younger generation. Recall that:

$$g(t) = \frac{M(t) - M(t-1)}{p(t)L(t)} = \frac{\mu m(t)}{1 + \mu}.$$

Substitute the above expression into equation 22c, which describes the quantity of real balances per worker demanded, and derive equation 24. It is the condition whereby the quantity of real balances in existence is equal to the quantity demanded. It is assumed that $m(t) < \bar{m}$, where $\bar{m}$ is the satiety level.

$$(24) \qquad m(t) = \frac{b_3 w(t)(1 + 1/\rho_t)}{1 - \frac{b_3 \mu}{1 + \mu}(1 + 1/\rho_t)} = M[k(t); \mu, n].$$

According to equation 12b, the real wage per worker $w(t)$ is a function of $k(t)$. The nominal rate of interest $\rho(t)$, defined by equation 17, depends upon $r^*(t + 1)$ and $\pi^*(t + 1)$. Assume that the expected rent per unit of capital is equal to its current value. The latter, according to equation 12c, depends upon the capital intensity $k(t)$. Therefore, $r^*(t + 1) = r(t) = r[k(t)]$. According to equation 20, the value of $\pi^*(t + 1)$ is assumed to be equal to the growth of the money supply per worker. On the basis of these relations the nominal rate of interest:

$$\rho(t) = (1 + r_t)\frac{(1 + \mu)}{(1 + n)} - 1$$

depends upon $k(t)$ and $(1 + \mu)/(1 + n)$.

$$(25) \qquad \rho(t) = \rho[k(t); \mu, n].$$

Using equations 12b and 25 in (24), it is seen that $m(t) = M[k(t); \mu; n]$. The quantity demanded of real balances per worker depends upon the capital intensity $k(t)$, the rate of monetary expansion μ, and the rate of growth of the labor force n.

The supply of, and demand for, real balances per member of the labor force must be equal in the Neoclassical model. There are only two ways in which to save: real capital $K(t + 1)$ and real balances $M(t)/p(t)$. If people are actually saving the desired quantity $K(t + 1) + M(t)/p(t)$ and are holding the desired stock of capital $K(t + 1)$, then they must be holding the desired stock of real balances $M(t)/p(t)$. Therefore, $m(t)$ in equation 24 represents both the quantity demanded and the quantity in existence.

B. THE DYNAMICS OF GROWTH

We can show that equation 11, concerning the capital intensity $k(t + 1)$, can be written as a first-order nonlinear difference equation in k; and equation 26 or 28 results. It is the fundamental dynamic equation in our monetary growth model which will now be discussed.

(26) $\qquad k(t + 1) = F[k(t); \mu, n]$.

From equation 11 we know that $k(t + 1)$ depends upon $w(t)$, $c_1(t)$, and $m(t)$. Equation 12b states that $w(t)$ depends upon $k(t)$. Equation 22a states that $c_1(t)$ depends upon real disposable income per worker $w(t) + g(t)$. Since real transfers per worker $g(t) = \mu m(t)/(1 + \mu)$, we must determine $m(t)$ if we wish to find the value of real disposable income. The previous discussion, summarized by equation 24, indicated that $m(t) = M[k(t); \mu, n]$. It follows that both $c_1(t)$ and $m(t)$ are functions of $k(t)$, μ, and n. That is:

(27a) $\qquad m(t) = M[k(t); \mu, n]$.

(27b) $\qquad c_1(t) = C[k(t); \mu, n]$.

Substituting (27a) and (27b) into (11), we derive:

(28) $\quad (1 + n)k(t + 1) = W[k(t)] - C[k(t); \mu, n] - \dfrac{M[k(t); \mu, n]}{1 + \mu}$,

which is equation 26 above. A complete and consistent monetary growth model has been formulated.

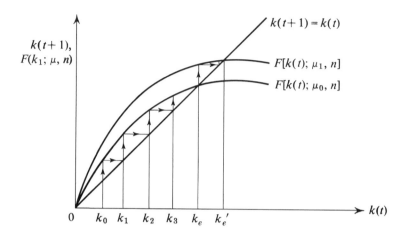

FIGURE 2. The dynamic process for the determination of the capital intensity. A rise in the rate of monetary expansion raises the steady state capital intensity from k_e to k_e' in a model where there is a unique stable equilibrium.

Figure 2 describes equation 26 in a dynamically stable case, where there is a unique stable equilibrium capital intensity k_e. By the equilibrium capital intensity k_e we mean the value of k such that:

(29) $$\infty > k_e = F[k_e; \mu, n] > 0.$$

This equilibrium will be locally stable if the absolute value of $F_1[k_e; \mu, n] < 1$, as Figure 2 indicates.

Function $F[k(t); \mu, n]$ will pass through the origin. If $k(t) = 0$, then there will be no output and nothing to accumulate. At this point the interest rate will be infinite given any positive value of $(1 + \mu)/(1 + n)$ since $r(0)$ is infinite. Capital will be valued very highly by the young savers.

Function $F(\cdot)$ will reach a maximum and fall to zero if the money supply grows at a slower rate than population. Why? The nominal rate of interest $\rho(t)$ is given by equation 25, repeated here.

(25) $$\rho(t) = [1 + r(t)]\frac{(1 + \mu)}{(1 + n)} - 1.$$

As $k(t)$ rises to plus infinity, $r(t)$ declines to zero. Accordingly, the nominal rate of interest would converge to $(\mu - n)/(1 + n)$. If the money supply per worker is not growing, then the nominal rate of interest becomes zero or negative. Real capital will not be held at a negative rate of interest. The yield on real balances would be higher and, if $m(t)$ were less than $\bar{m}$, may also produce a direct utility yield. Under these conditions for sufficiently large values of $k(t)$ or sufficiently low values of $r(t)$, the value of $k(t + 1)$ will not be positive. For these reasons we expect function $F(\cdot)$ to reach a maximum and fall to zero, if $\mu - n \leqq 0$.

Figure 2 may be used to describe the general case, regardless of the value of $\mu - n$, when there is a unique positive stable equilibrium k_e. A dynamic adjustment path $k_0, k_1, k_2, \ldots, k_e$ is described by the arrows. Given $k(t)$, μ, and n, the $F(\cdot)$ function determines $k(t + 1)$. This figure, or equation 26, implies the Neoclassical monetary growth model. When the rate of monetary expansion is μ_0, then the stable equilibrium capital intensity is k_e.

Several conclusions follow immediately:

1. If the money supply is not growing, that is, $1 + \mu \leqq 1$, then the nominal rate of interest (described in 21) will only be nonnegative if $r(k) \geqq n$. People will only choose to hold their wealth in the form of capital if the nominal rate of interest is positive. Under the condition that $\mu \leqq 0$ we know that the economy cannot permanently settle down with a capital intensity in excess of its Golden Rule value.

2. In general (contrary to Cass and Yaari) it is possible for r to be less than n and still have a positive interest rate ρ satisfying (18). A sufficiently high rate of inflation $(1 + \mu)/(1 + n) - 1$ will make capital as attractive as real balances as a store of value. Therefore, ρ can be positive and both stores of value will be held, although $(1 + r)$ is less than $(1 + n)$. The Cass-Yaari conclusion (that the mere existence of money guarantees efficiency) does not hold in this model where the money supply changes as a result of transfers to the younger generation.

III
THE EFFECT OF A RISE IN THE RATE
OF MONETARY EXPANSION

Harry Johnson (1967) criticized the Neoclassical monetary growth model's major conclusion that: a rise in the rate of monetary expansion (μ) will raise the steady state capital intensity (k_e). He argued that, when the utility yield of real balances is explicitly considered, the effects of a rise in μ upon k_e are ambiguous. On the basis of the intergeneration model of rational behavior described above, where real balances yield utility, it can be shown that there is no ambiguity. A rise in the rate of monetary expansion must raise the steady state capital intensity. However, Alvin Marty (1969) and others correctly indicate that a rise in the rate of monetary expansion may have an ambiguous effect upon the steady state capital intensity if output per worker is affected by real balances per worker, as well as by the capital intensity. Inflation may adversely affect the use of money as a medium of exchange; and the inefficiencies of a barter economy may reduce the productive capacity of the economy. In this chapter we ignore this important point and continue to focus upon real balances as an argument in the utility function.

The effect of a rise in μ upon k_e can be described tersely on an intuitive level. A rise in μ raises the expected rate of price change $\pi^*(t + 1)$. Given $k(t)$, the nominal rate of interest $\rho(t)$ rises, and the quantity of real balances demanded per worker declines. According to equation 11 or Tables 1–3, the decline in $m(t)$ means that a smaller amount of output is transferred from the younger generation to the older generation, which will consume it. The decline in the output transferred leaves a larger amount to be accumulated by the younger generation in the form of real capital, whose yield has increased relative to the yield on real balances. The crucial point to remember is that the older generation has absolutely no control over the rate of capital accumulation, as should be clear from the discussion concerning Table 3. The relevant variable is simply the younger generation's desired holdings of real balances.

When the rise in the expected rate of price change decreases the younger generation's desired purchase of real balances, there are two effects. Part of the reduction in the real transfer to the older generation will be reflected in a rise in the real consumption of the younger generation $C_1(t)$, and part of it will be used to increase $K(t + 1)$, the savings of the younger generation in the form of real capital. In this manner a rise in the rate of monetary expansion will shift the $F(\cdot)$ curve upward and lead to a rise in the steady state capital intensity. A mathematical analysis will now be given to justify this intuitive explanation. Contrary to Johnson, the Neoclassical monetary growth model is consistent with a theory of rational behavior.

What happens to the $F[k(t); \mu, n]$ function in Figure 2 as a result of a rise in the rate of monetary expansion? That is, using equation 11, what is:

$$(30) \qquad (1 + n)\frac{\partial k\,(t + 1)}{\partial \mu}\bigg|_{k(t) > 0} = -\frac{\partial c_1\,(t)}{\partial \mu} - \frac{\partial}{\partial \mu}\frac{m(t)}{1 + \mu}\,?$$

If it is positive, then the $F(\cdot)$ schedule in Figure 2 rises for positive values of $k(t)$; if it is negative, then the schedule declines for positive values of $k(t)$. It will be proved that the former occurs, and the dynamically stable equilibrium rises from k_e to k_e': the conventional Neoclassical result.

The demand for real balances per worker is equal to the stock of real balances per worker. Write, for simplicity of notation:

$$z(t) = \frac{1 + r(t)}{1 + n}.$$

Then, the quantity of real balances per worker $m(t)$ in equation 24 can be simplified as:

$$(31) \qquad m(t) = \frac{b_3 w(t)(1 + \mu)}{1 + \mu - 1/z(t) - b_3\mu}.$$

Using equations 22a and $g(t) = \mu m(t)/(1 + \mu)$, it follows that:

$$(32) \qquad \frac{\partial c_1\,(t)}{\partial \mu}\bigg|_{k(t) > 0} = b_1 \frac{\partial}{\partial \mu}\left[\frac{\mu m(t)}{1 + \mu}\right].$$

Substituting (32) into (30), we derive:

$$(33) \qquad (1 + n)\frac{\partial k\,(t + 1)}{\partial \mu}\bigg|_{k(t) > 0} = -b_1 \frac{\partial}{\partial \mu}\left[\frac{\mu m(t)}{1 + \mu}\right] - \frac{\partial}{\partial \mu}\left[\frac{m(t)}{1 + \mu}\right].$$

From equation 31 we derive:

$$(34) \qquad \frac{\partial}{\partial \mu}\frac{m(t)}{1 + \mu} = -\frac{b_3 w(1 - b_3)}{[1 + \mu - 1/z - b_3\mu]^2} < 0,$$

when the denominator is not zero. Substitute (34) into (33) and derive:

$$(35) \qquad (1 + n)\frac{\partial k\,(t + 1)}{\partial \mu}\bigg|_{k(t) > 0} = \frac{b_3 w[1 - b_1 - b_3 + b_1/z]}{[1 + \mu - 1/z - b_3\mu]^2} > 0.$$

This proves that the $F(\cdot)$ curve in Figure 2 rises as a result of a rise in the rate of monetary expansion. The younger generation transfers a smaller amount of its output to the older generation in exchange for money. Parts of this amount is consumed by the younger generation and part of it goes into the accumulation of capital. Therefore, the capital intensity rises from k_e to k_e' along the path described by the arrows in Figure 2. There is no ambiguity whatsoever about the effect of a rise in the rate of monetary expansion upon the steady state capital intensity in a dynamically stable system. This system has been constructed from a model of rational behavior where real balances yield utility. As long as the money supply does not rise, we can be sure that the equilibrium capital intensity will not exceed its Golden Rule value. By raising the rate of monetary expansion we can bring r down to the growth rate. Therefore, monetary policy can succeed in bringing the economy to the Golden Rule capital intensity. It may be impossible to satiate the economy with real balances, regardless of the number of instruments used. If the satiety level $\bar{m}$ is at least as great as the real wage, then the younger generation cannot purchase these real balances from the older generation and still consume.

🮑🮑🮑

CHAPTER THREE

The Keynes-Wicksell Model:
Behavioral Equations
and Conclusions

THE LONG RUN is the limit of a succession of short runs; and the connecting link between the short runs is the endogenous change in the capital stock resulting from the investment process. Dynamic short-run aggregative models generally assume (a) the existence of independent saving and investment functions and (b) that prices are changing if, and only if, there is market disequilibrium. By contrast, the Neoclassical monetary growth model assumes that planned investment is identically equal to planned savings and that all markets are always in equilibrium. What connection exists between these two sets of models? What unifying theory can be constructed which would be applicable to the short run as well as to the long-run aggregative economy? The subject of this chapter and the next is an analysis of the Keynes-Wicksell monetary growth model, which is designed to integrate the dynamic short-run aggregative model into the growth process.[1]

[1] A Keynes-Wicksell approach, characterized by assumptions (a) and (b) above was taken independently in 1966 by Rose and Stein and is similar to early work by Hahn (1960, 1961). This method has been developed in subsequent papers by Rose (1969), Stein ("Neoclassical and Keynes-Wicksell Monetary Growth Models," *Journal of Money, Credit and Banking*, May, 1969), Nagatani (1969), and Tsiang (1969). As a result of his criticisms of the Neoclassical model, Hahn (1969) also seems to lean in a Keynes-Wicksell direction. Cagan (May, 1969) implicitly thinks along these lines in the short run but not in the long run.

My aim has been to formulate a general dynamic macro-economic model which contains money in an essential way, regardless of whether it is inside or outside money. If the inputs of labor and capital were arbitrarily fixed, then it would look like a dynamic version of Don Patinkin's (1965) well-known short-run aggregative model. Alternatively this growth model would be the generalization of post-Keynesian dynamic macro-economics to a growing economy: where the input of capital is endogenously determined and growing over time. Long-run equilibrium is nothing other than the steady state solution of the short-run dynamic model with endogenous capital. Or, the short-run dynamic model is a special case of the general growth model. It has been used both in a full employment context and in the case of unemployment.[2]

This chapter is concerned with the assumptions and long-run conclusions of the Keynes-Wicksell model. A heuristic explanation of the results is presented; and the crucial assumptions, which distinguish it from the Neoclassical model, are identified. Technique is reserved for Chapter 4: wherein the dynamic operation of the Keynes-Wicksell model, in both the short run and the long run, is developed. Chapter 3 describes "the forest," and Chapter 4 contains the rigorous development of the general macro-economical model.

I

THE BEHAVIORAL EQUATIONS

How can the short-run aggregative model be generalized to a growing economy? A very brief review of the well-known Patinkin short-run aggregative model (1965, pp. 260–61) will set the stage for the development of the Keynes-Wicksell monetary growth model.

There are four basic equations in Patinkin's short-run dynamic model. First, full employment of labor and capital is always assumed to prevail where full employment must be defined in terms of given rates of input utilization. An aggregate production function relates the full employment inputs of labor and capital to capacity output Y_0; and capacity output is a synonym for full employment output at given rates of input

[2] See Nagatani (1969), Rose (Sept., 1966, and May, 1969), and Stein (1966, and "Neoclassical and Keynes-Wicksell Monetary Growth Models," *Journal of Money, Credit and Banking*, May, 1969).

utilization. Therefore, the available inputs of labor and capital determine capacity output.

Second, he assumed that the rate of price change is proportional to the excess demand for goods where the latter is equal to aggregate demand $F(\cdot)$ less capacity output Y_0. Aggregate demand is planned consumption plus planned investment plus government purchases of goods, in real terms. This sum is a function of three variables: capacity output, the rate of interest r, and real balances M_0/p. His equation for the rate of change of prices is:

(1) $$Dp = k_1[F(Y_0, r, M_0/p) - Y_0],$$

where $F(\cdot)$ is real aggregate demand, Y_0 is capacity output, M_0 is the exogenous money supply, r is the nominal rate of interest, and p is the price level.

Underlying most of his analysis are two assumptions: (i) the price of each good is expected with certainty to be the same in the future as it is in the present, and (ii) the money stock is exclusively a liability of the government.[3] There is: (a) no distinction between the real and the nominal interest rate since no price changes are anticipated, and (b) no inside money as a rule. The stock of money is an exogenous variable denoted by M_0.

Third, the interest rate changes as a result of an excess demand for, or excess supply of, bonds. The excess demand for bonds is a function of three variables: capacity output, the rate of interest, and real balances. He writes:

(2) $$Dr = -k_2 B(Y_0, 1/r, M_0/p),$$

where $B(\cdot)$ is the real excess demand for bonds.

Fourth, there is an identity or budget restraint, which states that the excess supply of real balances in a fully employed economy is equal to the excess demand for goods plus the excess demand for real bonds. Patinkin's equation is:

(3) $$[F(\cdot) - Y_0] + B(\cdot) \equiv M_0/p - L(Y_0, r, M_0/p),$$

where $L(\cdot)$ is the real demand for cash balances.

[3] This assumption is relaxed (Patinkin, 1965, pp. 295–310).

These four independent equations are used to determine: (i) capacity output, (ii) the rate of interest, (iii) real balances or, since the money supply is given, the absolute price level, and (iv) the quantity demanded of real balances. Using Lloyd Metzler's phase diagrams, the convergence of the system to equilibrium and the comparative statics of the system are examined. The steady state of the short-run dynamic system implies that the price level is constant, the bond market is in equilibrium, and the quantity demanded of real balances is equal to the quantity in existence. We shall work with the dynamic system and not be confined to the equilibrium solution. Let us now generalize the Patinkin model to a growing economy.

A. THE DYNAMICS OF PRICE CHANGE

The fundamental assumption which distinguishes between the Neo-classical and the Keynes-Wicksell model concerns the determinants of price change in continuous time. In the Keynes-Wicksell model, as in the dynamic version of the Patinkin model, prices are changing if, and only if, the aggregate demand for goods differs from capacity output. Excess aggregate demand is planned (real) consumption C plus planned (real) investment I less output Y. Assume that the government does not purchase goods. Since planned savings are $Y - C$, excess aggregate demand $C + I - Y \equiv I - S$. The proportionate rate of price change $\pi \equiv D \ln p$ is assumed to be a linear function of excess demand deflated by the stock of capital. A given real excess demand for goods will lead to a more rapid rate of inflation in a small economy (e.g., the United States in 1879) than in a large economy (for example, the United States in 1969). Therefore, in a growing economy the excess demand for goods per se is not a good index of inflationary pressure. For convenience we have deflated the (real) excess demand by the stock of capital. No essential difference would occur if we deflated $I - S$ by the size of the effective labor force.

The price change equation is:

(4) $$\pi = D \ln p = \lambda(I/K - S/K),$$

where λ is the speed of market adjustment and is assumed to be positive and finite. During periods of price change, planned savings and investment are not equal!

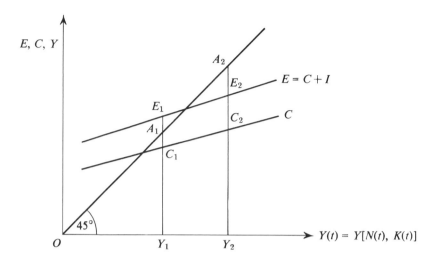

FIGURE 1. Sources of price change.

Figure 1 illustrates the difference in approach between the Neo-classical and Keynes-Wicksell models. Planned real consumption is C and planned real investment is I. Their sum is real aggregate demand E. Output $Y(t)$, in a full employment model is given by the production function and the available supplies of labor $N(t)$ and capital $K(t)$ such that $Y(t) = Y[N(t), K(t)]$.

Keynes-Wicksell models make the dynamic Walrasian assumption that, in purely competitive markets, prices are changing if, and only if, the markets are not in equilibrium. During inflationary periods the economy is at a point like Y_1, where Y_1 is the capacity output at a given time. Aggregate demand is $E_1 = C_1 + I_1$ and exceeds capacity output by A_1E_1. According to equation (4), the resulting rate of price change would be $\pi_1 = \lambda(A_1E_1)/K_1$ since it would be proportional to excess aggregate demand per unit of capital.

During deflationary periods aggregate demand is less than capacity output. The economy would be at a point like Y_2, where $Y_2 = Y[N_2, K_2]$ is capacity output at the given time. A deflationary gap A_2E_2 exists. As a result there is a rate of deflation equal to $\pi_2 = \lambda(A_2E_2)/K_2$ as producers seek to reduce the rate of growth of inventories of capital. Coefficient λ in equation 4 is the speed of adjustment. In the usual dynamic short-run models λ is assumed to be finite: for example, see equation 1 above (where k_1 is finite). A positive amount of time is required to equilibrate the market as a result of a disturbance. If λ were infinite, then equilibrium would be obtained immediately. This possibility of an infinite λ is excluded in the Keynes-Wicksell model, but λ may be very large.

Instantaneous equilibrium in all markets at all times is implied by the Neoclassical model. As the excess demand curves shift, the equilibrium prices change immediately. During an inflationary process everyone is always holding his desired stocks, and there is no excess demand for goods. Prices always rise instantly by the amount required to clear all markets. No sooner is the market cleared than the excess demand curve rises again; and a new and higher equilibrium price is established immediately. Stability in the Neoclassical model requires that price expectations change sluggishly:[4] for example, a sufficiently low adaptive expectations coefficient must be assumed.

Price change equation 4 is not necessarily implied by a competitive model.[5] It is possible that markets are organized by specialists who set prices on the basis of both the current state of excess demand $(I - S)/K$ and the specialists' expectations of the future state of excess demand. For example, the rate of price change set by the specialists may be described by equation 4a:

(4a) $\pi = \pi^* + \lambda(I/K - S/K).$

If there were market equilibrium at the present moment, then $I = S$; and I is certainly affected by the expected rate of price change, equation 9 below. Specialists anticipating a rate of price change π^* would mark prices up at this rate, even though there is no market disequilibrium at the present moment. On the other hand, even if specialists do not antici-pate price changes $(\pi^* = 0)$, they will mark prices up or down, depend-ing on whether there is excess demand or supply at present. There are two influences which directly affect the rate of price change in equation 4a. If equation 4a were used instead of equation 4, then the resulting model would be a synthesis of the Neoclassical and the Keynes-Wicksell model. Such a synthesis will be discussed in Chapter 5 below. At present we

[4] See Chapter 1, Section IE.
[5] I am indebted to Jürg Niehans for suggesting this approach.

shall use price change equation 4 in the development of the Keynes-Wicksell model.

B. PRODUCTION CONDITIONS

The same production conditions are assumed to prevail here as were assumed in the Neoclassical model. There is an aggregative production function in a single good economy subject to constant returns to scale, diminishing returns to substitution, and Harrod neutral-technical progress. Capacity output Y is a function of a given rate u^* of utilization of effective labor N and the stock of capital $Y(N, K)$ where Y is strictly concave. Suppose that the output of goods produced is a function of capacity output $Y(N, K)$ and the ratio of actual to capacity output $\varphi(u)$, where u is the rate of capacity utilization. It is assumed that φ is positively sloped ($\varphi' > 0$) and has an upper (as well as a lower) bound. Capacity, or full employment output, is defined as the output associated with a given rate u^* of input utilization such that $\varphi(u^*) \equiv 1$. It is consistent with the current usage of the term full employment.

(5) $$Y = Y(N, K)\varphi(u).$$

It is convenient to write the production function in intensive form (5a). Output per unit of capital $Y/K \equiv y$ depends upon the ratio of effective labor per unit of capital $N/K \equiv x$ and the rate of utilization.

(5a) $$y = y(x)\varphi(u).$$

Within the framework of a competitive economy the real wage of a unit of effective labor is equal to the marginal product of effective labor. Similarly, the rent per unit of capital is the marginal product of capital. If w is the real wage per unit of effective labor:

(6) $$w = y'(x)\varphi(u), \qquad y'' < 0.$$

If r is the rent per unit of capital:

(7) $$r = [y(x) - xy'(x)]\varphi(u) = r(x), \qquad r' > 0.$$

At any time the quantities of effective labor N and capital K are given. The rate of utilization u may either be fixed at the full employment level u^* such that $\varphi(u^*) = 1$, or we may consider a variant of the Keynes-Wicksell model which treats the rate of utilization as an endogenous variable subject to the constraint that $\varphi(u)$ lies within well-defined limits. Unless otherwise specified, we shall consider the full employment case. An endogenous rate of utilization is discussed later.

Given the full-employment rate of utilization u^*, output per unit of capital, the real wage of a unit of effective labor, and the rent per unit of capital are then determined by (5a), (6), and (7). Recall that $\varphi(u^*) \equiv 1$.

Effective labor is the product of the natural labor force N_1 and an index of technology A.

(8a) $N = AN_1.$

It is assumed that effective labor grows exogenously at proportionate rate n.

(8b) $DN/N = n;$

and the real wage adjusts instantly to absorb the existing quantity of effective labor at the full employment rate of utilization. At any time both u^* and $x(t) \equiv N(t)/K(t)$ are given. Thereby, output per unit of capital $y(x)$, the real wage $y'(x)$ and the rent per unit of capital are determined.

C. THE INVESTMENT FUNCTION

Firms are assumed to desire a ratio of capital to (effective) labor such that the expected yield on capital is equal to its opportunity cost. They are assumed to raise (lower) the existing ratio of capital to labor insofar as the expected yield on capital exceeds (is lower than) the opportunity cost of investment. When the expected yield is equal to the opportunity cost, then firms desire to maintain the ratio of capital to labor constant. Insofar as (effective) labor is growing at rate n, the desired rate of growth of capital would then be equal to the growth of effective labor.

The expected yield on capital is the sum of the expected rent per unit of capital and the expected rate of price change. The expected rent is assumed (for simplicity) to be equal to the current marginal product of capital $r(x)$. Denote the expected rate of price change by π^*. Firms anticipate a yield of $r(x) + \pi^*$ from the acquisition of an additional unit of capital.

The opportunity cost of acquiring additional capital is the nominal rate of interest on bonds, denoted by ρ. Even if the firm does not finance investment through borrowing, it could repay outstanding debt or lend funds in the market instead of accumulating capital. We assume that the desired rate of growth of the ratio of capital to labor is positively related to $r(x) + \pi^* - \rho$.

Assume that the desired rate of investment does not proceed at such a pace as to bring the marginal product of capital $r(x)$ and the real rate of interest (defined as) $\rho - \pi^*$ into equality immediately. An inside and an outside lag exist in the investment process. Time is required until the difference $r(x) - (\rho - \pi^*)$ is converted into a decision to alter the capital-labor ratio; and more time must elapse until the decision to invest is met by the receipt of the ordered capital goods. When $r(x) = \rho - \pi^*$, then firms desire to maintain the ratio of capital to labor constant. Desired capital would grow at the same rate as effective labor. Hence, we may write the desired rate of investment per unit of capital I/K as:

$$(9) \qquad I/K = n + r(x) + \pi^* - \rho,$$

where the implicit speed of response is defined as unity.[6] We could just as easily write $I/K = I(x, \pi^*, \rho; n)$, but we will use the more explicit formulation above.

This is a standard investment-demand schedule. Desired investment (per unit of capital) is positively related to: the (expected) rent per unit of capital[7] and the expected capital gain and is negatively related to the nominal rate of interest.

There is another way of viewing investment equation 9. The market value of an existing unit of capital is equal to the present value of its expected rents. Call this the capital value of the asset. Anyone wishing to acquire a unit of capital can either purchase an existing asset or demand a newly produced unit of output. If the capital value (that is, market price) of an existing unit of capital exceeds the price of a newly produced unit of capital (that is, a unit of output), then investors will demand newly produced output. On the other hand, if the capital value of an existing asset is less than the price of a newly produced unit of output, then investors will prefer used capital goods to newly produced capital goods.

The demand for newly produced goods to be used as capital depends

---

[6] Speed of response λ in equation 4 is, therefore, measured as a multiple of the implicit speed of response in equation 9.

[7] Since $y(x)$ is positively related to $r(x)$, one could say that I/K depends upon $y(x)$, π^*, ρ, and n.

upon the relation between the capital value of existing assets and the supply price, that is, the price of a newly produced unit of output.[8] The ratio of the capital value to supply price is described by equation 9a, where $R(\tau)$ is the expected marginal physical product of the unit of capital, $P^*(\tau)$ is the expected price of output, $P(0)$ is the supply (current) price of output, and ρ is the expected constant nominal rate of interest.

(9a) $$\frac{\text{capital value}}{\text{supply price}} = \int_0^\infty R(\tau) \frac{P^*(\tau)}{P(0)} e^{-\rho\tau} \, d\tau.$$

Assume that prices are expected to change at proportionate rate π^* such that $P^*(\tau) = P(0)e^{\pi^*\tau}$; and that, during the finite life of the investment, the marginal physical product $R(\tau)$ is equal to r. Therefore, 9a can be written as 9b.

(9b) $$\frac{\text{capital value}}{\text{supply price}} = r \int_0^\infty e^{-(\rho-\pi^*)\tau} \, d\tau = \frac{r}{\rho - \pi^*},$$

when the integral exists.[9] The capital value will exceed the supply price when r exceeds $\rho - \pi^*$, that is, when $r + \pi^*$ exceed ρ. If we assume that the demand for newly produced capital (i.e., investment) is positively related to the difference between the capital value of existing assets and the supply price of newly produced goods, then I/K is positively related to $r + \pi^* - \rho$.

If the capital value of an existing asset is equal to its supply price, then people should be indifferent between purchasing an existing asset or a newly produced unit of output. Suppose that effective labor were growing at proportionate rate n and firms expect demand to grow at this rate in the long run. Then they would demand both new and used equipment to keep pace with the expected growth in demand. Since the proportions of new and used capital demanded are constant when $r = \rho - \pi^*$, the growth of each type of capital would proceed at proportionate rate n. In this way, equation 9 is derived.

D. THE SAVINGS FUNCTION

Define (planned) savings as output less planned consumption. It is the distance between the 45-degree line and the consumption function

---

[8] This is the way Keynes (1930, 1936) and Tobin (Feb., 1969, pp. 15–29) look at the investment process.

[9] This ratio is precisely equal to Tobin's q in (February, 1969, pp. 19–21).

in Figure 1. Savings are not the planned change in private net worth or wealth since they exclude the desired increment of real net claims of the private sector upon the public sector. Aggregate private wealth (in a pure outside money economy with no government bonds) is $M/p + K$. The actual change in real private wealth is $DK + D(M/p)$, which differs from actual savings DK. Moreover, as Keynes taught us, planned savings are not identically equal to planned investment I desired by business firms. The Neoclassical model, on the other hand, assumes that planned investment is identically equal to planned savings.

Let us continue to use the same general consumption function as was used in most of Chapter 1. Assume that planned consumption is a function, homogeneous of degree one, in output and private wealth. The latter consists of capital K and real net claims of the private sector V_1. The components of V_1 are outside[10] money and the *net* interest bearing claims of the private sector on the public sector. If the public discounts completely the value of its government bonds in view of its expected tax liabilities, then V_1 would merely be the real value of outside money. Such an extreme assumption need not be made. It is convenient to define V_1 as a multiple θ of real balances M/p. Then θ represents the ratio of net claims of the private sector upon the public sector per dollar of money.

Using the definition $V_1 \equiv \theta M/p$ and the assumed homogeneity of the consumption function, desired consumption per unit of capital is:

(10) $C/K = C(y(x), \theta v)$,

where $v \equiv M/pK$ is real balances per unit of capital and $y(x)$ is output per unit of capital. Assume that the marginal propensity to consume out of output is a positive fraction $(1 > C_1 > 0)$ and that there is a positive marginal propensity to consume out of financial wealth $(C_2 > 0)$. Consumption function (10) is very similar to the ones used in Chapter 1.

Savings per unit of capital follows immediately: it is output per unit of capital less planned consumption per unit of capital.

(11) $S/K = y(x) - C(y(x), \theta v) = S(x, \theta v)$,

---

[10] In view of the discussion of inside money in Chapter 1, we should define outside money as that component of the total money supply which the public regards as wealth. Insofar as real balances are productive services, the real value of money (or its contribution to wealth) is its ability to produce a net increment to the flow of output. The distinction between liabilities of all of the people and of some of the people would not be relevant.

where $S_1 = y'(x)(1 - C_1) > 0$ and $S_2 = -C_2 < 0$. The conventional result is obtained: savings are positively related to output and negatively related to real private financial wealth. Very little is lost by assuming that savings are interest inelastic; and there is a substantial gain in simplicity.

Real aggregate demand per unit of capital is the sum of equations 10 and 9:

$$n + r(x) + \pi^* - \rho + C(y(x), \theta v).$$

It is a generalization of Patinkin's $F(Y_0, r, M_0/p)$ to a growing economy.

E. THE RATE OF CAPITAL FORMATION

During inflationary periods the demand for output $C + I$ exceeds the capacity of a fully employed economy $Y = Y(N, K)$, where N and K are the currently available input quantities and the rate of utilization u^* of K and N is constant.[11] Consider Figure 1 above. When output is $Y_1 = Y(N_1, K_1)$, then planned consumption C_1 plus planned investment $E_1 - C_1$ exceeds capacity output. Households plan to save $A_1 - C_1$, but firms would like to use $E_1 - C_1 > A_1 - C_1$ of output for investment. Since $C + I - Y = I - (Y - C) = I - S$ is positive, the question arises: How much output will actually be allocated for consumption and how much will be allocated for investment? Clearly both consumers and firms cannot be satisfied simultaneously during periods of excess aggregate demand. Will the actual rate of capital formation be equal to $C_1 A_1 = Y_1 - C_1$ planned savings, that is, output less planned consumption? Or will the actual rate of capital formation be equal to planned investment $C_1 E_1$? We assume that the actual rate of capital formation DK during periods of excess aggregate demand will be less than firms desire (I) but more than consumers plan to save (S). Neither investment plans nor consumption plans are fully realized in periods of excess aggregate demand. Everyone is partially frustrated. The actual rate of growth of capital DK will be such that $I > DK > S$. Specifically, assume that the actual rate of growth of capital DK will be a linear combination of planned savings and planned investment: equation 12.

(12) $DK/K = aI/K + (1 - a)S/K.$

Coefficient a is institutionally determined such that $1 > a > 0$ during

---

[11] A different situation exists when the rate of capacity utilization is endogenous. See section IIC of this chapter.

periods of excess aggregate demand. Even if there were perfect foresight that $C + I$ would exceed Y, not everyone could be satisfied. Which demands are frustrated and which demands are satisfied has to be determined by the institutional structure.

No such problem exists during deflationary periods when there is sufficient output such that consumption plans can be and are fully realized. Such a situation is described by point $Y_2 = Y(N_2, K_2)$ in Figure 1. Consumers are able to consume $Y_2 C_2$. Capital formation is $Y_2 - C_2$, that is, $a = 0$; and there is more capital formation than is desired by firms. Firms find that they have not been operating on their investment demand schedules since $I = C_2 E_2$ differs from $DK = C_2 A_2$ in periods of price change. During deflationary periods the full employment assumption may be questionable. For this reason we shall generally confine our analysis to inflationary periods when the rate of utilization is fixed at the full employment level u^*.

Using equation 4, which states that the rate of price change π is proportional to excess demand per unit of capital, the rate of capital formation is:

$$(13) \qquad DK/K = a\pi/\lambda + S/K; \qquad 1 > a > 0 \quad \text{when} \quad \pi > 0,$$
$$a = 0 \quad \text{when} \quad \pi \quad 0.$$

"Forced savings" per unit of capital, $a\pi/\lambda$, occurs during inflationary periods and reflects the fact that consumers acquire less output than they planned. It is based upon the assumption that if $C + I > Y$, then consumers will find that their actual consumption-output ratio is less than their desired consumption-output ratio. To be sure, firms will find that the actual rate of capital formation is less than the planned rate.

F. THE DEMAND FOR REAL BALANCES

Money in this model is held as a medium of exchange and store of value. If all yields were known with certainty, then money would be held exclusively for transactions purposes. Since the yields on real capital and bonds are stochastic variables, there will also be a precautionary demand for money if people think that it is the safest store of value.[12]

The transactions demand for real balances depends upon planned real expenditures by households and firms: $E = C + I$. Since planned

[12] See Tobin (1958).

consumption is $Y - S$, planned real expenditure is $E = Y + I - S$. Using price change equation 4, the transactions demand for real balances per unit of capital is closely related to planned real expenditures per unit of capital[13] E/K:

$$E/K = y + \frac{I - S}{K} = y + \frac{\pi}{\lambda}.$$

The demand for real balances per unit of capital, both for transactions purposes and as an asset, also depends upon the opportunity costs of holding wealth in the form of money. One alternative to holding wealth in the form of money is to hold bonds. The money rate of interest on bonds ρ is an opportunity cost of holding money. It is assumed that the expected value of the capital gain or loss on bonds is zero, such that ρ is the expected return on bonds. Another alternative to holding wealth in the form of money is the expected return on real capital. There are two components of the yield on real capital: its expected marginal product $r(x)$ and the expected proportionate rate of change of the price level π^*, which is the expected capital gain or loss resulting from inflation or deflation. The quantity demanded of real balances per unit of capital is negatively related to the opportunity costs $r(x) + \pi^*$ and ρ and is positively related to the transactions demand $y(x) + \pi/\lambda$. Finally, let real balances per unit of capital be complementary with real net private financial wealth per unit of capital θv. Then the demand for real balances per unit of capital is:

(14) $L = L[y(x) + \pi/\lambda, r(x) + \pi^*, \rho, \theta v]$,

where $L_1 > 0$, $L_2 < 0$, $L_3 < 0$. Assume that a unit rise in real balances and an equivalent rise in net real claims of the private sector upon the public sector is associated with an excess supply of real balances, $1 > L_4\theta > 0$.

G. PRICE EXPECTATIONS

Price expectations π^* can profoundly affect the stability of any dynamic system. There is a variety of functions that can be used, each of which has a different effect upon the stability of the system.

Three different expectations functions will be used in the course of

---

[13] I am indebted to S. C. Tsiang for this point.

this book. When our concern is exclusively with dynamically stable systems, which are simple to handle analytically, we shall usually use the same price expectations function as was used in the previous chapters. People are assumed to be intelligent insofar as their expectations are assumed to be based upon historical experience and what is occurring at present. In any dynamically stable model the actual rate of price change converges asymptotically to the growth of the money supply per worker. Price expectations should be based upon this knowledge or historical experience. Moreover, the difference between the current rate of price change π and its equilibrium value $\mu - n$ should also be taken into account. A reasonable expectations function would be:

(15a) $\qquad D\pi^* = g(\mu - n - \pi); \qquad g' > 0, g'' < 0.$

As long as π exceeds $\mu - n$, the rate of price change is expected to decline; and as long as π is less than $\mu - n$, the rate of price change is expected to rise. The magnitude of the expected change is related to the deviation between the present magnitude and its equilibrium value.

For simplicity (that is, to save a differential equation), we shall often assume that price expectations are of the simple form (15b). People always expect prices to change at a rate equal to the equilibrium rate of price change, regardless of the difference between π and $\mu - n$. No difference in results occurs through the use of the simpler function insofar as the steady state is concerned.

(15b) $\qquad\qquad\qquad \pi^* = \mu - n.$

Another price expectations function is based upon adaptive expectations, equation 16.

(16) $\qquad\qquad\qquad D\pi^* = b(\pi - \pi^*).$

Expectations are revised in proportion to the previous forecasting error $(\pi - \pi^*)$, where b is the factor of proportionality. The stability of a dynamic system will be affected by the magnitude of the factor of proportionality b. If the expected rate of price change π^* is always equal to the current rate π, regardless of the rate of price change, then b is implicitly infinite. That is:

(16a) $\qquad\qquad \pi^* = \pi - D\pi^*/b = \pi, \quad \text{for all} \quad D\pi^*,$

implies that b is infinite. Unless other frictions (such as λ in equation 4) are introduced into the model, the system would be dynamically unstable. An example of this phenomenon was provided in Chapter 1.

Still another price expectations function is:

(17) $\pi^* = g(\pi), \qquad g' > 0$

(17a) $\pi_e^* = \pi_e.$

The expected rate of price change is positively related to the current rate. In the steady state, however, they must be equal. Subscript e denotes that the variable is at its equilibrium value. When we wish to work with models, which may be dynamically unstable, either price expectations function (16) or (17) will be used.

H. WALRAS' LAW

Walras' law[14] is based upon the budget restraint and relates the excess demands for goods, bonds, and money. Continue to assume that the labor market is always in equilibrium. Table 1 describes the typical family's sources and uses of funds during a period of length τ. It enters the period with $M(t - \tau)$ of money balances and a value of bonds $B(t - \tau)$. In most models the money supply grows as a result of unexpected transfers from the government. Therefore, the transfer from the government is $M(t) - M(t - \tau)$. Let the instantaneous rate of nominal income flow produced per unit of time be Z. Then, during a period of length τ, the nominal income earned by the family is $Z\tau$. The sources of funds available to the family at time t is the sum of items (1)–(4) in the table.[15]

TABLE 1. SOURCES AND USES OF FUNDS

Sources	Uses
1. Income $Z\tau$	5. Expenditures $E\tau$
2. Money $M(t - \tau)$	6. Money $L^*(t)$
3. Bonds $B(t - \tau)$	7. Bonds $B(t)$
4. Transfers $M(t) - M(t - \tau)$	

[14] I have been influenced by Patinkin (1965, pp. 515–23).

[15] The net acquisition of capital goods can be subsumed under item (5) expenditures. Alternatively $K(t - \tau)$ would be a source and $K(t)$ would be a use of funds.

Funds are used in three ways. A quantity of goods is acquired at the end of the period. If the instantaneous rate of nominal purchases is E, then $E\tau$ dollars of goods were acquired during a period whose length is τ. Desired money balances are $L^*(t)$, and desired holdings of bonds are $B(t)$. The budget constraint in nominal terms is equation 18: the nominal excess demand for goods is equal to the nominal excess supply of money and bonds.

(18) $(E - Z)\tau = M(t) - L^*(t) + B(t - \tau) - B(t).$

Deflate the variables by the price level and the stock of capital. Then the real excess demand for goods per unit of capital over the period is identically equal to the real excess supply of real balances per unit of capital

$$\frac{M(t)}{p(t)K(t)} - \frac{L^*(t)}{p(t)K(t)},$$

plus the real excess supply of bonds per unit of capital.

If the period is of length τ, then the flow excess demand for goods per unit of capital $(E - Z)/p(t)K(t)$ is equal to:

(18a) $\dfrac{E - Z}{p(t)K(t)} = \dfrac{1}{\tau}\left[\dfrac{M(t)}{p(t)K(t)} - \dfrac{L^*(t)}{p(t)K(t)}\right] + B_s,$

where B_s is the real excess flow supply of bonds per unit of capital

$$\frac{1}{\tau}\left[\frac{B(t - 1) - B(t)}{p(t)K(t)}\right].$$

For the planning period the flow excess supply of real balances per unit of capital can be written as $h[v - L(\cdot)]$. According to equation 4, the excess demand for goods per unit of capital is π/λ. Solving for the real excess flow supply of bonds per unit of capital, Walras' Law is:

(18b) $B_s = \dfrac{\pi}{\lambda} + h[v - L(\cdot)].$

It is often convenient to assume that the speed of response in the bond market is infinite, such that the excess demand for bonds is eliminated immediately. Then, in the aggregate, the excess demand for goods per unit of capital must be equal to the flow excess supply of real balances per unit of capital. Walras' law becomes:

(19) $$\frac{\pi}{\lambda h} = v - L\left[y(x) + \frac{\pi}{\lambda}, r(x) + \pi^*, \rho, \theta v\right],$$

where λh is finite and positive and $v \equiv M/pK$ is real balances per unit of capital.

I. THE SUPPLY OF MONEY

What determines the rate of monetary expansion DM/M denoted by μ? Several different institutional arrangements can be considered: a mixed inside-outside money system and one version of an inside money system.

1. An Inside-Outside Money System.[16] Define the money supply M as currency C, a liability of the monetary authority, plus deposits D, a liability of a privately owned banking system.

(20) $$M \equiv C + D.$$

The total claims of the private sector upon the public sector consists of high-powered money H and that quantity of government bonds that is not discounted against tax liabilities. High-powered money H is the sum of four elements: (a) gold coins and certificates, (b) Treasury currency, including silver dollars, silver certificates, subsidiary silver, minor coins, and national bank notes, (c) Federal Reserve notes, and (d) Federal Reserve deposits. Prior to the establishment of the Federal Reserve System in 1914, only items (a) and (b) were relevant. Define currency as that part of items (a), (b), and (c) held by the nonbank public. Define reserves R as item (d) plus that part of items (a), (b), and (c) held by the private banking system.

(21) $$H \equiv C + R.$$

It is convenient to denote the desired ratio of currency (held by the public) to their deposits in banks as δ.

(22) $$C^* = \delta D,$$

where C^* is desired currency holdings and δ is a function of several

---

[16] See Cagan (1965) and Friedman and Schwartz (1963).

variables. Similarly, let γ denote the desired ratio of (bank) reserves to deposits.

(23) $$R^* = \gamma D,$$

where R^* is desired reserves and γ is a function of several variables.

Using equations 21 and 22, there is a negative relation between actual bank reserves and deposits. Given the quantity of high-powered money, a rise in deposits leads to a rise in the public's holdings of currency. Bank reserves are thereby reduced. This is described by curve HR in Figure 2. Desired reserves are positively related to deposits, given γ, and are described by curve OR^*.

Whenever deposits (inside money) are less than D_1, actual reserves exceed desired reserves. Banks are induced to expand deposits and thereby reduce the excessive reserves defined here as $R - R^*$. A very quick way for the banks to achieve this goal is to purchase bonds in exchange for deposits. Bond prices or interest rates will be affected thereby, and there will be repercussions upon the desired rate of investment.

Alternatively, if deposits were greater than D_1, banks have less reserves than they desire. They attempt to sell off some of their portfolio of bonds to the public; and the public pays for these purchases with either currency or deposits. In the process of offering the bonds for sale, bond

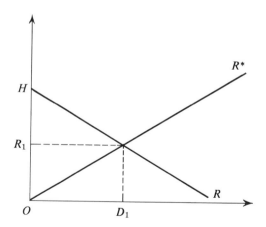

FIGURE 2. Determinants of inside money D (deposits).

prices are depressed and interest rates rise. Planned investment by firms will be affected by the rise in nominal rates of interest.

Suppose that banks react to a discrepancy between actual and desired reserves so quickly that they are brought into equality almost immediately:[17] equation 24.

(24) $R = R^* = R_1$ (in Figure 2).

Then the resulting level of deposits will be D_1:

(25) $$D_1 = \frac{1}{\delta + \gamma} H;$$

and the money supply $C + D$ will be:

(26) $$M = \frac{(1 + \delta)}{(\gamma + \delta)} H.$$

The proportionate rate of change of the money supply will depend upon (a) the proportionate rate of change of high-powered money, (b) the change in the currency-deposit ratio desired by the public, and (c) the change in the ratio of reserves to deposits desired by the banks. This is the classification used by Cagan, Friedman, and Schwartz.

If all government bonds are discounted by the public against future tax liabilities, then H represents net claims of the private sector upon the public sector. Variable θ, used in connection with the savings function above, is:

(27) $$\theta = \frac{\gamma + \delta}{1 + \delta}.$$

Neither δ nor γ is constant. Let us now drop assumption (24). If we assume that δ is roughly approximated over the long run by the actual currency-deposit ratio and γ is roughly approximated by the actual reserve-deposit ratio, then they clearly have not been constant during the past century.

Table 2 shows that, in the long run, increases in high-powered money accounted for 90 per cent of the growth of the money stock. The contributions of γ and δ largely offset each other over the long run. Over

---

[17] We only make this assumption for illustrative purposes here. It is not carried over into the rest of this chapter.

TABLE 2. SOURCES OF THE RATE OF CHANGE IN THE MONEY STOCK:
1875–1955 AND OVER BUSINESS CYCLES 1880–1951

	Average Rate (per cent per year) Contributed by Sources:			
	Total Money	High Powered	Currency Ratio	Reserve Ratio
All years 1875–1955	5.7	5.2	0.5	0.1
War years	16.0	16.3	−5.5	6.0
Nonwar years	4.9	4.3	1.0	−0.3
Pre-March 1917	6.3	4.3	1.6	0.6
Post-Nov. 1918	3.2	4.4	0.2	−1.4
Period between specific cycle bases, centered peaks				
Nov. 1880–Dec. 1885	6.8	4.7	2.0	0.1
Dec. 1885–Dec. 1889	4.7	2.2	1.7	0.8
Dec. 1889–Dec. 1891	8.1	5.3	1.8	1.0
Dec. 1891–Dec. 1894	0.5	1.1	0.4	−1.0
Dec. 1894–Dec. 1898	3.6	1.4	1.4	0.8
Dec. 1898–Dec. 1900	20.7	13.3	3.1	4.3
Dec. 1900–Dec. 1904	7.9	5.3	1.6	1.0
Dec. 1904–Nov. 1908	3.7	3.8	1.3	−1.5
Nov. 1908–Oct. 1911	5.6	1.0	2.8	1.8
Oct. 1911–Dec. 1916	6.1	4.5	0.9	0.7
Dec. 1916–Dec. 1918	23.3	25.1	−5.1	3.4
Dec. 1918–April 1922	2.4	−1.5	2.6	1.3
April 1922–Aug. 1925	5.5	2.4	2.4	0.7
Aug. 1925–Nov. 1927	4.7	0.9	2.9	0.9
Nov. 1927–April 1936	−2.0	4.5	−2.8	−4.0
April 1936–June 1943	12.3	15.8	−1.2	−2.4
June 1943–July 1951	6.6	5.0	−0.1	1.7

Source: Cagan (1965), Tables 2, F-4.

business cycles, however, variations in the ratios γ and δ accounted for significant variations in the growth of the money supply.

In view of the long-run significance of variations in the quantity of high-powered money in accounting (arithmetically) for the largest source of the growth of the money supply, we shall ignore the variations in δ and γ in our study of growth. Variable θ will be treated either as an endogenous variable or as a policy parameter.

2. An Inside Money Model. The Keynes-Wicksell model is also able to explain the short-run and long-run effects of changes in the rate of monetary expansion in an economy where all of the money supply consists of liabilities of the private sector.

Suppose that a group were given the franchise to print the medium of exchange (currency).[18] The output produced by the owners of the franchise (which shall be called the bank) is DM in nominal terms and DM/p in real terms.[19] Nominal output DM is exchanged for DM/p of goods with the nonbank public, which desires currency for the usual reasons.

The real value of the flow of output per worker produced by the bank is:

(28a) $$DM/pN = (DM/M)M/pN = \mu m,$$

where m is real balances per worker and μ is the rate of monetary expansion. If people were always holding their desired stocks of real balances (an assumption which will be dropped very shortly), then m is equal to the quantity demanded.

If the marginal cost of producing currency is zero, then the rate of monetary expansion $\mu = \mu_0$, which will maximize the real revenue (per worker) per unit of time of the bank (DM/pN), will be such that:

(28b) $$\frac{d}{d\mu}(\mu m) = \mu \frac{dm}{d\mu} + m = 0 \quad \text{or}$$

(28c) $$\frac{\mu}{m}\frac{dm}{d\mu} = -1.$$

At the maximum profit rate of monetary expansion μ_0, the demand for real balances per worker will have a unit total elasticity of demand with respect to the rate of monetary expansion. If there is a strictly positive marginal cost of currency creation, then the rate of monetary expansion will differ from μ_0. In either case μ_0 is the rate of monetary expansion produced by the owners of the franchise. Its derivation is not essential to my argument.

Suppose that the franchise owners try to sell their output in exchange for interest-bearing debt; and they plan to use their future interest receipts to purchase consumer goods. The sellers of the debt are business firms which would use the acquired currency to demand output in the form of investment goods. The investment-demand function may be of the form

---

[18] This example was inspired by Cagan (1969, unpublished), who must be absolved from any responsibility for the views expressed here.

[19] $D \equiv d/dt$.

described by equation 9, repeated here. The desired proportionate rate of change of the ratio of capital per effective worker $I/K - n$ (where I is desired investment) is assumed to be proportional to the difference between the expected yield on capital $r + \pi^*$ and the nominal rate of interest ρ on debt.

(9) $\qquad I/K - n = r(x) + \pi^* - \rho = r - (\rho - \pi^*).$

The franchise owners use their newly produced money to purchase debt in the market, thereby lowering the nominal interest rate on debt. At this lower nominal rate of interest there will be a rise in planned investment by firms since the expected yield on capital $r + \pi^*$ has risen relative to ρ, the nominal rate of interest.

The decline in the nominal rate of interest ρ leads to an excess demand for goods: planned investment has increased without a corresponding decline in the demand for consumption! In the Neoclassical model, on the other hand, there is no independent investment function; and planned investment is identically equal to planned savings by consumers.

There is an excess demand for goods resulting from the attempt of the franchise owners to sell their output. What will happen to the rate of capital formation? The Keynes-Wicksell model shows how the rate of monetary expansion, produced by the franchise owners or the monetary authority, will affect the capital intensity $k(t) = 1/x(t)$ in both the short run and in the long run (steady state). No real balance effect in the savings function is necessary for this result.

J. THE DYNAMIC EQUATIONS

Finally, there are two differential equations for the growth of $x \equiv N/K$ and $v \equiv M/pK$.

(29) $\qquad Dx/x = n - DK/K = -Dk/k.$
(30) $\qquad Dv/v = \mu - \pi - DK/K.$

There are eleven equations to determine the eleven variables:

(i) output per unit of capital y
(ii) effective labor per unit of capital x
(iii) rent per unit of capital r
(iv) planned savings per unit of capital S/K
(v) planned investment per unit of capital I/K

(vi) the growth of capital DK/K
(vii) real balances per unit of capital v
(viii) the quantity demanded of real balances per unit of capital L
(ix) the nominal rate of interest ρ
(x) the actual rate of price change π
(xi) the expected rate of price change π^*

in terms of exogenous variables M and N and policy variable θ.

II
A HEURISTIC EXPOSITION OF THE STEADY STATE
PROPERTIES OF THE KEYNES-WICKSELL MODEL

There are at least two versions of the Keynes-Wicksell model. In one there is forced savings during inflationary periods: the actual rate of capital formation exceeds planned savings but is less than planned investment. In the other the rate of utilization varies positively with the rate of price change. Both versions imply monetary nonneutrality, even if there is no real balance effect in the savings function. Our main interest will be with the former since the latter may be based upon a shortrun rather than a longrun relationship.

It is desirable to describe the operation of the Keynes-Wicksell models in a heuristic manner before we discuss the dynamic processes in detail. In this manner the reader will better appreciate the distinction between the Neoclassical and the Keynes-Wicksell model. Chapter 4 will stress the technical dynamic aspects of the model in both the short run and long run, whereas only a heuristic account of the long run implications of the models will be presented here.

A. THE POSSIBILITY OF FORCED SAVINGS DURING INFLATIONARY PERIODS

During inflationary periods the demand for output $C + I$ exceeds the capacity of a fully employed economy $Y = Y(N, K)$, where N and K are the currently available input quantities, and the rate of utilization of K and N is u^*. What determines the actual rate of capital formation? Is it planned savings S or planned investment I? We assumed that everyone is partially frustrated: the actual growth of capital DK will be a linear combination of planned savings and planned investment, equation 12 repeated here. Coefficient a is institutionally determined such that $1 > a > 0$ during periods of excess aggregate demand.

(12) $$DK/K = aI/K + (1 - a)S/K.$$

Using equation 4, which states that the rate of price change π is proportional to excess demand per unit of capital, the rate of capital formation is equation 13, repeated here.

(13) $$DK/K = a\pi/\lambda + S/K, \quad 1 > a > 0 \quad \text{when} \quad \pi > 0$$
$$a = 0 \quad \text{when} \quad \pi \leqq 0.$$

Forced savings per unit of capital $a\pi/\lambda$ occurs during inflationary periods because there is excess aggregate demand, and will exist in a steady state of inflation, even with perfect foresight among competitive units.

The proportionate rate of change of the ratio of effective labor per unit of capital Dx/x is n minus DK/K. Variable π and S/K are endogenous[20] and contain x and v as arguments.

(29) $$Dx/x = -Dk/k = n - (S/K + a\pi/\lambda).$$

The growth of real balances per unit of capital Dv/v is equal to the growth of the money supply less the growth of the price level π less the growth of capital, equation 30 repeated here.

(30) $$Dv/v = \mu - \pi - DK/K.$$

In the steady state x and v are constant at x_e and v_e, respectively. Therefore, (a) capital and labor grow at exogenous rate n, and (b) the equilibrium rate of price change π_e is equal to the proportionate rate of change of the money supply per (effective) worker:

(31) $$(DK/K)_e = n.$$

(32) $$\pi_e = \mu - n.$$

Figure 3 describes the steady state when planned savings per unit of capital are primarily a function of output per unit of capital. Then, the S/K function is positively sloped with respect to $Y/K = y(x)$. If there were price-level stability, then there would be no forced savings. Planned savings per unit of capital would be equal to the growth of effective labor

---

[20] See Chapter 4 for this derivation.

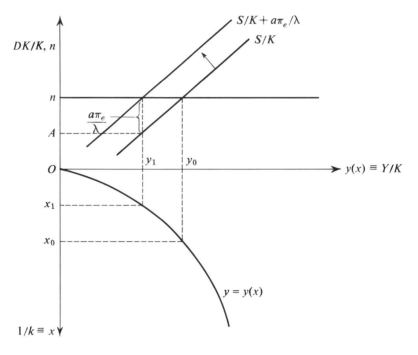

FIGURE 3. The effect of variations in the rate of monetary expansion upon the steady state values in the Keynes-Wicksell model. A rise in the rate of monetary expansion raises the steady state capital intensity (that is, lowers the ratio of effective labor per unit of capital).

at capital intensity $k_0 \equiv 1/x_0$. The lower half of the figure relates output per unit of capital y to (effective) labor per unit of capital x. The real wage, per unit of effective labor, is $y'(x)$.

When prices are stable ($\pi = 0$), the rate of capital formation is equal to planned savings. At output per unit of capital y_0, capital and labor grow at the same rate. Let the rate of monetary expansion rise above the growth of effective labor. Inflation raises the rate of capital formation for two reasons. First, if there is a real balance effect in the savings function, a rise in the rate of inflation reduces real balances and thereby raises planned savings. Second, there will be forced savings per unit of capital $a\pi_e/\lambda$ since the driving force behind inflation is the difference between planned investment and planned savings. (Recall our example where the franchise owners were purchasing debt with their output of currency.) The curve DK/K shifts to $S/K + a\pi/\lambda$. No real balance effect in the savings function is required for this effect. For simplicity of exposition, assume that there is a negligible real balance effect in the savings function.

Since the growth of capital has increased relative to the growth of (effective) labor, output per unit of capital tends to fall toward y_1. Consequently, planned savings per unit of capital declines from On to OA.

Equilibrium is attained when planned savings per unit of capital declines by the amount of forced savings per unit of capital $a(\mu - n)/\lambda = a\pi_e/\lambda$. Here, the equilibrium ratio of effective labor per unit of capital x_e is negatively related, or the equilibrium capital intensity $k_e \equiv 1/x_e$ is positively related, to the rate of monetary expansion. The original Neoclassical result was obtained in a different manner.

B. REVERSE RESULTS ARE POSSIBLE WHEN SAVINGS PLANS ARE REALIZED

If the savings function (S/K) depend upon x and v, and consumption plans were always realized (i.e., $a = 0$), a rise in $\mu - n$ can conceivably lower the steady state capital intensity in a dynamically stable model. The proof will be given in Chapter 4. An intuitive explanation can be given for this result if we consider an economy with no bonds: there are just goods and money. Then, the excess demand for goods is equal to the flow excess supply of real balances. Walras' law, equation 19, in a two asset model would be:

$$(33) \qquad \frac{\pi}{\lambda h} = v - L'(x, \pi^*),$$

where $L'(x, \pi^*)$ is an abbreviated way of writing the demand for real balances per unit of capital in such an economy.

If savings plans are always realized $(a = 0)$, then the growth of capital DK/K is equal to planned savings per unit of capital: equation 34. For simplicity assume that $\theta = 1$ so that all money is of the outside type and there are no (net) government bonds.

$$(34) \qquad n = S(x, v); \qquad S_1 > 0, \qquad S_2 < 0.$$

In the steady state $\pi_e^* = \pi_e = \mu - n$. Using this relation in (33) and substituting (33) into (34), we obtain equation 35.

$$(35) \qquad n = S\left[x, \frac{\mu - n}{\lambda h} + L'(x, \mu - n)\right] = \frac{DK}{K}.$$

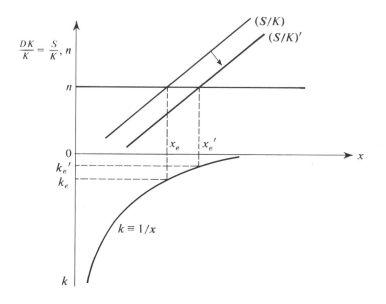

FIGURE 4. A rise in the rate of inflation may lower the steady state capital intensity in a Keynes-Wicksell model when savings plans are always realized.

When equation 35 is satisfied, then both capital and effective labor grow at rate n. This is graphed in Figure 4, where S/K is positively related to x since $S_1 + S_2 L_1 > 0$ for stability.

A rise in the rate of monetary expansion $\mu = \pi_e + n$ is associated with a rise in the excess supply of real balances per unit of capital, equation 33 in the steady state. At any given capital intensity, the quantity demanded will decline, that is $L_2' < 0$. But the actual quantity of real balances per unit of capital in existence will change by:

$$(1/\lambda h + L_2') \Delta \mu.$$

With a slow speed of response of price the rise in the rate of monetary expansion will raise $M(t)$ faster than $p(t)$, and therefore v rises. If real balances v rises, then S/K declines to $(S/K)'$ in Figure 4. The decline in savings per unit of capital raises x from x_e to x_e' (or reduces the steady state capital intensity from k_e to k_e').

Analytically, this result is obtained by differentiating (35) with respect to μ and solving for $dx_e/d\mu$.

(36)
$$\frac{dx_e}{d\mu} = \frac{(-S_2)(1/\lambda h + L_2')}{(S_1 + S_2 L_1')},$$

where for stability

$$(S_1 + S_2 L_1') > 0; \qquad S_2 < 0 \quad \text{and} \quad L_2' < 0.$$

If $(1/\lambda h + L_2') > 0$, then a rise in μ raises v and lowers S/K. Hence, $dx_e/d\mu > 0$: the equilibrium shifts from x_e to x_e' (or from k_e to k_e'). The Neoclassical model assumes that λh is infinite, but that is an arbitrary assumption and is counter to the usual practice in short run dynamics. An important conclusion that emerges from the Keynes-Wicksell model is that a rise in the rate of monetary expansion can either raise or lower the steady state capital intensity in a dynamically stable system. It is implicitly assumed that the rate of inflation is not sufficiently great as to interfere with the productivity of the economy; hence, the effects of inflation upon capacity output are ignored.

C. VARIATIONS IN CAPACITY UTILIZATION

The Keynes-Wicksell model does not need to rely upon the existence of forced savings, or disequilibrium in the money market, to produce the result that a rise in the rate of monetary expansion can affect the steady state capital intensity. A variable rate of capacity utilization and an empirical "law of markets" will suffice; and it will cover the deflationary case in a symmetrical manner. It would be applicable to a highly developed economy such as the United States, rather than to an economy with under-developed financial institutions where a reduction in real balances may affect the productive capacity of the economy.

Suppose that the rate of utilization u in production function (5a), repeated here, were an endogenous variable.

(5a)
$$y = \frac{Y}{K} = y(x)\varphi(u),$$

where $\varphi' > 0$; and $\varphi(u)$, the ratio of actual to capacity output, is bounded from above (as well as from below).

Aggregate demand $C + I$ is assumed to be satisfied at all times, but there may have to be substantial variations in the rate of capacity utilization (u) in the short run to produce the equality between aggregate demand and supply.

(37) $$\frac{C + I}{K} = y(x) \cdot \varphi(u)$$

describes this assumption. Capital intensity $k \equiv K/N \equiv 1/x$ does not imply in this model, the rates at which these inputs are being utilized. Assume, in this section, that equation 37 has a solution. That is, $\varphi(u)$ is below its upper bound.

The crucial assumption is described by equation 38a. Assume that there is a behavioral equation, a law of markets, which states that the rate of price change $\pi = D \ln p$ is proportional to the percentage difference between actual output and capacity output. Inflationary periods imply that utilization rate u exceeds u^*; and deflationary periods imply that rate u is less than u^*. This assumption is consistent with the data from 1948–1968 and is taken as a behavioral equation. It is an attempt to introduce some empirical facts into this very abstract subject. Consider equations 38a and 38b as a description of the way markets function in the aggregate: a "Phillips" curve for the commodity market.

(38a) $$\pi = \lambda[\varphi(u) - 1]$$

or

(38b) $$\varphi(u) = 1 + \pi/\lambda.$$

A positive relation exists between the rate of price change (π) and the ratio of actual to capacity output $\varphi(u)$. This is the key to this model.

Table 3 presents the data which suggest that, certainly in the 1948–1968 period, there has been a positive relation between the utilization rate of manufacturing output and the rate of price change of an index of all industrial commodities. In parentheses are the rankings of each element in the column.

The Spearman rank-correlation coefficient between columns (1) and (2) is 0.51, which is significantly different from zero at almost the one per cent level. Columns (1) and (3) are very highly correlated: high rates of capacity utilization are associated with high rates of labor utilization, that is, low rates of unemployment. It follows that high rates of price change (Column 2) are associated with low rates of unemployment (Column 3), that is, high rates of labor utilization over the twenty-year period covered. We have, therefore, assumed that in highly competitive

TABLE 3. THE RELATION BETWEEN RATES OF UTILIZATION AND RATES
OF PRICE CHANGE: 1948–1968

Year	Utilization Rate of Manufacturing Output (1)		Rate of Change of the Price Index of All Industrial Commodities (2)		Unemployment Rate: Blue Collar Workers (3)	
1948	89.7%	(7)	8.5%	(2)	4.2%	(16.5)
1949	80.2	(19)	−2.1	(20)	8.0	(3)
1950	90.4	(5)	3.6	(4)	7.2	(8.5)
1951	94.0	(2)	10.4	(1)	3.9	(19)
1952	91.3	(3)	−2.3	(21)	3.6	(20)
1953	94.2	(1)	0.7	(12)	3.4	(21)
1954	83.5	(14)	0.4	(14)	7.2	(8.5)
1955	90.0	(6)	2.2	(7)	5.8	(12)
1956	87.7	(9)	4.4	(3)	5.1	(14)
1957	83.6	(13)	2.8	(5)	6.2	(11)
1958	74.0	(21)	0.3	(15)	10.2	(1)
1959	81.5	(17)	1.8	(9)	7.6	(4)
1960	80.6	(18)	0	(16.5)	7.8	(5)
1961	78.5	(20)	−0.5	(19)	9.2	(2)
1962	82.1	(16)	0	(16.5)	7.4	(6)
1963	83.3	(15)	−0.1	(18)	7.3	(7)
1964	85.7	(10)	0.5	(13)	6.3	(10)
1965	88.5	(8)	1.3	(11)	5.3	(13)
1966	90.5	(4)	2.1	(8)	4.2	(16.5)
1967	85.3	(11)	1.5	(10)	4.4	(15)
1968	84.4	(12)	2.5	(6)	4.1	(18)

Source: Economic report of the President, January, 1969. Column 1 is based on Table B-38, and Column 2 is based upon Table B-48. Column 3 is based upon Table B-24.

markets the rate of price change is positively associated with the rate of capacity utilization. What are the implications of this assumption for the growth process?

Planned savings per unit of capital is primarily a function of actual output per unit of capital $Y/K = y(x)\varphi(u)$ and real balances per unit of capital v, such that $S/K = S[y(x) \cdot \varphi(u), v]$. Assume that the rate of utilization, which can satisfy equation 37, is less than its upper bound $\bar{u}$.

The actual rate of growth of capital DK/K is assumed to be equal to planned savings per unit of capital. Therefore:

(39a)
$$\frac{Dx}{x} = n - S[y(x) \cdot \varphi(u), v] = -\frac{Dk}{k}$$

is the differential equation of this growth model. As usual, assume that savings are positively related to output ($S_1 > 0$) and negatively related to real balances ($S_2 < 0$).

Use equation 38b in 39a to obtain differential equation 39b.

(39b) $$\frac{Dx}{x} = n - S[y(x)(1 + \pi/\lambda), v] = -\frac{Dk}{k}.$$

Figure 5 describes this equation. Equilibrium is initially at $x_0 \equiv 1/k_0$, where capital and labor grow at rate n. Let the rate of monetary expansion rise. In equilibrium the actual (equals the expected) rate of price change will rise by an equal amount. Two effects will occur.

First, the rise in the equilibrium rate of price change will reduce the quantity of real balances demanded per unit of capital at any ratio of effective labor per unit of capital. As a result, planned savings per unit of capital will rise. This is the usual Neoclassical result.

Second, the rise in the equilibrium rate of price change will raise the rate of capacity utilization. That is, the rate of capacity utilization will rise

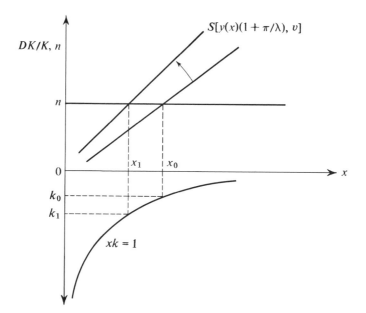

FIGURE 5. The effect of a variable rate of capacity utilization.

to raise the rate of output toward the level of a higher aggregate demand. The resulting rise in output per unit of capital will raise savings per unit of capital ($S_1 > 0$). The net effect is to shift the $S(\cdot)$ curve upward in Figure 5 and thereby raise the steady state ratio of capital per unit of effective labor from k_0 to k_1.

If the rate of capacity utilization were initially at its upper bound $\bar{u}$ when the rate of monetary expansion rose, then there would be excess aggregate demand. That is, it may be impossible to satisfy equation 37 with a permissible level of utilization. Then the model described in section IIA, involving forced saving, would be relevant rather than the one described here.

D. CONCLUSION

Monetary growth theory can be made to yield a variety of qualitatively different results depending upon which model is used. Both the Neoclassical and the Keynes-Wicksell model imply that in the steady state (a) the expected and actual rates of price change are equal ($\pi_e{}^* = \pi_e$) and (b) the actual rate of price change π_e is equal to the growth of the money supply per worker $\mu - n$. For expository purposes assume that there is secular inflation in the steady state. The models differ with respect to the underlying short-run dynamic models; and this difference carries over to the steady state characteristics of the model. The steady state must be the asymptotic solution of the short-run dynamic mode : it cannot be brought in as a deus ex machina.

Instantaneous equilibrium in all markets at all times is implied by the Neoclassical model. As the excess demand curves shift, the equilibrium prices change immediately. During an inflationary process everyone is always holding his desired real balances, and there is no excess demand for goods. Prices always rise instantly by the amount required to clear all markets. No sooner is the market cleared than the excess demand curve rises again; and a new and higher equilibrium price is established instantly. Stability in the Neoclassical model requires that price expectations change sluggishly, for example, a sufficiently low adaptive expectations coefficient must be assumed.

A very different approach is taken in the first version of the Keynes-Wicksell model (section IIA). It is assumed that prices rise if, and only if, there exists excess demand. Expectations by themselves do not raise prices, but expectations working through excess demands produce price changes. Markets are not always cleared. At any time, rising prices imply disequilibrium, that is, unsatisfied demands. A Walrasian dynamic price adjustment process is postulated; and there is no presumption that prices move in precisely the manner postulated by the Neoclassical model. Prices do not change too rapidly in response to changes in excess demand. A stable economy converges to a steady state in terms of variables deflated by the growing stock of capital or the growing size of the labor force. In this steady state there is inflation which is anticipated $\pi_e^* = \pi_e = \mu - n$. Prices do not rise in a dynamically stable model just because people expect them to do so. They rise steadily because there is permanent excess demand. A natural bridge is created between the short run and the steady state in this set of models. The Patinkin model is a special case of the Keynes-Wicksell model developed here.

The second version (IIB) of the Keynes-Wicksell model relies upon a variable rate of utilization for its results. A higher rate of utilization is associated with a higher rate of price change. This is taken as an empirical regularity: a law of markets. Therefore, if the inflation raises the utilization rate and also raises savings, a rise in the rate of monetary expansion must raise the capital intensity.

A possible synthesis of the Neoclassical and Keynes-Wicksell models could be made if the price-change equation were:

(4a) $\pi = Dp/p = \pi^* + \lambda(I/K - S/K).$

In a perfectly competitive market firms must take the market price as a datum, and production is adjusted accordingly. If there is excess demand (that is, $I > S$), then there is some market-bidding process that produces a rise in prices. Expectations of rising prices affect $I - S$ and only thereby affect the rate of price change. This was the rationale underlying equation 4. On the other hand, it is possible that firms may have some power to set prices or that markets are organized by specialists who take the expected rate of price change into account in setting prices. The actual rate of price change may then be the sum of two elements: the specialists' expectations of price changes and the actual state of excess demand, as described by equation 4a.

If equation 4a were the correct price-determination equation, then the Keynes-Wicksell model (to be discussed further in Chapter 5), would describe the growing economy outside of the steady state. As the economy approaches the steady state, π approaches π^* and I/K approaches S/K. Then (a) all markets would be in equilibrium, and (b) the actual rate of growth of capital will be equal to S/K. Monetary policy would be able to affect the steady state capital intensity with this synthesis only if there were a real balance effect in the consumption (savings) function or in the net production function. The crucial question is: Which is the correct monetary growth model?

%%%%

CHAPTER FOUR

The Short-Run
and Long-Run Operation of the
Keynes-Wicksell Model

THE KEYNES-WICKSELL MODEL differs from the Neoclasical model insofar as it drives a wedge between saving and investment during periods of price change. Prices do not adjust instantly to clear markets. When prices are rising, the amount of unfilled orders is rising. If inflation exists in the steady state, then the quantity of unfilled orders grows at the same rate as the stock of capital. The ratio of unfilled orders per unit of capital converges to a constant which is proportional to the rate of inflation.

A rise in the rate of monetary expansion can either raise or lower the steady state capital intensity.[1] If prices respond quickly to excess demands, then a rise in the rate of monetary expansion will reduce the ratio of real balances per unit of capital. Planned savings per unit of capital will tend to rise relative to the growth of labor since planned savings are negatively related to real balances. Consequently, the steady state capital intensity will rise. Other results, however, are possible. When the rate of monetary expansion increases, prices may respond slowly to the resulting excess demand. The ratio of real balances per unit of capital will rise since the rate of monetary expansion has initially increased faster than the rate of inflation. In turn, the rise in real balances will induce a subsequent rise in the rate of inflation. The ratio of real balances per unit of capital will

---

[1] There is a summary (section IV) at the end of this chapter.

continue to rise until the rate of inflation has caught up to the rate of monetary expansion per unit of capital. This phenomenon could not occur in the Neoclassical model, which assumed that the stock of real balances is equal to the quantity demanded, even during inflationary periods. In the Keynes-Wicksell model, however, inflation implies an excess supply of real balances.

If the ratio of real balances per unit of capital rises, then there are two different effects. Planned savings tend to decline; and this decline tends to reduce the rate of capital formation. But planned investment tends to rise since the rise in real balances is associated with a higher rate of anticipated (and actual) inflation. If the actual rate of capital formation were primarily determined by planned savings, the capital intensity will fall. If the actual rate of capital formation were primarily determined by planned investment, the capital intensity will rise. A wide range of results is logically possible in the Keynes-Wicksell model.

I

THE SHORT-RUN MODEL

Four equations describe the short run, wherein the ratio of effective labor per unit of capital $x(t)$ is assumed to be fixed. Since these equations were discussed in the previous chapter, only a brief discussion is necessary.

First, the rate of price change $\pi \equiv Dp/p$ is proportional to the excess aggregate demand for goods per unit of capital: that is, to planned investment less planned savings per unit of capital.[2] It is assumed that markets are highly competitive, and prices rise when there are more buy orders than there are sell orders. The rate at which prices rise depends upon the excess of buy orders over sell orders. One could think of the excess demand for goods as the change in unfilled orders. Then equation 1 states that the proportionate rate of price change π is related to the change in unfilled orders per unit of capital.

$$(1) \qquad\qquad \pi = \lambda(I/K - S/K),$$

where coefficient λ depends upon the structure of the competitive market.

[2] A different assumption is made in Chapter 5, which synthesizes the Neoclassical and Keynes-Wicksell models.

Planned investment per unit of capital depends positively upon the anticipated growth of the economy n and the relation between the capital value of an existing asset and its supply price (or reproduction cost). It was shown in the previous chapter that the ratio of the capital value of an existing asset to its supply price is positively related to the rent per unit of capital r plus the anticipated capital gain π^* less the nominal rate of interest ρ. When $r + \pi^* - \rho$ rises, the capital value of an existing asset rises relative to its reproduction cost. Firms demand newly produced capital goods in preference to existing assets; and planned investment rises per unit of capital. Substituting the planned savings and investment equations[3] into equation 1, equation 1a is derived.

(1a) $\qquad \dfrac{\pi}{\lambda} = n + r(x) + \pi^* - \rho - S(x, \theta v).$

Second, according to Walras' law, the real excess flow supply of bonds per unit of capital B_s is equal to the real excess flow demand for goods per unit of capital plus the real excess flow demand for real balances per unit of capital. Walras' law states that:[4]

(2a) $\qquad \dfrac{\pi}{\lambda} + h\left\{ L\left[y(x) + \dfrac{\pi}{\lambda}, r(x) + \pi^*, \rho, \theta v \right] - v \right\} = B_s.$

Assuming that the bond market comes into equilibrium very quickly, such that $B_s = 0$, Walras' law can be written as:

(2b) $\qquad \dfrac{\pi}{\lambda} + h\left\{ L\left[y(x) + \dfrac{\pi}{\lambda}, r(x) + \pi^*, \rho, \theta v \right] - v \right\} = 0.$

Third, some price expectations function π^* must be chosen. A choice will be made from among equations 15b, 16, or 17 in Chapter 3.

Fourth, the proportionate rate of change of real balances per unit of capital $v \equiv M/pK$ is equal to the proportionate rate of change of the money supply μ less the proportionate rate of change of the price level π less the proportionate rate of change of capital. By definition, the short run is a span of time in which the ratio of effective labor per unit of capital is assumed to be constant. Since $x = x_0$:

(3) $Dv/v = \mu - \pi - DK/K = \mu - \pi - n + Dx/x = \mu - \pi - n$

is the short-run differential equation for the change in v.

---

[3] See equations 4, 9, and 11 in Chapter 3.
[4] See equation 19 in Chapter 3.

A. SHORT-RUN EQUILIBRIUM ANALYSIS

The implied short-run equilibrium of the Keynes-Wicksell model will turn out to be a very familiar system. Part B of this section will then lead us from the familiar to the unfamiliar.

When real balances per unit of capital are constant, that is, $Dv = 0$, then the rate of price change will be equal to the rate of monetary expansion per effective worker. Assume $x = x_0$.

$$(4) \qquad \pi_s = \mu - n,$$

where π_s is the short-run equilibrium rate of price change.

Regardless of which price expectations function is used (15b, 16, or 17 in Chapter 3), the equilibrium expected rate of price change π_s^* will be equal to the actual rate of price change π_s. It follows that:

$$(5) \qquad \pi_s^* = \pi_s = \mu - n$$

in short-run equilibrium (that is, when the ratio of effective labor per unit of capital is fixed).

Substitute equation 5 into equations 1 and 2 and derive equations 6 and 7, the basic short-run equilibrium macro-economic model. The given ratio of effective labor per unit of capital is denoted by x_0.

$$(6) \qquad \pi_s/\lambda = n + r(x_0) + \pi_s - \rho - S(x_0, \theta v).$$

$$(7) \qquad \pi_s/\lambda h = v - L[y(x_0) + \pi_s/\lambda, r(x_0) + \pi_s, \rho, \theta v].$$

Equation 6 will be called the SIS (short-run equilbrium IS) curve and is graphed in Figure 1. It relates the nominal rate of interest ρ to real balances per unit of capital v such that the rate of price change $\pi_s = \mu - n$ is proportional to the inflationary (or deflationary) gap $I/K - S/K = \pi_s/\lambda$. The speed of adjustment λ could be as large or as small as we wish to make it without affecting the argument at this stage.

The SIS curve will be positively sloped. If the rate of price change were zero, as is the usual case in short-run macro-economic equilibrium models, then planned investment is equal to planned savings (per unit of capital). A rise in the nominal rate of interest ρ lowers planned investment. Real balances per unit of capital v must, therefore, rise to raise planned consumption, that is, lower planned savings. A positive relation would exist between ρ and v. Similarly, if prices are changing at rate $\pi_s = \mu - n \neq 0$, then there is a gap between planned investment and planned savings

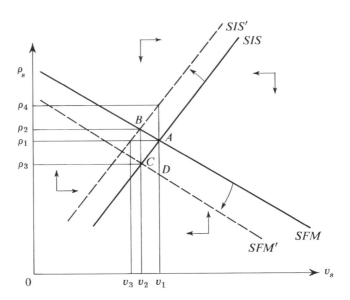

FIGURE 1. Short-run macro-economic equilibrium. A rise in the rate of Harrod neutral technical change shifts the *SIS* curve to *SIS'*. A decline in liquidity preference (relative to bonds) shifts the *SFM* curve to *SFM'*.

(per unit of capital). The size of the gap is π_s/λ. To be sure, the faster the speed of adjustment (that is, the larger λ), the smaller will be the inflationary or deflationary gap. A rise in ρ will lower planned investment and thereby decrease the (say) inflationary gap. To offset the effect of a rise in the nominal rate of interest, real balances (per unit of capital) v must rise to restore the gap to π_s/λ. The *SIS* curve is the set of ρ and v such that an inflationary or deflationary gap of π_s/λ is produced. With a finite speed of response λ, price stability will occur in short-run equilibrium only if the stock of money per effective worker is constant ($\mu - n = 0$). The *SIS* curve must be positively sloped:

(8)
$$\left. \frac{\partial \rho}{\partial v} \right|_{x_0,\mu} = (-S_2\theta) > 0,$$

regardless of the speed of response.

Along the *SIS* curve planned investment per unit of capital minus planned savings per unit of capital is equal to π_s/λ, that is, there is a constant inflationary gap. If the rate of interest rose above the *SIS* curve, then planned investment would decline relative to planned savings. As a result, the rate of price change π would decline. The proportionate rate of change of real balances M/p would therefore rise when the rate of price change declined. The movement of v is to the right when the nominal rate of interest is above the *SIS* curve. Similarly, suppose that the nominal rate of interest were below the *SIS* curve. Then planned investment will rise relative to planned savings, and the rate of price change will rise along with the inflationary gap. When the rate of price change increases, the quantity of real balances M/p declines. The movement of v is to the left when the nominal rate of interest is below the *SIS* curve. Horizontal arrows in Figure 1 indicate the movement of v for points off the *SIS* curve.

Equation 7 is also graphed in Figure 1 and is referred to as the *SFM* (short-run equilibrium financial market) curve. It represents the relation between the short-run equilibrium nominal rate of interest and the short-run equilibrium real balances per unit of capital when Walras' law is satisfied and the bond market is in equilibrium. The *SFM* curve has the characteristics of a liquidity preference curve. If the rate of price change were zero, as is usually the case in short-run macro-economic models, the supply of and demand for real balances are equal: that is, $v = L(\cdot)$ in equation 7. A decline in the nominal rate of interest ρ raises the quantity of real balances demanded $L(\cdot)$; and the quantity of real balances in existence must adjust to satisfy $v = L(\cdot)$ when $\mu - n = 0$.

Similarly, if there is a nonzero of price change $\pi_s = \mu - n$, then equation 7 states that there must be a constant gap $\pi_s/\lambda h$ between the stock v and the quantity demanded (assuming that the speeds of response λh are finite). A decline in the nominal rate of interest ρ will raise the quantity of real balances demanded. To preserve a constant gap between the supply of and demand for real balances, v must rise. Our *SFM* curve is a generalized liquidity preference curve. The slope of the *SFM* curve is:

$$(9) \qquad \left.\frac{\partial \rho_s}{\partial v_s}\right|_{x_0,\mu} = \frac{1 - L_4\theta}{L_3} < 0.$$

Along the *SFM* curve the bond market is in equilibrium. Suppose that the rate of interest were below the curve. Then the excess demands for real balances and for goods would rise; and the excess supply of bonds would also increase to satisfy Walras' law. A rise in the excess supply of bonds would lower bond prices or raise the interest rate on bonds. When the interest rate on bonds is below the *SFM* curve, there develops an excess supply of bonds; and the interest rate tends to rise. Similarly, if the interest rate were above the *SFM* curve, there would be declines in the excess demands for goods and for real balances. As a result of the disequilibrium in the bond market, bond prices would rise and interest rates would decline. When the nominal rate of interest is above the *SFM* curve, an excess demand for bonds develops; and interest rates tend to decline. The vertical arrows in Figure 1 indicate the directions of movement of the interest rate.

Figure 1 describes the determination of the short-run equilibrium rate of interest ρ_s and real balances per unit of capital v_s, given the ratio of effective labor per unit of capital. The inflationary gap $\pi_s/\lambda = (\mu - n)/\lambda$ is equal to the excess flow supply of real balances $h[v - L(\cdot)]$, and the actual and expected rates of price change are equal to the rate of monetary expansion per effective worker $\pi_s = \pi_s{}^* = \mu - n$ at the equilibrium point. The vertical and horizontal arrows indicate the path to equilibrium.

We examine the effects of three standard disturbances upon the short-run macro-economic equilibrium. Continue to assume that the rate of monetary expansion is constant at $\mu \gtreqless 0$, thereby producing an inflationary (or deflationary) gap of:

$$\pi_s/\lambda = (\mu - n)/\lambda = I/K - S/K.$$

Initially, equilibrium is at point $A = (v_1, \rho_1)$.

First, suppose that firms revise upward their expected rate of Harrod neutral technical change without any change in the equilibrium rate of price change: that is, $\Delta\mu = \Delta n$. Since effective labor is expected to grow at a faster rate than before, planned investment will rise relative to planned savings. The *SIS* curve will shift upward to the left to *SIS'* as a result of this expectation. Why? To preserve the inflationary (or deflationary) gap of $\pi_s/\lambda = (\mu - n)/\lambda$, either planned investment will have to revert to its original level or planned savings per unit of capital will have to rise. A rise in the nominal rate of interest to ρ_4, given planned savings $S(x_0, \theta v_1)$, will reduce planned investment to the original level, and the inflationary (deflationary) gap of $(\mu - n)/\lambda$ will be restored. Therefore, the *SIS* curve must shift upward. Alternatively, if ρ_s remained at ρ_1, then planned savings (per unit of capital) must rise to offset the higher investment demand. If real balances per unit of capital declined to v_3, then planned savings would rise. The SIS curve must shift to the left.

Originally the economy was at point $A = (v_1, \rho_1)$; then the higher expected rate of technical progress raised the SIS curve to SIS'. What happens? At interest rate ρ_1 there is a greater inflationary gap than before. Prices rise at a rate in excess of $\pi_s = \mu - n$, thereby reducing real balances per unit of capital. The reduction in v and the rise in the transactions demand for real balances raise the rate of interest above ρ_1. The rate of planned investment is diminished as a result of the rise in ρ. Moreover, the decline in v reduces aggregate demand directly by raising planned savings per unit of capital. Short-run equilibrium will occur at point $B = (v_2, \rho_2)$, with a higher nominal rate of interest and lower real balances per unit of capital. The short-run equilibrium rate of price change will be $\pi_s = \mu - n$, as before.

Second, suppose that there were a switch away from money and into bonds. People decide to hold a smaller fraction of their wealth in the form of money and a correspondingly larger fraction in the form of bonds. No direct effect is assumed to occur in the commodity market. What will happen?

No change will occur in the SIS curve since we postulated that no shift has occurred in the savings and investment functions. A downward shift occurs in the SFM curve to SFM'. Why? As a result of the switch in preferences from money to bonds, there is an excess demand for bonds. Equilibrium can only occur in the bond market at a lower rate of interest. Therefore, the SFM curve declines.

Equilibrium will shift from A to C as a result of the decision to change the composition of portfolios from money to bonds. There is an initial decline in interest rates resulting from the excess demand for bonds. Planned investment will rise relative to planned savings as a consequence of the decline in nominal rates of interest. The inflationary gap $I/K - S/K$ will widen (or the deflationary gap will narrow), thereby raising the rate of price change π above $\pi_s = \mu - n$. Since prices are now rising at a faster pace than the rate of monetary expansion, real balances per unit of capital will decline. The decline in v will tend to raise the rate of savings, thereby moderating the rate of inflation. A rise will occur in the nominal rate of interest relative to point D: the rate that occurred immediately after the switch from money to bonds. Planned investment will decline and planned savings will tend to rise. Equilibrium will be restored when the economy reaches $C = (v_2, \rho_3)$. Then the inflationary gap $I/K - S/K$ will again be equal to $(\mu - n)/\lambda$, and the rate of price change π_s will be equal to $\mu - n$, the rate of monetary expansion per effective worker. Both the nominal rate of interest and the level of real balances per unit of capital will be reduced relative to point $A = (v_1, \rho_1)$. The portfolio choice between money and bonds will affect the short-run equilibrium rate of interest.

Third, suppose that there were a change (rise) in the stock of money at $t = 0$ but that from then on the money stock continued to grow as proportionate rate μ. The trend line of the logarithm of M against time is raised without changing its slope. What will happen?

Neither the *SIS* curve nor the *SFM* curve, relating ρ_s to v_s, has changed as a result of the parallel (upward) displacement of the trend line of the logarithm of M against time. If equilibrium were initially at A, the initial rise in the stock of money temporarily raises v above v_1. The excess supply of money will raise the demand for bonds and lower the rate of interest. The rise in v would decrease planned savings, that is, increase consumption. As a result planned investment would rise relative to planned savings, and the inflationary gap would widen. With the increase in the inflationary gap $I/K - S/K$ above $(\mu - n)/\lambda$, the rate of price change would exceed μ, the rate of monetary expansion. Real balances per unit of capital would decline until v reverted to v_1 and the rate of interest returned to ρ_1. Equilibrium would again occur at point A. Since real balances per unit of capital are constant, the rate of price change π_s will equal the rate of monetary expansion per effective worker. However, the trend line of the logarithm of p against time would eventually shift upward without changing its slope.

The object of this section has been to show that, when the ratio of labor to capital is arbitrarily fixed, the Keynes-Wicksell model reduces to the familiar short-run macro-economic model.

B. THE SHORT-RUN EFFECT OF A RISE IN THE RATE OF MONETARY EXPANSION

1. An Economic Explanation of Paradoxical Results. In the Neo-classical model a rise in the rate of monetary expansion unambiguously reduced the ratio of real balances per unit of capital. The line of reasoning was direct and is based upon the assumption that the supply of and demand for real balances per unit of capital are equal. A rise in the rate of monetary expansion μ raises the equilibrium rate of price change π. Certainly in equilibrium, the expected rate of price change π^* must equal the actual rate. When the expected rate of price change increases, the quantity of real balances demanded per unit of capital declines. Therefore, the actual stock of real balances per unit of capital also declines since money-market equilibrium must prevail. This short-run phenomenon has significant long-run implications for the capital intensity. Savings per unit of capital are negatively related to real balances per unit of capital. When real balances per unit of capital are reduced, savings per unit of capital rise. The growth of the capital-labor ratio is equal to savings per unit of capital less the growth of labor. Consequently, the decline in real balances per unit of capital raises the growth of the capital-labor ratio. Equilibrium will be reached when the higher capital-labor ratio lowers savings per unit of capital back to the growth of labor.

A different situation exists in the Keynes-Wicksell model. Insofar as prices are changing, there is market disequilibrium. Neither the market for goods nor the money market is in equilibrium during periods of price change. A rise in the rate of price change will lower the quantity of real balances demanded per unit of capital, but it may either raise or lower the stock of real balances in existence per unit of capital. We assumed that the existence of inflation implies that there is an excess demand for goods (per unit of capital). Since the bond market is assumed to adjust very quickly, the excess demand for goods (per unit of capital) π_s/λ is equal to the excess flow supply of real balances (per unit of capital), $h[v - L(\cdot)]$, that is:

(a) $$\pi/\lambda = h[v - L(\cdot)]$$

or

(b) $$v = \pi/\lambda h + L(\cdot).$$

A rise in the rate of monetary expansion raises the short-run equilibrium rate of price change $\pi_s = \mu - n$. Therefore, $\pi_s/\lambda h$ must rise. We know that the greater rate of inflation will lower the quantity demanded $L(\cdot)$. Will the quantity demanded $L(\cdot)$ decline by more, or by less, then $\pi_s/\lambda h$ rises in equation b above? It can be shown that either result is possible.

Therefore, a rise in the rate of monetary expansion can either raise or lower the short-run equilibrium values of v_s.

An intuitive (and oversimplified) explanation of this phenomenon will precede a mathematical proof. In short-run equilibrium the actual and expected rates of price change are equal. Suppose that $\pi_s{}^*$ rose by one unit when the actual rate of monetary expansion per effective worker $\mu - n$ rose by one unit. Will enough excess demand be generated to raise the actual rate of price change by one unit when v_s is constant? A unit rise in $\pi^* = \mu - n$ will raise the rate of investment per unit of capital by one unit and thereby raise excess demand per unit of capital by the same amount. As a result the rate of price change rises by λ units. If $\lambda < 1$, then a rise in price expectations will not be justified at a constant v. However, the value of real balances per unit of capital will rise since the rate of monetary expansion rose by one unit but the rate of price change rose by $\lambda < 1$ units. With the rise in v, aggregate demand per unit of capital will increase. Short-run equilibrium will only be attained when v has increased sufficiently to raise the actual rate of price change to the new rate of monetary expansion per effective worker. This result could not occur in the Neoclassical model.

On the other hand, if $\lambda > 1$, then the unit rise in $\pi_s{}^* = \mu - n$ will raise the actual rate of price change by more than one unit. Real balances per unit of capital will therefore decline since $\mu - n$ is less than π. This decline in real balances per unit of capital will decrease aggregate demand and thereby mitigate the rate of price change. Short-run equilibrium will only be attained when v has decreased sufficiently to lower the actual rate of price change to the new rate of monetary expansion per effective worker.

We have shown in an intuitive manner that a rise in the rate of monetary expansion per effective worker will:

(a) *raise* the short-run equilibrium level of real balances per unit of capital if a unit rise in price expectations leads to a smaller rise in the actual rate of price change;

(b) *lower* the short-run equilibrium level of real balances per unit of capital if a unit rise in price expectations leads to a larger rise in the actual rate of price change. A proof of these statements follows.

2. A Proof of the Proposition that a Rise in the Rate of Monetary Expansion May Either Raise or Lower the Equilibrium Ratio of Real Balances Per Unit of Capital. The short-run dynamic model consists of equations 1a, 2b, 3, and a price expectations function. Suppose price expectations are formed according to the adaptive expectations equation 10.

(10) $$D\pi^* = b(\pi - \pi^*).$$

We shall solve equations 1a and 2b for the rate of price change π and the nominal rate of interest ρ in terms of variables π^* and v and obtain equations 11 and 12, respectively.

(11) $$\pi = f(\pi^*, v).$$
(12) $$\rho = g(\pi^*, v).$$

Substituting equation 11 in (10) and (3), a short-run dynamic system[5] is obtained, described by equation 13 and 14.

(13) $$D\pi^* = b[f(\pi^*, v) - \pi^*].$$
(14) $$Dv/v = \mu - n - f(\pi^*, v).$$

In equilibrium, π^* and v are constant; and equations 13 and 14 are equal to zero. It follows that, in equilibrium:

(15) $$\pi_s^* = \pi_s = f(\pi_s^*, v_s) = \mu - n.$$

The actual and expected rates of price change are equal to the growth of the money supply per effective worker.

The relation between the rate of price change $\pi_s = \pi_s^*$ and the short-run equilibrium level of real balances per worker v_s can be obtained from (15a), which is based upon (15).

(15a) $$\pi_s = f(\pi_s, v_s).$$

Differentiate (15a) with respect to $\pi_s = \pi_s^* = \mu - n$ and solve for $dv_s/d\pi_s$, We obtain:

(16) $$\frac{dv_s}{d\pi_s} = \frac{1 - f_1}{f_2}.$$

Partial derivative f_1 describes the effect of a unit rise in price expectations upon the actual rate of price change $(\partial\pi/\partial\pi^*)$ when real balances

---

[5] This dynamic system can be solved in the manner described in the next chapter. The only change is that, in the Keynes-Wicksell model, f_1 can be less than unity. In that case the PP' curve (Chapter 5, Figures 2 and 3) will be upward sloping. A rise in μ will raise v_s and π_s^*.

per unit of capital are constant. It will be shown in part C1 that f_2 is positive: namely, a rise in the level of real balances per unit of capital will raise the rate or price change. Therefore:

(i) a rise in $\pi_s = \pi_s{}^* = \mu - n$ will *raise* the short-run equilibrium level of real balances per unit of capital if $1 > f_1$; and

(ii) a rise in $\pi_s = \pi_s{}^* = \mu - n$ will *lower* the short-run equilibrium level of real balances per unit of capital if $1 < f_1$.

II

A BRIDGE TO THE LONG RUN

Two differential equations describe the growth path of the economy (if we temporarily ignore the adaptive expectations equation). Equation 17 describes the change in the ratio of effective labor per unit of capital (the reciprocal of the capital intensity); and equation 18 describes the change in real balances per unit of capital.

(17) $$Dx/x = n - DK/K = -Dk/k.$$

(18) $$Dv/v = \mu - \pi - DK/K.$$

The growth of capital[6] DK/K is the sum of planned savings per unit of capital[7] $S/K = S(x, \theta v)$ and, during inflationary periods, unintended or forced savings per unit of capital $a\pi/\lambda$.

(19) $$DK/K = S(x, \theta v) + a\pi/\lambda.$$

Using equation 19 above for the growth of capital, differential equations 20 and 21 may be derived from equations 17 and 18.

(20) $$Dx/x = n - a\pi/\lambda - S(x, \theta v).$$

(21) $$Dv/v = \mu - \pi - a\pi/\lambda - S(x, \theta v).$$

To solve the model of a growing economy, described by differential equations 20 and 21, the rate of price change π must be expressed in terms of state variables x and v. The relation between the rate of price change π and state variables x and v can be derived from equations 1a and 2b. A

---

[6] See equation 13, Chapter 3.

[7] See equation 11, Chapter 3.

graphic analysis in terms of *IS* and *FM* curves and then a mathematical approach will be used to derive this relation. Unlike the analysis in section IA of this chapter, we do not assume that the rate of price change is equal to the rate of monetary expansion per unit of effective labor: that is, we are not confining ourselves to short-run equilibria. A more general analysis is employed; and the situation described in section IA is a special case of the analysis presented here.

Equation 1a will be called an *IS* curve. It relates rates of inflation[8] ($\pi > 0$) to nominal rates of interest given three parameters: (a) the ratio of effective labor per unit of capital x, (b) real balances per unit of capital v, and (c) the expected rate of price change π^*. The reason for calling it an *IS* curve is that equation 1a states that the rate of price change is proportional to the difference between planned investment per unit of capital and planned savings per unit of capital. Clearly this curve is negatively sloped: a decline in the nominal rate of interest will raise planned investment relative to planned savings. The excess demand for goods per unit of capital rises. Since the rate of price change π is proportional to the excess demand for goods per unit of capital, the decline in ρ will raise π. The slope of the *IS* curve is:

$$(22) \qquad \left. \frac{\partial \rho}{\partial \pi} \right|_{x,v,\pi^*} = -1/\lambda < 0 \qquad IS$$

for a finite positive speed of response λ.

Equation 2b will be called the *FM* (financial market) curve. It too relates π to ρ, given parameters π^*, x, and v. This equation expresses Walras' law under the assumption that the bond market is always in equilibrium: the excess demand for goods is equal to the excess flow supply of real balances. A positive relation exists between the rate of price change and the nominal rate of interest when the bond market is always in equilibrium. Why? Let the rate of price change rise. This implies that there has been an increase in the excess demand for goods per unit of capital π/λ. Moreover, the transactions demand for real balances per unit of capital (which depends upon $y(x) + \pi/\lambda$) has increased since people want to finance a larger real expenditure. Together, the rise in the excess

---

[8] If $\pi < 0$, then $a = 0$; and the rate of capital formation $DK/K = S(x, \theta v)$. Mathematically we treat the general case $\pi \gtreqless 0$. In the literary and graphic analysis it is expositionally convenient to deal with the case of inflation.

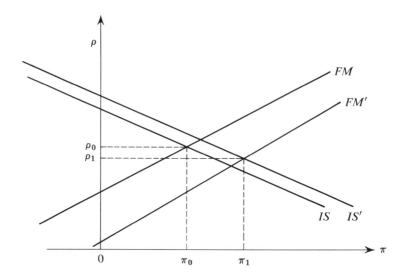

FIGURE 2. A rise in parameter v shifts both the IS and FM curves to the right. A rise in parameter π^* shifts both curves to the right. The effect of a rise in parameter x upon each curve is ambiguous.

demand for goods and real balances imply a rise in the excess supply of bonds (according to Walras' law). To equilibrate the bond market, the nominal rate of interest must rise. Equation 2b implies that ρ and π are positively related. The slope of the FM curve is:

$$(23) \qquad \frac{\partial \rho}{\partial \pi}\bigg|_{x,v,\pi^*} = \frac{1}{-\lambda L_3}(L_1 + 1/h) > 0 \qquad FM.$$

These curves are drawn in Figure 2, where x, v, and π^* are treated as parameters. The short-run (but not necessarily the short-run equilibrium) solutions for the nominal rate of interest ρ and the rate of price change π are described by the intersection of the two curves. Formally, the short-run solutions are (24) and (25), based upon (1a) and (2b).

$$(24) \qquad\qquad \pi = f(\pi^*, v, x; n, \theta).$$

$$(25) \qquad\qquad \rho = g(\pi^*, v, x; n, \theta).$$

Our interest is in the partial derivatives of these two equations. What will be the effects of variations in x, v, and π^* upon the short-run solutions?

These partial derivatives are presented in Table 1. A literary discussion of the signs of these partial derivatives will be helpful in understanding the subsequent mathematics. We have already seen that the values $1 - f_1$ and f_2 have economic significance. They determine the effect of a rise in the rate of monetary expansion upon the short-run equilibrium ratio of real balances per unit of capital.

1. Changes in Real Balances per Unit of Capital. Suppose that v rose but the other parameters were unchanged. Both the *IS* and *FM* curves would shift, raising the rate of price change to $\pi_1 > \pi_0$. Consider the *IS* curve. The rise in real balances per unit of capital v will raise the demand for consumption, that is, reduce planned savings if there is a real balance effect in the savings function. If the nominal rate of interest were unchanged at ρ_0, then the excess demand for goods would rise, and there would be an increase in the rate of price change. The rise in v shifts the *IS* curve to the right to *IS'*. Alternatively, the rise in v requires a rise in the nominal rate of interest, which would decrease planned investment if the rate of price change is to remain unchanged.

The rise in v will also shift the *FM* curve. When the ratio of net private wealth to money θ is constant, then net private financial wealth must change in the same proportion. Assume that a rise in v (and, therefore, a rise in θv, real net financial wealth per unit of capital) is associated with a rise in the excess supply of real balances per unit of capital: that is, $1 > L_4\theta$. Given the rate of price change π, which is proportional to the excess demand for goods, what must happen to the nominal rate of interest such that Walras' law is satisfied? A rise in the excess supply of real balances implies a rise in the excess demand for bonds when there is no change in the excess demand for goods. To equilibrate the bond market, the nominal rate of interest must decline. The *FM* curve shifts downward as a result of the rise in v. Alternatively, if the nominal rate of interest were given, the excess demand for goods must rise to offset a rise in the excess supply of real balances. Since π is proportional to the excess demand for goods, the *FM* curve will shift to the right when v rises.

The net effect of a rise in parameter v is to raise the rate of price change, to π_1, that is, $f_2 > 0$ as was claimed in connection with equation 16. The effect on the nominal rate of interest, however, is ambiguous. Both the shift in the *IS* curve and in the *FM* surve lead to an excess demand for goods and tend to raise the rate of price change. However, the shift of the

IS curve resulting from the wealth effect ($\theta \, \Delta v$) tends to raise the nominal rate of interest by decreasing planned savings; whereas the shift of the *FM* curve resulting from the monetary effect (Δv) tends to lower the nominal rate of interest. (See part 4 of this section.)

2. *Changes in the Expected Rate of Price Change.* A rise in the expected rate of price change π^* will shift both the *IS* and *FM* curves, given parameter x and v.

At a given nominal rate of interest a rise in the expected rate of price change raises planned investment relative to planned savings. Alternatively, we may say that the rise in π^* has initially lowered the real rate of interest (defined as) $\rho - \pi^*$. Or the rise in π^* raises the capital value of existing assets relative to their supply price and thereby stimulates a demand for newly produced investment goods. As a result the excess demand for goods, planned investment minus planned savings, increases; and there is a proportional rise in the rate of price change $\pi = \lambda(I - S)/K$. The *IS* curve will shift upward to the right in Figure 2. Alternatively, if the desired rate of investment is to remain constant, the nominal rate of interest will have to rise by the amount of the rise in π^*. To preserve a constant inflationary gap, or rate of inflation, the *IS* curve will have to shift upward.

A shift will also occur in the *FM* curve as a result of a rise in the expected rate of price change. The rise in π^* raises the expected yield on real capital $r(x) + \pi^*$ and thereby decreases the quantity of real balances demanded. According to Walras' Law, the rise in the excess supply of real balances (resulting from the rise in π^*) must be met by an increase in the excess demand for goods and bonds. Equation 2 is Walras' law under the assumption that the bond market is always in equilibrium. If the nominal rate of interest were given at ρ_0, then the rise in real balances would be met with an increase in the excess demand for goods. This means that the *FM* curve would shift to the right: the rate of price change would rise.

As a result of a rise in the expected rate of price change, both the *IS* and the *FM* curve would shift to the right, thereby raising the actual rate of price change.

3. *Changes in the Ratio of Effective Labor per Unit of Capital.* The effects of changes in parameter x, the ratio of effective labor per unit of capital, upon ρ and π can be traced in a similar manner. Consider the *IS* curve, equation 1. A rise in x will raise the rent per unit of capital $r(x)$ and output per unit of capital $y(x)$. Desired savings per unit of capital

will rise by S_1 and desired investment per unit of capital will rise by $r'(x)$, given the values of the other parameters. If the demand for savings (that is, investment) rises by more than the supply of savings, that is, $r'(x) > S_1(x, \theta v)$, then the real excess demand for goods per unit of capital would rise. According to the dynamic Walrasian equation $\pi = \lambda(I/K - S/K)$, there would be an increase in π the rate of price change. At any nominal rate of interest ρ, the IS curve would shift to the right.

On the other hand, if the supply of savings rose by more than the demand for savings, that is, $r'(x) < S_1(x, \theta v)$, the excess demand for goods per unit of capital would decline. Consequently, the rate of price change would decline: the IS curve would shift to the left. A priori, it is not obvious whether the IS curve shifts to the right or to the left as a result of a rise in x, given the value of v. The usual Keynesian assumption is that a rise in output and employment will raise planned savings relative to planned investment such that the IS curve shifts to the left. But that is an arbitrary assumption.

Ambiguity also surrounds the shift of the FM curve, given a rise in x. When x rises, there is an income effect and a substitution effect. The rise in x raises $y(x)$, output per unit of capital; the transactions demand for real balances per unit of capital rises by $L_1 y'(x)$. On the other hand, the rise in $r(x)$ raises the yield on real capital relative to real balances; and the quantity demanded of real balances per unit of capital changes by $L_2 r'(x)$. The question is whether there has been a net increase or decrease in the demand for real balances per unit of capital as a result of the rise in x (given v).

If the income (transactions) effect dominates $L_1 y'(x) + L_2 r'(x) > 0$, then a rise in x raises the excess demand for real balances or increases the real excess supply of bonds. To equilibrate the bond market, the interest rate must rise (that is, bond prices fall). The FM curve shifts upward, if the income (transactions) effect dominates.

On the other hand, the substitution effect may dominate: $L_1 y'(x) + L_2 r'(x) < 0$. Then a rise in x is associated with a decline in the quantity of real balances demanded. Given the nominal rate of interest ρ, the decline in the quantity of real balances demanded will be directed to the market for goods. The rise in the excess demand for goods will lead to a rise in the rate of price change. A rightward shift will occur in the FM curve. If the decline in the quantity of real balances demanded is offset by a rise in the quantity of bonds and goods demanded, then the nominal rate of interest will tend to fall and the rate of price change will tend to rise. If the substitution effect is dominant, the FM curve shifts downward to the right.

There are four possibilities resulting from a change in parameter x. The most inflationary case occurs when a rise in x raises planned investment relative to planned savings $(r' > s_1)$ and the substitution effect is dominant $(L_1y' + L_2r' < 0)$. Then the IS curve shifts upward to the right; and the FM curve shifts downward to the right. The most deflationary case occurs when a rise in x raises planned savings relative to planned investment $(r' < S_1)$ and the transactions effect is dominant $(L_1y' + L_2r' > 0)$. Then the IS curve shifts downward to the left; and the FM curve shifts upward to the left. Keynes must have had this second case in mind when he considered the stability of "unemployment equilibrium." A rise in employment above the equilibrium would raise planned savings relative to investment, thereby producing an excess supply of goods. Moreover, the rise in output would raise the transactions demand for money; thereby, interest rates would be raised. The net effect would be to produce a deflationary gap. Consequently, the initial rise in employment could not be sustained.

The remaining two cases, where one curve shifts to the right and the other shifts to the left, yield ambiguous results concerning the effect of changes in x upon π.

4. *Summary: Mathematical Analysis.* The previous discussion can be summarized mathematically. Take the differentials of equations 1a and 2b and derive equation 26, written in matrix notation.

$$
(26) \quad \begin{pmatrix} \dfrac{1}{\lambda} & 1 \\[2ex] \dfrac{1}{\lambda}\left(\dfrac{1}{h} + L_1\right) & L_3 \end{pmatrix} \begin{pmatrix} d\pi \\[1ex] d\rho \end{pmatrix}
$$

$$
= \begin{pmatrix} r' - S_1 \\[1ex] -L_1y' - L_2r' \end{pmatrix} dx + \begin{pmatrix} -S_2\theta \\[1ex] 1 - L_4\theta \end{pmatrix} dv + \begin{pmatrix} 1 \\[1ex] -L_2 \end{pmatrix} d\pi^*.
$$

The determinant $J \equiv \dfrac{1}{\lambda}[L_3 - (1/h + L_1)]$ is unambiguously negative.

Table 1 presents the relevant partial derivatives derived from equation 27.

TABLE 1. RELEVANT PARTIAL DERIVATIVES IN EQUATIONS 15 AND 16

With Respect to Changes in:	Change in Variable	
	π	ρ
x	$\dfrac{1}{J}[L_3(r' - S_1) + (L_1y' + L_2r')]$	$-\dfrac{1}{\lambda J}\left[(L_1y' + L_2r') + (r' - S_1)\left(\dfrac{1}{h} + L_1\right)\right]$
v	$\dfrac{1}{J}[(-S_2\theta)L_3 - (1 - L_4\theta)] > 0$	$\dfrac{1}{\lambda J}\left[(1 - L_4\theta) + S_2\theta\left(\dfrac{1}{h} + L_1\right)\right]$
π^*	$\dfrac{1}{J}(L_2 + L_3) > 0$	$-\dfrac{1}{\lambda J}\left[L_2 + \left(\dfrac{1}{h} + L_1\right)\right] > 0$

$$J = \frac{1}{\lambda}\left[L_3 - \left(\frac{1}{h} + L_1\right)\right] < 0.$$

Compare the literary discussion in parts 1, 2, and 3 above with Table 1. The variety of possible effects is quite apparent. Several examples can be cited.

First, what will be the effect of a rise in v upon π and ρ, given the values of the other parameters? According to row 2 of the table, the rate of price change must rise $\partial\pi/\partial v > 0$. Both the *IS* and *FM* curves shift to the right. The effect on the nominal rate of interest is ambiguous. The rise in v tends to lower ρ via liquidity preference. However the wealth effect $S_2\theta$ decreases savings and tends to raise the rate of interest. A weak wealth effect, that is, a small value of θ, will imply that ρ declines.

Second, what will be the effect of a rise in x upon π and ρ, given the values of the other parameters. According to row 1 of the table, both effects are ambiguous. If the rise in x raises planned investment relative to planned savings ($r' > S_1$), then the rate of price change tends to rise. If the substitution effect between real balances and capital is dominant ($L_1y' + L_2r' < 0$), then the rate of price change tends to rise. Of course, there is no reason why the *IS* and *FM* curves must shift in the same direction with respect to the π axis. A similar ambiguity exists with respect to $\partial\rho/\partial x$. If the transactions effect is dominant ($L_1y' + L_2r' > 0$), then the interest rate tends to rise. Similarly, if the investment demand schedule rises relative to the savings schedule ($r' > S_1$), then the nominal rate of interest tends to rise. But these effects need not occur. The rate of savings may rise relative to the rate of investment; and the substitution effect could be dominant. In this case the nominal rate of interest would decline.

Third, what are the effects of a rise in the expected rate of price change π^* upon the values of π and ρ, given the values of the other parameters? According to row 3 of the table, the actual rate of price change must rise. When π^* rises, there must be a substitution of goods for money, and the excess demand for goods per unit of capital rises. Both the IS and FM curves shift to the right. The rate of price change π is proportional to the excess demand for goods per unit of capital, and hence $\partial\pi/\partial\pi^*$ is positive.

The value of $\partial\pi/\partial\pi^*$, referred to as f_1, could be greater than or less than unity. From Table 1:

$$(27) \qquad f_1 = \frac{\partial\pi}{\partial\pi^*} = \frac{(L_2 + L_3)\lambda}{L_3 - (1/h + L_1)}.$$

The greater the transactions demand for real balances ($1/h + L_1$) and the slower the speed of price response (λ), the lower will be the value of f_1. On the other hand, the greater the substitutability between real balances and capital ($-L_2$), the greater will be the value of f_1.

Formally, the effect upon the nominal rate of interest is ambiguous. Equation 2 views the excess real supply of bonds per unit of capital as the sum of the excess demand for goods per unit of capital plus the excess demand for real balances per unit of capital. A rise in π^* raises the excess demand for goods but lowers the excess demand for real balances. It would seem that the effect upon the bond market could go either way.

Ambiguity can be dispelled if we focus directly upon the bond market. A rise in π^*, given the nominal rate of interest, induces firms to offer more bonds to finance the purchase of real capital. The supply of bonds rises. But the rise in the expected rate of price change makes the purchase of bonds less attractive than before, relative to real capital, given the nominal rate of interest. The demand for bonds falls. The net effect of a rise in π^* is to increase the excess supply of bonds; and the nominal rate of interest must rise: $\partial\rho/\partial\pi^* > 0$.

III
THE LONG-RUN SOLUTION[9]

Now the complete model of a growing economy can be solved. The assumption that the ratio of capital to labor is fixed is relaxed; and no artificial dichotomy between the short run (with a fixed ratio of effective labor to capital) and the long run (with an endogenously determined capital intensity) is necessary. The only change in the behavioral equations that will be made (for expositional simplicity) concerns the price expectations function. In the steady state with an endogenously determined stock of capital, the rate of price change π_e will equal the growth of the money supply per worker. This can be seen by setting $Dx = 0$ and $Dv = 0$ in equations a and b below, based upon equations 17 and 18.

(a) $\qquad Dx/x = n - DK/K = 0.$

(b) $\qquad Dv/v = \mu - \pi - DK/K = 0.$

Therefore, the (long-run) steady state rate of price change denoted by π_e is:

(28) $\qquad\qquad \pi_e = \mu - n.$

Instead of the adaptive expectations function, assume that the expected rate of price change π^* is always equal to the equilibrium rate of price change; but it is the long-run equilibrium π_e that is now appropriate. No dichotomy is made between the long run and the short run.

(29) $\qquad\qquad \pi^* = \pi_e = \mu - n.$

To remind us that we are assuming price expectations function (29), rather than the adaptive expectations function, we shall write equation 24 as equation 30. Parameter θ will not be written explicitly for the sake of notational simplicity, but it is implicit in the analysis. Instead of (24), $\pi = f(\pi^*, v, x)$, write:

(30) $\qquad\qquad \pi = \pi(x, v; \mu, n),$

where $\pi_x = f_3$, $\pi_v = f_2$, and $\pi_\mu = f_1$.

[9] This is a development of my paper "Neoclassical and Keynes-Wicksell Monetary Growth Models," *Journal of Money, Credit and Banking*, I, No. 2 (May, 1969).

The long-run growth model is described by equations 31a and 31b, and they are based upon equations 20, 21, 24, and 29.

(31a) $\qquad Dx/x = n - \dfrac{a}{\lambda}\,\pi(x, v; \mu, n) - S(x, v) \equiv F(x, v; \mu, n).$

(31b) $\qquad Dv/v = \mu - \left(1 + \dfrac{a}{\lambda}\right)\pi(x, v; \mu, n) - S(x, v) \equiv G(x, v; \mu, n).$

These differential equations in x and v constitute the dynamic Keynes-Wicksell monetary growth model. We shall assume that for the set of (μ, n) under consideration, there are strictly positive steady state values (x_e, v_e) such that $F(x_e, v_e; \mu, n) = 0$ and $G(x_e, v_e; \mu, n) = 0$ in equations 31a and 31b.

First, the model consisting of (31a) and (31b) will be solved mathematically. This analysis is purely formal. Second, an economic interpretation of these results is given in part B of this section. Some readers may prefer to go directly to part B, which discusses the economics, and then return to the mathematical section, part A.

A. THE MATHEMATICAL SOLUTION OF THE KEYNES-WICKSELL MODEL

Define $x_1 = x - x_e$ as the deviation of x from its steady state value and $x_2 = v - v_e$ as the deviation of v from its steady state value. Then a linear expansion of (31a) and (31b) around the equilibrium yields differential equations 32 and 33.

(32) $\qquad\qquad Dx_1 = x_e F_1 \cdot x_1 + x_e F_2 \cdot x_2,$

(33) $\qquad\qquad Dx_2 = v_e G_1 \cdot x_1 + v_e G_2 \cdot x_2;$

where the matrix

$$\begin{pmatrix} F_1 & F_2 \\ G_1 & G_2 \end{pmatrix} \equiv (-1)\begin{pmatrix} \dfrac{a}{\lambda}\pi_x + S_x & \dfrac{a}{\lambda}\pi_v + S_2 \\[2mm] \pi_x\left(1 + \dfrac{a}{\lambda}\right) + S_x & \pi_v\left(1 + \dfrac{a}{\lambda}\right) + S_2 \end{pmatrix}.$$

Stability from any direction requires that the inequalities (34a) and (34b) be satisfied.

(34a) $\qquad\qquad\qquad x_e F_1 + v_e G_2 < 0.$

(34b) $\qquad\qquad\qquad x_e v_e (F_1 G_2 - F_2 G_1) > 0.$

Using these stability conditions we ask: What will be the effect of a change in the rate of monetary expansion μ upon the steady state values of x_e and v_e? In the steady state $Dx = Dv = 0$. Then, from (31a) and (31b), the steady state is described by (35) and (36).

(35) $\qquad\qquad F(x_e, v_e; \mu, n) = 0.$

(36) $\qquad\qquad G(x_e, v_e; \mu, n) = 0.$

The first equation states that capital and labor both grow at rate n: that is, $n = \dfrac{a}{\lambda}\pi(x_e, v_e; \mu, n) + S(x_e, v_e)$. The second equation states that real balances per worker are constant. Hence, the growth of the money supply per worker $\mu - n$ will equal the steady state rate of inflation π_e.

Solving (35) and (36) for $dx_e/d\mu$ and $dv_e/d\mu$, equations 37 and 38 are derived. Stability (34b) requires that their denominators be positive, but the sign of the numerator is ambiguous.

(37) $\qquad\qquad \dfrac{dx_e}{d\mu} = \dfrac{-F_\mu G_2 + F_2 G_\mu}{F_1 G_2 - F_2 G_1}.$

(38) $\qquad\qquad \dfrac{dv_e}{d\mu} = \dfrac{-F_1 G_\mu + F_\mu G_1}{F_1 G_2 - F_2 G_1}.$

From the definitions of F_1 and G_1, equation 37 can be written as equation 37a.

(37a) $\qquad\qquad \dfrac{dx_e}{d\mu} = \dfrac{(-S_v)(1 - \pi_\mu) - (a/\lambda)\pi_v}{F_1 G_2 - F_2 G_1}.$

The denominator of (37), (38), and (37a) must be positive in a dynamically stable system. Therefore, the sign of $dx_e/d\mu$ must be the same as the sign of the numerator. From the previous analysis we know that $(-S_v)$ and π_v are positive. Quantity $1 - \pi_\mu$ is just $1 - f_1$ used in the short-run analysis. If $1 - \pi_\mu$ is positive, a rise in μ raises the short-run equilibrium level of real balances; if $1 - \pi_\mu$ is negative, a rise in μ lowers the short-run equilibrium level of real balances. When a rise in μ lowers the short-run equilibrium level of real balances (that is, $1 - \pi_\mu$ is negative), then a rise in the rate of monetary expansion must raise the long-run capital intensity $k_e \equiv 1/x_e$. On the other hand, if $1 - \pi_\mu$ is positive, then a rise in the rate of monetary expansion could either raise or lower the long-run equilibrium capital intensity. Let us now turn to the economics of the growth process and interpret these results

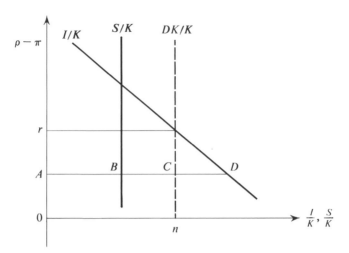

FIGURE 3. Inflation $\pi = \mu - n$ implies an inflationary
gap BD. The real rate of interest OA is less than the
rent per unit of capital Or. The growth rate is AC.

B. AN ECONOMIC INTERPRETATION OF THE VARIETY OF POSSIBLE RESULTS
What is going on in this model in economic terms? A diagram will
be helpful in interpreting the mathematics. In Figure 3 the planned savings
and investment functions are plotted against the real rate of interest.[10]
All functions are evaluated at the steady state solution x_e, v_e, π_e, and ρ_e.

*1. Inflation Implies That the Rent per Unit of Capital Exceeds the
Real Rate of Interest.* The existence of inflation $\pi = \mu - n$ implies that
planned investment per unit of capital exceeds planned savings per unit of
capital. That is, $BD = \pi/\lambda$ in the figure. Since there is excess demand, the
growth of capital $DK/K = n$ is a linear combination of planned savings
and planned investment per unit of capital $(1 > a > 0)$. There is no
presumption that either firms or consumers obtain their desired demands.
Everyone is partially frustrated.

The growth of capital is equal to the growth of labor but, when
$1 > a > 0$, desired investment per unit of capital AD exceeds the growth
of capital AC. This implies that the rent per unit of capital Or exceeds the
real rate of interest OA during inflationary periods. The gap Ar, between

[10] This diagram was suggested to me by James Tobin.

the marginal return on capital and the real rate of interest,[11] is the driving force behind the inflation in the Keynes-Wicksell mode l

Figure 3 was derived on the basis of the following considerations.

(a) $$\pi = \lambda(I/K - S/K)$$

and

(b) $$DK/K = aI/K + (1 - a)S/K \quad \text{when} \quad \pi > 0.$$

The growth of capital is:

(39) $$DK/K = I/K - (1 - a)\pi/\lambda = (n + r(x) + \pi^* - \rho) - (1 - a)\pi/\lambda.$$

In the steady state:

(c) $$DK/K = n$$

(d) $$\pi_e^* = \pi_e.$$

Using (c) and (d) with (39), we derive equation 40, describing the gap between the rent per unit of capital $r(x_e)$ and the real rate of interest $\rho_e - \pi_e$.

(40) $$r(x_e) - (\rho_e - \pi_e) = (1 - a)\pi_e/\lambda$$

or

(41) $$\rho_e = r(x_e) + \pi_e - (1 - a)\pi_e/\lambda.$$

A rise in the steady state rate of inflation, where $\pi_e = \pi_e^* = \mu - n$ and DK/K equals n, will change the nominal rate of interest in a manner described by (42).

(42) $$\frac{d\rho_e}{d\pi_e} = r'(x_e)\frac{dx_e}{d\pi_e} + \left[1 - \frac{(1 - a)}{\lambda}\right].$$

As a rule we cannot expect the money rate of interest to change by exactly the change in the rate of inflation. The relation between the interest rate ρ and the rate of inflation is more profound than a casual reading of Fisher's *The Theory of Interest* would suggest. To sustain inflation in the steady state, the real rate of interest must be below the rent on capital if $1 > a > 0$.

2. *Why a Rise in the Rate of Monetary Expansion Has an Ambiguous Effect upon the Steady State Capital Intensity.* Why can a rise in the rate

[11] Or, it is the gap between the capital value of existing assets and the supply price of newly produced capital goods.

of monetary expansion (μ) exert an ambiguous effect upon the steady state value of x (the reciprocal of the capital intensity)? Let us trace several possible effects of a rise in the rate of monetary expansion upon the growth path of the economy.

The rise in the rate of monetary expansion is interpreted by the economic agents as a harbinger of a greater rate of inflation. A rise in the demand for capital assets occurs as a result of these price expectations. Insofar as the capital value of existing assets rises relative to the supply price of newly produced goods, there is an increase in the desired rate of investment in newly produced capital goods. To be sure, there will be an excess supply of bonds resulting from the new price expectations. Equilibrium in the bond market will require that the nominal rate of interest rise; but the interest rate will not rise by as much as the rise in the expected capital gain. Aggregate demand for goods will increase and will raise the actual rate of price change. The chain of causation has run from the expected to the actual rate of price change. How quickly will prices respond to the pressure of excess demand?

If prices respond slowly such that the actual rate of price change rises at a slower rate than the rate of monetary expansion, several effects will occur. (1) The level of real balances M/p must rise since μ has increased relative to π. (2) There will be a rise in the volume of unfilled orders per unit of capital since aggregate demand has increased relative to aggregate supply.

As a result of the rise in real balances per unit of capital, planned consumption per unit of capital will increase, and the inflationary gap will be aggravated. The rate of price change is positively related to the inflationary gap ($I/K - S/K$), and the rise in consumption demand will raise the rate of inflation. There are two stabilizing forces. One is the rigidity of price expectations $\pi^* = \mu - n$. The second is the real balance effect. As long as (π), the rate of price change, is less than $\mu - n$, real balances per worker rise; and the rise in real balances raises π further. Eventually, the growth in real balances will raise π until it is equal to the growth of the money supply per effective worker. At that point the rate of price change will not rise further (given the expectations function $\pi^* = \mu - n$ and the capital intensity).

The rise in the level of real balances has two countervailing effects upon the rate of capital formation. On the one hand, it raises planned consumption or decreases planned savings. This effect tends to lower the capital intensity by decreasing the growth of capital. On the other hand, the rise in the rate of price change stimulates investment. This effect tends to raise the rate of capital formation, and thereby tends to raise the capital intensity. A priori, either effect could dominate. If the rate of capital formation is primarily determined by planned savings (that is, coefficient a in equation 20 is small), then the rate of capital formation per unit of capital will decline. The net effect will be to lower the steady state ratio of capital to labor, the reverse of the Neoclassical result.[12]

Other consequences are logically possible. The rate of capital formation could be primarily determined by the rate of planned investment (that is, coefficient a in equation 20 could be close to unity). Then the rise in planned investment per unit of capital raises the rate of capital formation per unit of capital. As a result the capital intensity rises when the rate of monetary expansion per worker increases. The conventional Neoclassical result concerning the capital intensity could be obtained although the level of real balances per unit of capital has increased.[13]

There is another possibility that may occur if prices respond very quickly to the pressure of excess demand. The rise in price expectations, resulting from a rise in the rate of monetary expansion per worker, raises aggregate demand in the manner described above. Prices may rise at a faster rate than the rate of monetary expansion (that is, $f_1 = \pi_\mu > 1$). As a result of the rise in the rate of price change in excess of the rate of monetary expansion, the level of real balances will be reduced. Consumption, which is positively related to real balances, will be reduced. Thereby, the rate of inflation will be reduced. Moreover, the decline in real balances will tend to raise the nominal rate of interest. In addition to this effect there will be an upward pressure upon interest rates exerted by the greater transactions demand for money. The net effect of the rise in interest rates and the decline in real balances will be to reduce the level of excess aggregate demand. The rate of inflation will be reduced as a

---

[12] In terms of equation 39, $1 - \pi_\mu$ was assumed to be positive: that is, prices were assumed to respond slowly to the pressure of excess demand. Insofar as the rate of capital formation is primarily determined by the savings behavior of the economy, a is assumed to be small. Therefore, the sign of $dx_e/d\mu$ is given by $(-S_v)(1 - \pi_\mu)$. Hence, the steady state value of x_e rises or the equilibrium capital intensity $k_e \equiv 1/x_e$ declines.

[13] This was the conclusion in my study "Money and Capacity Growth," *Journal of Political Economy*, LXXIV (1966).

result. As long as the rate of price change π exceeds the growth of the money supply per worker $\mu - n$, the value of v will decline, and the rate of price change will be reduced. The level of v will decline until the rate of price change declines to the value of the growth of the money supply per effective worker.

If the rate of capital formation is primarily determined by planned savings, then the decline in real balances per unit of capital will raise the rate of capital formation per unit of capital. The capital intensity rises and the level of real balances per unit of capital declines as a result of the rise in the rate of monetary expansion. This is the Neoclassical result.

It is possible that the rate of planned investment is the primary determinant of the rate of capital formation during periods of excess aggregate demand. The rate of price change π in the Keynes-Wicksell model is proportional to I/K less S/K. We know that π and S/K have increased. Therefore, I/K must have increased. Hence, the growth of capital rises relative to the growth of effective labor, and (again) the capital intensity has increased.[14]

Finally, the Keynes-Wicksell model implies that the ratio of unfilled orders per unit of capital is proportional to the rate of inflation. Eventually, unfilled orders grow at the same rate as the economy. The proof is straightforward Excess aggregate demand is equal to the change in unfilled orders The rate of price change π_e is proportional to excess aggregate demand per unit of capital Therefore, the change in unfilled orders per unit of capital is proportional to the rate of inflation π_e.

Formally, let $DU = I - S$ be the change in unfilled orders (DU). Then:

$$(43) \qquad\qquad DU/K = \pi/\lambda,$$

follows from equation 1. In the steady state, $\pi = \pi_e = \mu - n$; the stock of capital grows at proportionate rate n. Therefore:

$$(43a) \qquad\qquad DU = \frac{\pi_e}{\lambda} K(T) e^{n(t-T)},$$

---

[14] In terms of equation 39, $1 - \pi_\mu$ is assumed to be negative. Therefore, the sign of $dx_e/d\mu$ is unambiguously negative. A rise in the rate of monetary expansion must lower x_e or raise the steady state capital intensity, regardless of whether the rate of capital formation is primarily determined by savings or by investment decisions.

where T is the date at which balanced growth first occurs. The ratio of unfilled orders per unit of capital U/K converges to a constant which is proportional to the rate of inflation.

(44)
$$\lim_{t \to \infty} \frac{U}{K} = \frac{\pi_e}{\lambda n} = \frac{\mu - n}{\lambda n} .$$

In the Keynes-Wicksell model inflation implies disequilibrium, even in the steady state. The magnitude of the disequilibrium is proportional to the rate of inflation. Prices do not change except insofar as there is excess demand or supply in this model; and this ostensibly innocuous assumption has generated a wider set of results than were obtained from the Neoclassical model.

IV

SUMMARY

The long run is the limit of a succession of short runs; and the connecting link between the short runs is the endogenous change in the capital stock resulting from the investment process. Dynamic short-run macro-economic models generally assume (a) the existence of independent savings and investment equations and (b) that prices are changing in a competitive economy if, and only if, there is a market disequilibrium. By contrast, the Neoclassical monetary growth model assumes that planned investment is identically equal to planned savings and that all markets are always in equilibrium. What connection exists between these two sets of models? What unifying theory can be constructed which would be applicable to the short-run as well as the long-run aggregative enonomy? The Keynes-Wicksell model is designed to integrate the usual dynamic short-run aggregative model into the growth process. Long-run equilibrium is nothing other than the steady state solution of the dynamic model with endogenous capital. Or, the short-run dynamic model is a special case of the general growth model.

In the Keynes-Wicksell model prices are changing in a competitive economy if, and only if, the aggregate demand for goods differs from capacity output. Excess aggregate demand is planned consumption plus planned investment less capacity output. Since planned savings are output less planned consumption, excess aggregate demand is equal to planned investment less planned savings. The proportionate rate of price change is assumed to be related directly to the real excess demand for goods deflated by the stock of capital. A given real excess demand for goods will lead to a more rapid rate of inflation in a small economy (for example, the United States in 1879) than in a larger economy (for example, the United States in 1970). In a growing economy the excess demand for goods per se is not a satisfactory index of inflationary pressure. For convenience, the real excess demand for goods is deflated by the stock of capital. No essential difference would occur if it were assumed that the proportionate rate of price change is directly related to the real excess demand for goods per worker.

The existence of inflation implies that planned investment per unit of capital exceeds planned savings per unit of capital. Wicksell would have said that the natural rate of interest exceeds the market rate of interest. In the steady state of this model the existence of inflation implies that the marginal efficiency of capital, which is the expected rent per unit of capital plus the expected capital gain, exceeds the nominal rate of interest. Alternatively, the existence of inflation implies that the rent per unit of capital exceeds the real rate of interest, where the latter is defined as the nominal rate of interest less the expected rate of price change. It is the gap between the rent per unit of capital and the real rate of interest that is the driving force behind the inflation.

When savings and investment are not equal, what will be the rate of capital formation? We assume that it will be less than firms desire but more than households plan to save. The rate of capital formation will be a linear combination of planned savings and planned investment during periods of excess aggregate demand. Even though the inflation is anticipated, not all the demands can be satisfied during periods of excess demand. Unfilled orders rise during such periods.

All growth models imply that, in the steady state, the actual and expected rates of price change are equal to the growth of the money supply per worker. A rise in the rate of monetary expansion per worker can produce a variety of results in the Keynes-Wicksell model. Let us trace several possible effects of a rise in the rate of monetary expansion upon the growth path of the economy. Assume that the expected rate of price change is equal to the steady state value: the rate of monetary expansion per (effective) worker.

The rise in the rate of monetary expansion is interpreted by the economic agents as a harbinger of a greater rate of inflation. A rise in the demand for capital assets occurs as a result of these price expectations. Insofar as the capital value of existing assets rises relative to the supply price of newly produced goods, there is an increase in the desired rate of investment in newly produced capital goods. To be sure, there will be an excess supply of bonds resulting from the new price expectations. Equilibrium in the bond market will require that the nominal rate of interest rise; but the interest rate will not rise by as much as the rise in the expected capital gain. Aggregate demand for goods will increase and will raise the actual rate of price change. The chain of causation has run from the expected to the actual rate of price change. How quickly will prices respond to the pressure of excess demand?

If prices respond slowly such that the actual rate of price change rises at a slower rate than the rate of monetary expansion, several effects will occur. (1) The level of real balances must rise since the rate of monetary expansion has increased relative to the rate of price change. (2) There will be a rise in the volume of unfilled orders per unit of capital since aggregate demand has increased relative to aggregate supply.

As a result of the rise in real balances per unit of capital, planned consumption and investment per unit of capital will increase, and the inflationary gap will be aggravated. The rate of price change is positively related to the inflationary gap, planned investment less planned savings per unit of capital; and the rise in consumption and investment demand will raise the rate of inflation. There are two stabilizing forces. One is the assumed rigidity of price expectations. The second is the real balance effect. As long as the rate of price change is less than the rate of monetary expansion per worker, real balances per worker rise; and the rise in real balances raises the rate of price change further. Eventually, the growth in real balances will raise the rate of price change until it is equal to the growth of the money supply per effective worker. At that point the rate of price change will not rise further (given the expectations function and the capital intensity).

The rise in the level of real balances has two countervailing effects upon the rate of capital formation. On the one hand, it raises planned consumption or decreases planned savings. This effect tends to lower the capital intensity by decreasing the growth of capital. On the other hand, the rise in the rate of price change stimulates investment by lowering the real rate of interest. This effect tends to raise the rate of capital formation and thereby tends to raise the capital intensity. A priori, either effect could dominate. If the rate of capital formation is primarily determined by planned savings, then the rate of capital formation per unit of capital will decline. The net effect will be to lower the steady state ratio of capital to labor, the reverse of the Neoclassical result.

Other consequences are logically possible. The rate of capital formation could be primarily determined by the rate of planned investment. Then the rise in planned investment per unit of capital raises the rate of capital formation per unit of capital. As a result the capital intensity rises when the rate of monetary expansion per worker increases. The conventional Neoclassical result concerning the capital intensity could be obtained, although the level of real balances per unit of capital has increased.

There is another possibility that may occur if prices respond very quickly to the pressure of excess demand. The rise in price expectations, resulting from a rise in the rate of monetary expansion per worker, raises aggregate demand in the manner described above. Prices may rise at a faster rate than the rate of monetary expansion. As a result of the rise in the rate of price change in excess of the rate of monetary expansion, the level of real balances will be reduced. Consumption, which is positively related to real balances, will be reduced. Thereby, the rate of inflation will be reduced. Moreover, the decline in real balances will tend to raise the nominal rate of interest. In addition to this effect, there will be an upward pressure upon interest rates exerted by the greater transactions demand for money. The net effect of the rise in interest rates and the decline in real balances will be to reduce the level of excess aggregate demand. The rate of inflation will be reduced as a result. As long as the rate of price change exceeds the growth of the money supply per worker, the rate of inflation will decline: that is, the rate of price change will be reduced. Eventually, the level of real balances per unit of capital will decline until the rate of price change will have declined to equal the growth of the money supply per effective worker.

If the rate of capital formation is determined primarily by planned savings, then the decline in real balances per unit of capital will raise the rate of capital formation per unit of capital. The capital intensity rises and the level of real balances per unit of capital declines as a result of the rise in the rate of monetary expansion. This is the Neoclassical result derived from a Keynes-Wicksell model.

It is possible that the rate of planned investment is the primary determinant of the rate of capital formation during periods of excess aggregate demand. The rate of price change, in the Keynes-Wicksell model, is proportional to planned investment per unit of capital less planned savings per unit of capital. We know that the rate of price change and planned savings per unit of capital have increased. Therefore, planned investment per unit of capital must have increased. It follows that the growth of capital rises relative to the growth of (effective) labor and the capital intensity rises.

Finally, the Keynes-Wicksell model implies that the ratio of unfilled orders per unit of capital is proportional to the rate of inflation. Eventually, unfilled orders grow at the same rate as the economy when there is inflation. The reasoning is straightforward. Excess aggregate demand is equal to the change in unfilled orders. The rate of price change is proportional to excess aggregate demand per unit of capital. Therefore, the change in unfilled orders is proportional to the rate of inflation multiplied by the stock of capital. Since capital grows at the same rate as labor, unfilled orders also grow at that rate. Only when prices are constant are unfilled orders per unit of capital equal to zero.

CHAPTER FIVE

░░░░

A Synthesis of Neoclassical and Keynes-Wicksell Models

TWO SEPARATE QUESTIONS are immediately suggested by the previous chapters. First, are the Neoclassical and Keynes-Wicksell models of growth mutually exclusive? Is it possible that both views are correct? The Neoclassical model ignores the developments in aggregative economics associated with the name of Keynes, and it does not appear to be a useful technique for short-run analysis. On the other hand, the Keynes-Wicksell model implies that market disequilibrium must exist in the steady state if there is secular inflation or deflation. Many economists feel uneasy with that conclusion. Is a reconciliation of the two approaches possible? A model which synthesizes these two views is formulated in section I of this chapter. The resulting synthesis has the properties of a Keynes-Wicksell model outside the steady state but becomes a Neoclassical model in the steady state.[1]

Another question is: How useful are the previous models in explaining observed empirical regularities? Two phenomena are not easily explainable by the conventional models. (A) Year-to-year changes in the nominal rate of interest are negatively related to year-to-year changes in the rate of monetary expansion and to year-to-year changes in the money-wealth ratio. (B) A positive association exists between the nominal

---

[1] A summary (section IV) is found at the end of the chapter.

interest rate and the index of prices during periods of rising and falling prices: the Gibson paradox. Section II of this chapter explains phenomenon (A), and section III of this chapter explains phenomenon (B). Although the explanations are in terms of the Synthesis model developed in section I, the pure Keynes-Wicksell model (Chapters 3 and 4) is also capable of explaining these phenomena in about the same way.

I

A MODEL SYNTHESIZING

THE TWO APPROACHES

The Neoclassical and Keynes-Wicksell models can be synthesized if it is assumed that the rate of price change π is affected directly, as well as indirectly, by price expectations.[2] Assume that the rate of price change $\pi \equiv D \ln p$ is the sum of two components. First, the specialists who make markets initially change prices at a rate equal to the expected rate of price change π^*. Second, prices are changed further at a rate proportional to the excess demand for goods per unit of capital, as in the Keynes-Wicksell model. This important assumption is stated as equation 1.

(1) $$\pi = \pi^* + \lambda(I/K - S/K).$$

No other assumption is required to convert the Keynes-Wicksell model into one which implies the Neoclassical results in the steady state (long-run equilibrium).

The IS curve is equation 2, which differs from the IS curve in the Keynes-Wicksell model by the addition of the direct effect of price expectations upon the actual rate of price change.[3]

(2) $$\pi = \pi^* + \lambda[n + r(x) + \pi^* - \rho - S(x, \theta v)].$$

The FM curve of the Keynes-Wicksell model[4] is changed somewhat in the Synthesis model. The transactions demand for real balances per unit of capital depends upon planned real expenditures per unit of capital: $(C + I)/K = (Y + I - S)/K$. In the Keynes-Wicksell model, when price

---

[2] Jurg Niehans suggested this assumption to me. See also P. Cagan (May, 1969, pp. 207–27).
[3] Compare equation 1 in Chapter 4.
[4] Compare equation 2 in Chapter 4.

expectations only have an indirect effect upon aggregate demand:

$$Y/K + (I - S)/K = y(x) + \pi/\lambda.$$

On the other hand, in the Synthesis model, equation 1 implies that:

$$Y/K + (I - S)/K = y(x) + (\pi - \pi^*)/\lambda.$$

Consequently, the FM curve becomes:[5]

(3) $$\frac{\pi - \pi^*}{\lambda h} = v - L\left[y(x) + \frac{(\pi - \pi^*)}{\lambda}, r(x) + \pi^*, \rho, \theta v \right]$$

instead of equation 2 in Chapter 5.

The growth of capital DK/K will continue to be a linear combination of planned investment and planned savings per unit of capital in inflationary periods.

(4a) $$\frac{DK}{K} = a\frac{I}{K} + (1 - a)\frac{S}{K}; \quad 1 > a > 0 \quad \text{when} \quad \pi > 0$$

$$a = 0 \quad \text{otherwise.}$$

Using equation 1 in (4a), the growth of capital is described by equation 4

(4) $$\frac{DK}{K} = \frac{a}{\lambda}(\pi - \pi^*) + S(x, \theta v).$$

Therefore, the proportionate rate of change of the ratio of effective labor per unit of capital $x \equiv N/K$ is equal to the growth of effective labor n less the growth of capital DK/K.

(5) $$\frac{Dx}{x} = n - \frac{a}{\lambda}(\pi - \pi^*) - S(x, \theta v).$$

The proportionate rate of growth of real balances per unit of capital $v \equiv M/pK$ is simply:

(6) $$\frac{Dv}{v} = \mu - \pi - \frac{DK}{K},$$

where the growth of capital is described by equation 4.

In the steady state the actual and expected rates of price changes are equal, regardless of the model studied. We could assume that the expected

---

[5] When the bond market is in equilibrium, Walras' law is: $\dfrac{I - S}{K} = h(v - L)$. Since $\dfrac{\pi - \pi^*}{\lambda} = \dfrac{I - S}{K}$, equation 3 follows.

rate of price change is always equal to the steady state rate of price change, as was done in the previous chapters for both the Neoclassical and the Keynes-Wicksell models. Instead of that assumption, we shall use the adaptive expectations equation relating the expected to the actual rate of price change: equation 7.

$$(7) \qquad\qquad D\pi^* = b(\pi - \pi^*).$$

Expectations are revised at a rate proportional to the difference between the actual and expected rates of price change. Although the form of the price expectations function has no effect upon the steady state solution, it affects the path to the long-run equilibrium.

Equations 2-7 constitute a dynamic model in six unknowns: the nominal rate of interest (ρ), the rate of price change (π), the expected rate of price change (π^*), real balances per unit of capital (v), the ratio of effective labor per unit of capital (x), and the growth of capital (DK/K).

Two aspects of the model will be considered. Part A of this section examines the steady state solution, and the Tobin Neoclassical results are obtained. A rise in the rate of monetary expansion will unambiguously raise the steady state capital intensity $k_e \equiv 1/x_e$ and will lower the steady state real balances per unit of capital v_e. The nominal rate of interest ρ_e is the sum of the marginal product of capital $r(x_e)$ and the rate of price change π_e. In every model the steady state rate of price change is equal to the growth of the money supply per effective worker $\mu - n$. Therefore, the steady state nominal rate of interest $\rho_e = r(x_e) + (\mu - n)$.

Part B of this section is concerned with the short-run dynamic solution of the model when the ratio of effective labor per unit of capital is fixed. It is a generalized short-run macro-economic model. Endogenous variables are the rate of interest ρ, real balances per unit of capital, and rates of price change π and π^*. It is assumed, however, that the ratio of effective labor per unit of capital is fixed. The results of this section are used, in Sections II and III, to explain some empirical results concerning the nominal rate of interest.

A. THE STEADY STATE SOLUTION

Long-run equilibrium implies that the ratios of effective labor per unit of capital and real balances per unit of capital are constant. Moreover, the expected rate of price change will be constant, but not necessarily zero, in the steady state. This implies that:

(8a) $$Dx/x = n - DK/K = 0$$

or

(8b) $$DK/K = n.$$

Capital and effective labor grow at the same rate n.
Constancy of real balances per unit of capital implies that:

(9a) $$Dv/v = \mu - \pi - DK/K = 0$$

or

(9b) $$\mu - \pi = DK/K.$$

Since capital and labor grow at rate n, constancy of real balances per unit of capital implies that the steady state rate of price change π_e is equal to the growth of the money supply per worker.

(9c) $$\mu - \pi_e = n$$

or

(9d) $$\pi_e = \mu - n.$$

When the expected rate of price change π^* is constant, then:

(10a) $$D\pi^* = b(\pi - \pi^*) = 0.$$

This implies that the actual and expected rates of price change are equal in the steady state.

(10b) $$\pi_e = \pi_e^*.$$

Equation 1 implies that, when the actual and expected rates of price change are equal $\pi_e^* = \pi_e$, then planned savings are equal to planned investment. There is no disequilibrium in the market for goods in the steady state, within the context of this model which synthesizes the Neoclassical and Keynes-Wicksell approaches.

(11a) $$\pi_e - \pi_e^* = 0 = \lambda(I/K - S/K).$$

Anticipations of price changes lead specialists to mark up prices at a rate $\pi_e^* = \pi_e = \mu - n$, without any concomitant excess demand for goods. Since these expectations are correct in the steady state, the price changes are of exactly the correct amount to preserve equilibrium in the market for goods.

The condition of equilibrium in the market for goods, that is, the equality of planned savings and investment, implies that:

(11b)
$$n + r(x_e) + \pi_e - \rho_e = S(x_e, \theta v_e),$$

where equation 11b is based upon equations 2 and 11a.

Planned savings and investment are equal in the steady state. Therefore, the growth of capital is equal to planned savings per unit of capital (see equation 4). Since the growth of capital is equal to the growth of labor:

(11c)
$$n + r(x_e) + \pi_e - \rho_e = S(x_e, \theta v_e) = n.$$

Equation 11c implies that the nominal rate of interest in the steady state is equal to the marginal rate of return on capital: its rent plus the capital gain.

(12)
$$\rho_e = r(x_e) + \pi_e.$$

Steady state inflation does not require that the rent per unit of capital $r(x_e)$ exceed the real rate of interest $\rho_e - \pi_e$, as was the case in the Keynes-Wicksell model.

A simultaneous determination of the steady state values of effective labor per unit of capital (x_e) and real balances per unit of capital (v_e) will allow us to infer that a rise in the rate of monetary expansion will lower both x_e and v_e. No ambiguity exists in this Synthesis model, which is Keynes-Wicksell at any moment of time but Neoclassical in the steady state.

Two basic equations describe the steady state solution. First, planned savings per unit of capital are equal to the growth of effective labor.

(13)
$$S(x_e, \theta v_e) = n,$$

which is based upon equation 11c. If there were no real balance effect in the savings function $(S_2 \theta = 0)$, then the steady state value of effective labor per unit of capital would be determined directly from equation 13. Monetary policy would not be able to influence the steady state values of the real variables. Assume, instead, that there is a real balance effect in the savings function $(S_2 \theta < 0)$.

Second, in the steady state, the quantity demanded of real balances per unit of capital is equal to the stock of real balances per unit of capital. This follows from the FM curve, using equation 11a. If the excess demand for goods and bonds is zero, there will be a zero excess demand for real balances.

(14a) $$v_e = L[y(x_e), r(x_e) + \pi_e, \rho_e, \theta v_e].$$

Equation 12 states that the yield on bonds is equal to the yield on real capital. It follows that:

(14b) $$v_e = L[y(x_e), r(x_e) + \pi_e, r(x_e) + \pi_e, \theta v_e]$$

is the *FM* curve in the steady state.

Equations 13, 14b, and 9d enable us to solve for the steady state values of x_e, v_e, and π_e in terms of parameters μ, n, and θ. A graphic solution will be employed.

1. A Graphic Presentation of the Long-Run Solution. Define the *LX* curve as the set of (x_e, v_e) such that planned savings per unit of capital $S(x_e, \theta v_e)$ are equal to the growth of effective labor. It is the graph of equation 13. Suppose that x_e rose. What must happen to v_e to preserve equilibrium $n = S(x_e, \theta v_e)$? When x_e rises, it raises output per unit of capital. Savings per unit of capital are positively related to output per unit of capital. Therefore, a rise in x_e raises planned savings per unit of capital. What must happen to real balances per unit of capital v_e if planned savings per unit of capital are to remain equal to the growth of effective labor n? Real balances per unit of capital must change in such a manner as to offset the rise in planned savings per unit of capital (that resulted from the rise in the ratio of effective labor per unit of capital).

Savings per unit of capital are negatively related to real balances per unit of capital. Real balances per unit of capital must, therefore, rise to offset the rise in savings (that was induced by the rise in x). For this reason the *LX* curve is positively sloped. Equation 15a describes the exact value of this slope (when $S_2\theta < 0$).

(15a) $$\frac{dv_e}{dx_e} = \frac{S_1}{-S_2\theta} > 0 \qquad (LX \text{ curve})$$

Define the *LV* curve as the graph of equation 14b. It is the set of (x_e, v_e) such that the supply of, and demand for, real balances per unit of capital are equal. Along this curve money-market equilibrium is preserved in the steady state. The slope of this curve is ambiguous and is described by equation 15b.

(15b) $\quad \dfrac{dv_e}{dx_e} = \dfrac{1}{(1 - L_4\theta)}\,[L_1 y' + (L_2 + L_3)r']$ $\quad$ (LV curve).

Ambiguity arises because of the conflict between the transactions and substitution effects, which were discussed in Chapter 4. Suppose that money-market equilibrium prevailed, $v_e = L(\cdot)$, and x_e increased. What must happen to v_e to preserve long-run money-market equilibrium? It will depend upon what happens to the quantity demanded of real balances per unit of capital as a result of the rise in x.

When x_e rises, output per unit of capital increases, and more real balances are demanded for transactions purposes. On the other hand, the rise in x_e raises the yield on capital, and the yield on bonds must equal the yield on capital in the steady state. Therefore, the rise in x_e raises the yields on both of the substitute assets and thereby decreases the quantity demanded of real balances per unit of capital.

On balance, which effect will be dominant? If the transactions effect $L_1 y'$ dominates the substitution effect $(L_2 + L_3)r'$, then a rise in x_e will increase the quantity demanded of real balances per unit of capital. A positively sloped LV curve will result. When the substitution effect is dominant, then a rise in x_e lowers the quantity demanded of real balances per unit of capital. A negatively sloped LV curve results if the substitution effect is dominant.

Stability of equilibrium requires that the LX curve have the greater slope, but it makes no difference to our present argument whether the LV curve is positively or negatively sloped. In Figure 1 it was arbitrarily assumed that the transactions effect is dominant. The reader will have no difficulty in repeating the analysis when the substitution effect is dominant: that is, when the LV curve is negatively sloped. A heuristic explanation of the dynamic processes at work is found in part 3 of this section. The comparative steady state analysis will first be proved algebraically in part 2 of this section; and then the nature of the economic forces at work will be discussed in part 3.

2. An Algebraic Analysis of the Effect of a Change in the Rate of Monetary Expansion upon the Steady State Values of x and v. How will a

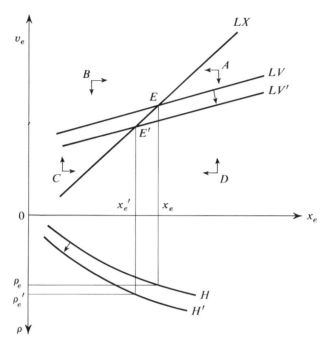

FIGURE 1. The determination of long-run equilibrium values of effective labor per unit of capital (x_e) and real balances per unit of capital (v_e) in the Synthesis model. The LX curve is equation 13 and the LV curve is equation 14b. A rise in the rate of monetary expansion shifts the LV curve to LV' and the H curve to H'.

change in the rate of monetary expansion μ affect the equilibrium point E in Figure 1? Is there any ambiguity concerning the effects of a rise in μ upon the steady state values of the ratio of effective labor per unit of capital $x_e \equiv 1/k_e$ (the reciprocal of the capital intensity) and real balances per unit of capital?

In the steady state the rate of price change $\pi_e = \pi_e^*$ is equal to the growth of the money supply per worker (see equations 9d and 10b). We may reformulate our question and ask: What will happen to x_e and v_e as a result of a rise in $\pi_e = \mu - n$?

Differentiate equation 13, the LX curve, and equation 14b, the LV

curve, with respect to π_e. Equations 16a and 16b are obtained.

(16a)
$$S_1 \frac{dx_e}{d\pi_e} + S_2\theta \frac{dv_e}{d\pi_e} = 0$$

(16b)
$$-[L_1 y' + (L_2 + L_3)r'] \frac{dx_e}{d\pi_e} + (1 - L_4\theta) \frac{dv_e}{d\pi_e} = (L_2 + L_3).$$

The values of $dx_e/d\pi_e$ and $dv_e/d\pi_e$ are given by equations 17 and 18, respectively.

(17)
$$\frac{dx_e}{d\pi_e} = \frac{-(S_2\theta)(L_2 + L_3)}{J} < 0.$$

(18)
$$\frac{dv_e}{d\pi_e} = \frac{S_1(L_2 + L_3)}{J} < 0.$$

The value of J is described by equations 19a and 19b. In the latter $\sigma(X)$ refers to the slope of the LX curve and $\sigma(V)$ refers to the slope of the LV curve. Stability requires that the LX curve have the greater slope; therefore, $\sigma(X) - \sigma(V)$ is positive. It follows that J is positive in a dynamically stable system.

(19a) $$J = S_1(1 - L_4\theta) + S_2\theta[L_1 y' + (L_2 + L_3)r']$$

(19b) $$J = (-S_2\theta)(1 - L_4\theta)[\sigma(X) - \sigma(V)] > 0.$$

The substitution effect $(L_2 + L_3)$ is negative. Therefore, the rise in π_e unambiguously lowers the steady state values of x_e and v_e. Equilibrium point E is shifted downward and to the left. No ambiguity concerning the steady state exists in the Synthesis model.

3. *A Heuristic Account of the Dynamic Economic Processes at Work.* Figure 1 can be used to describe the economic processes which determine the signs of derivatives (17) and (18) above.[6] First, the convergence of the economy to equilibrium will be described. Second, the figure will be used to explain the effects of a rise in the rate of monetary expansion upon the steady state values of x_e and v_e.

[6] Strictly speaking, the use of Figure 1 to describe a dynamic process is technically incorrect. A phase diagram in the (x, v, π^*) space should be used, corresponding to differential equations 5, 6, and 7. This is difficult to do and would defeat our purpose. An algebraic solution (along the lines presented in Chapter 4) can be given, and the stability conditions can be determined from the Routh-Hurwitz inequalities. For the sake of simplicity and clarity, technical rigor has been sacrificed. Our aim is to describe the nature of the underlying economic processes.

Suppose that the economy were shifted to the right (left) of the LX curve to points A or D (C or B). Along the LX curve capital and effective labor are both growing at rate n. An increase (decrease) in x will raise (lower) planned savings per unit of capital, and thereby the growth of capital will exceed (be less than) the growth of effective labor. As a result the value of x will decrease (rise) in the direction of the LX curve. This is a stabilizing force which has been described by the arrows in the horizontal direction through points A, B, C, and D.

This system is assumed to be dynamically stable, and (x, v) will converge to the equilibrium point[7] E. Suppose, for example, that the economy were at point A. Capital is growing more rapidly than effective labor since A is to the right of the LX curve. In addition, the stock of real balances per unit of capital exceeds the quantity demanded since A is above the LV curve. Therefore, the rate of price change exceeds the growth of the money supply per unit of capital. The values of x and v continue to decline as long as the economy is inside region $(LX)E(LV)$. Equilibrium is attained at point E, where equations 13, 14b, and 9d are satisfied. A similar argument applies to point C.

If the economy started from points B or D, the convergence to equilibrium point E need not be monotonic. However, in Figure 1, the economy always converges to the equilibrium point.

What will be the effect of a rise in the rate of monetary expansion $\mu = \pi_e + n$ (or a rise in the steady state rate of price change $\pi_e = \pi_e{}^* = \mu - n$) upon the steady state values of x_e and v_e?

No change will occur in the LX curve (equation 13) as a result of a rise in π_e. On the other hand, the LV curve will shift downward (for any value of x) when π_e rises. An increase in the rate of price change raises the yields on capital and bonds relative to the yield on money. As a result of the substitution effect, the quantity demanded of real balances per unit of capital declines, and the LV curve shifts downward. The magnitude of the shift is:

(20)
$$\frac{\partial v}{\partial \pi_e} = \frac{(L_2 + L_3)}{(1 - L_4\theta)} < 0,$$

based upon the equation for the LV curve.

---

[7] Stability will only be assured if the value of the adaptive expectations coefficient b is sufficiently small. 1B discusses the dynamics of the short-run version of the model and the stability conditions in a rigorous manner.

If the economy were initially at point E, the downward shift of the LV curve throws the economy out of equilibrium. Although capital and effective labor are growing at rate n (since the economy is on the LX curve), the money market is out of equilibrium. There is an excess supply of real balances per unit of capital since the economy is above the LV curve. Prices rise at a faster rate than before, and the value of v tends to decline. A reduction in real balances per unit of capital raises planned savings per unit of capital, and capital is now growing more rapidly than effective labor. The economy is drawn off the LX curve into region $(LX)E'(LV')$.

Equilibrium is attained at point E', where again capital grows at rate n. At E', the rate of price change is equal to the new rate of monetary expansion per worker. Both the ratio of effective labor per unit of capital x_e and real balances per unit of capital v_e have been reduced.

The Synthesis model, whereby $\pi = \pi^* + \lambda(I/K - S/K)$, implies that the Tobin Neoclassical results occur in the steady state. There is no ambiguity about the effects of a rise in the rate of monetary expansion upon the steady state solution.

What happens to the nominal rate of interest in the steady state? According to equation 12, graphed in the lower half of Figure 1, the nominal rate of interest is the sum of the steady state rent per unit of capital $r(x_e)$ and the steady state rate of price change π_e.

The rise in the rate of price change shifts the H curve, which describes the equation $\rho_e = r(x_e) + \pi_e$, to H'. On the other hand, the decline in the rent per unit of capital from $r(x_e)$ to $r(x_e')$ constitutes a movement along the H' curve. It is believed that $r(x)$ changes by less than π_e. Therefore, the steady state nominal rate of interest is expected to rise from ρ_e to ρ_e' in Figure 1. Conventional results are obtained from the Synthesis model in the steady state.

B. SHORT-RUN DYNAMICS

By definition, the short run is a span of time in which the ratio of effective labor per unit of capital is relatively constant. During such a period of time, what will be the effects of variations in the rate of monetary expansion upon the nominal rate of interest ρ, real balances per unit of capital v, the expected rate of price change π^*, and the actual rate of price change π. This set of questions was considered in the previous chapter in terms of the Keynes-Wicksell model. An important conclusion was that the effect of a rise in the rate of monetary expansion upon the short-run equilibrium level of real balances per unit of capital v_s was ambiguous.

Within the context of the Synthesis model, a different conclusion emerges. A rise in μ will unambiguously lower the short-run equilibrium level of real balances per unit of capital and raise the short-run equilibrium nominal rate of interest. Nevertheless, at any moment in time, there will probably be a negative relation between changes in the nominal rate of interest and changes in the rate of monetary expansion.

Four equations constitute the short-run dynamic model: an *IS* curve, an *FM* curve, the differential equation describing the proportionate rate of change of real balances per unit of capital, and a price expectations function. These were precisely the equations used to describe the short-run dynamic process in the previous chapter. To facilitate a comparison between the Keynes-Wicksell and the Synthesis models, a Kronecker δ will be used: it assumes the value of 1 in the Synthesis model and a value of 0 in the Keynes-Wicksell model.

Since the four equations were discussed earlier in this chapter, they will be repeated with no additional explanation, and they will be renumbered for the reader's convenience.

The *IS* curve is equation 21a, the *FM* curve is equation 21b, and the price expectations function is 21c. The growth of real balances per unit of a fixed amount of capital is equation 21d.

(21a) $\quad \dfrac{\pi - \delta\pi^*}{\lambda} = n + r(x_0) + \pi^* - \rho - S(x_0, \theta v).$

(21b) $\quad \dfrac{\pi - \delta\pi^*}{\lambda h} = v - L\left[y(x_0) + \dfrac{\pi - \delta\pi^*}{\lambda}, r(x_0) + \pi^*, \rho, \theta v\right].$

(21c) $\quad D\pi^* = b(\pi - \pi^*).$

Since Dx is defined to be approximately zero in the short run, the growth of real balances per unit of capital is equal to the growth of real balances per unit of effective labor.

(21d) $\qquad\qquad \dfrac{Dv}{v} = \mu - \pi - DK/K$

$\qquad\qquad\qquad\quad = \mu - \pi - n + Dx/x$

$\qquad\qquad\qquad\quad = \mu - \pi - n.$

If $\delta = 0$, then the Keynes-Wicksell model is obtained. With the exception of the price expectations equation, it is precisely the model discussed in Section I of the previous chapter. By assuming that $\delta = 1$, the Synthesis model is obtained.

To solve the dynamic model described by equations 21a–21d, endogenous variables π and ρ must be expressed in terms of state variables π^* and v. Then two differential equations in π^* and v would be obtained. Once we know the time profiles of π^* and v, the time profiles of the nominal rate of interest ρ and the rate of price change π can be determined.

The *IS* and *FM* curves, equations 21a and 21b, are solved for ρ and π in terms of π^* and v. The graphic analysis is the same as was described in Figure 2 of Chapter 4; thus, it need not be repeated. Taking the differentials of (21a) and (21b) with respect to π^* and v, since x is held constant at $x = x_0$ in the short run, matrix equation 22 is derived. Obviously it is the same as equation 17 in the previous chapter if $\delta = 0$.

$$(22) \quad \begin{bmatrix} 1/\lambda & 1 \\ (1/\lambda)(1/h + L_1) & L_3 \end{bmatrix} \begin{bmatrix} d\pi \\ d\rho \end{bmatrix}$$
$$= \begin{bmatrix} 1 + \delta/\lambda \\ (\delta/\lambda)(1/h + L_1) - L_2 \end{bmatrix} d\pi^* + \begin{bmatrix} -S_2\theta \\ 1 - L_4\theta \end{bmatrix} dv + \begin{bmatrix} 1 \\ 0 \end{bmatrix} dn.$$

By solving explicitly for differentials $d\pi$ and $d\rho$, equations 23 and 24 are derived. Quantity $J = (1/\lambda)[L_3 - (1/h + L_1)]$ is negative.

$$(23) \qquad d\pi = f_1 \, d\pi^* + f_2 \, dv + f_3 \, dn$$

and

$$(24) \qquad d\rho = g_1 \, d\pi^* + g_2 \, dv + g_3 \, dn,$$

where the partial derivatives f_i, g_i are defined as follows.

$$(23a) \qquad f_1 = \frac{\partial \pi}{\partial \pi^*} = \delta + \frac{(L_2 + L_3)\lambda}{(L_3 - 1/h - L_1)} > 0$$

$$(23b) \qquad f_2 = \frac{\partial \pi}{\partial v} = -\frac{1}{J} [S_2\theta L_3 + (1 - L_4\theta)] > 0$$

$$(23c) \qquad f_3 = \partial \pi / \partial n = L_3/J > 0.$$

$$(24a) \qquad g_1 = \frac{\partial \rho}{\partial \pi^*} = -\frac{1}{\lambda J} (L_1 + 1/h + L_2)$$

$$(24b) \qquad g_2 = \frac{\partial \rho}{\partial v} = \frac{1}{\lambda J} [(1 - L_4\theta) + (1/h + L_1)S_2\theta]$$

$$(24c) \qquad g_3 = \frac{\partial \rho}{\partial n} = -\frac{1}{\lambda J} (1/h + L_1) > 0.$$

When $\delta = 1$ in the Synthesis model, a rise in π^* by one unit tends to raise the actual rate of price change by more than one unit. This is described by equation 23a. Why does this occur? A rise in π^* by one unit has a direct effect upon π resulting from the initial behavior of specialists who raise π by one unit. Moreover, the rise in π^* raises the excess demand for goods and thereby adds to the initial rise in π^*. The net effect in the Synthesis model is to make $f_1 > 1$. A rise in the expected rate of price change by one unit initially tends to raise the actual rate of price change by more than one unit. In the presence of such an instability element, some friction must be introduced to stabilize the system. It will come as no surprise that a sufficiently sluggish price expectations function must be invoked to stabilize the system.

From equations 23 and 24, we may write:

(25a) $$\pi = f(\pi^*, v; n)$$

(25b) $$\rho = g(\pi^*, v; n).$$

Substituting these equations into differential equations 21c and 21d, a pair of differential equations in π^* and v is obtained. Equations 26a and 26b represent the dynamic short-run Synthesis model: $\delta = 1$. If $\delta = 0$, the Keynes-Wicksell model would be obtained.

(26a) $$D\pi^* = b[f(\pi^*, v) - \pi^*]$$

(26b) $$Dv/v = \mu - f(\pi^*, v) - DK/K = \mu - n - f(\pi^*, v),$$

since $Dx = 0$ in the short run.

Both an algebraic and a graphic solution of this system will be offered. By starting with an algebraic solution, the stability conditions will be found directly. Using these stability conditions, the phase diagrams will be constructed for the stable case.

1. An Algebraic Solution. Denote the deviations from short-run equilibrium (π_s^*, v_s) by:

(27a) $$x_1 \equiv \pi^* - \pi_s^*,$$

(27b) $$x_2 \equiv v - v_s.$$

The equilibrium π_s^* is equal to $\mu - n$; and the equilibrium v_s is derived from the equation $\pi_s^* = \pi_s = \mu - n = f(\mu - n, v_s)$.

A linear expansion of equations 26a and 26b around the short-run equilibrium yields equations 28a and 28b.

(28a) $$Dx_1 = [b(f_1 - 1)] \cdot x_1 + [bf_2] \cdot x_2.$$
(28b) $$Dx_2 = [-v_s f_1] \cdot x_1 + [-v_s f_2] \cdot x_2.$$

Necessary and sufficient conditions for stability of this system are that the sum of the characteristic roots (T) be negative and their product (det) be positive.

(29a) $$T = b(f_1 - 1) - v_s f_2.$$
(29b) $$(\det) = bf_2 v_s > 0.$$

The product of the roots is always positive since f_2 is positive (equation 23b). We continue to assume that the monetary effect of a rise in v exceeds the wealth effect: that is, $1 > L_4 \theta$.

Two countervailing effects are operative. On the one hand, a rise in the actual rate of price change $\pi(t)$ by one unit raises the expected rate of price change $\pi^*(t)$ by b units. In the Synthesis model a rise in the expected rate of price change by b units raises the actual rate of price change by $bf_1 > b$ units. Therefore, inflation or deflation tends to be cumulative: that is, the system tends to be dynamically unstable. On the other hand, a rise in the actual rate of price change $\pi(t)$ by one unit lowers real balances per unit of capital. Total spending is positively related to real balances. When real balances tend to decline, excess demand for goods also declines, and the rate of price change resulting from the excess demand for goods tends to decline. This real balance effect is a stabilizing force.

The net effect of these countervailing forces constitutes T in equation 29a. If the price expectations effect dominates, T is positive and the system is explosive. Stability can only occur if the real balance effect dominates: that is, T is negative. A sufficiently small adaptive expectations coefficient b, which is equivalent to a sufficiently large amount of friction, is required to stabilize the system.

In the Keynes-Wicksell model the value of f_1 is less than the value that prevails in the Synthesis model. The reason is that, in the Keynes-Wicksell model, price expectations only affect the actual rate of price change indirectly: whereas they affect π directly in the Synthesis model. For this reason the Keynes-Wicksell model is more likely to be dynamically stable than is the Synthesis model.

2. A Solution with Phase Diagrams. Equations 26a and 26b can be solved graphically using phase diagrams. Define the price expectations PP' curve as the set of π^* and v such that the expected rate of price change is constant. This curve satisfies equation 30.

(30) $$D\pi^* = b[f(\pi^*, v) - \pi^*] = 0.$$

A negative relation would exist between π^* and v along this curve. Differentiating equation 30 with respect to π^*, the slope of the PP' curve is derived.

(30a) $$\frac{dv}{d\pi^*} = \frac{1 - f_1}{f_2} < 0.$$

On the basis of equation 23a the value of f_1 exceeds unity in the Synthesis model, where $\delta = 1$. Moreover, deviations from the PP' curve tend to be cumulative. Price change expectations tend to be self-justifying (when $\delta = 1$). This is seen in equation 30b, based upon equation (30).

(30b) $$\frac{\partial(D\pi^*)}{\partial\pi^*}\bigg|_v = b(f_1 - 1) > 0.$$

The horizontal vectors in Figure 2 describe the fact that deviations in π^* from PP' are cumulative.

Define the VV' curve as the set of π^* and v such that real balances per unit of capital are constant. At each point on the curve the actual rate of price change $\pi = f(\pi^*, v)$ is equal to the growth of the money supply per effective worker $\mu - n$. Equation 31 describes this curve, and equation 31a describes its slope.

(31) $$\frac{Dv}{v} = \mu - n - f(\pi^*, v) = 0.$$

(31a) $$\frac{dv}{d\pi^*} = -\frac{f_1}{f_2} < 0.$$

An intuitive explanation for the negative slope is based upon the *IS* and *FM* curves. A rise in the expected rate of price change shifts both the *IS* and *FM* curves (discussed in Chapter 4) to the right, thereby raising the actual rate of price change. To preserve the equality between the actual rate of price change π and the growth of the money supply per worker $\mu - n$, what must happen to v? Obviously, v must change in such a way as to reduce the actual rate of price change. A decline in v will shift the IS and FM curves to the left and offset the effect of a rise in π^*. For this reason the VV' curve is negatively sloped.

Unlike the PP' curve, deviations of v from the VV' curve tend to be eliminated. If v exceeded the amount required to keep the rate of price change equal to the growth of the money supply per effective worker, then the level of real balances would be reduced. This phenomenon is described by equation 31b; it is illustrated by the vertical vectors in Figure 2.

(31b) $$\left. \frac{\partial(Dv/v)}{\partial v} \right|_{\pi^*} = -f_2 < 0.$$

Algebraically, the PP' curve has a greater slope than the VV' curve. The slope of the PP' curve is $(1 - f_1)/f_2$, whereas the slope of the VV' curve is $-f_1/f_2$.

Stability of equilibrium depends upon the relative strengths of the expectations and real balance effects, summarized in equation 29a. On the one hand, in the Synthesis model, price change expectations are self-justifying. A rise in the expected rate of price change π^* raises the actual

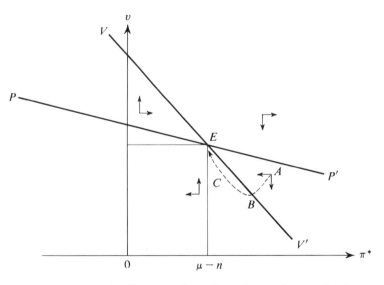

FIGURE 2. Short-run dynamics, when ratio x is fixed. Stability of equilibrium is assumed. From point A the movement to equilibrium is $ABC \cdots E$.

rate of price change both directly, and indirectly by raising the excess demand for goods. A unit rise in π^* raises the actual rate of price change by $f_1 > 1$; and the gap between the actual and expected rate of price change increases by $(f_1 - 1)$. On the basis of the adaptive expectations equations, the change in π^* is proportional to the change in the error $f(\pi^*, v) - \pi^*$. When the error rises by $(f_1 - 1)$ units, the expected rate of price change rises by $b(f_1 - 1)$ units. A dynamically unstable situation tends to develop.

Offsetting this effect (to some extent) is the decline in real balances that results from the rise in the rate of price change. When v declines, then aggregate demand for goods is reduced: the IS and FM curves shift to the left. With the decline in aggregate demand, the rate of price change is reduced. This effect tends to reduce the expected rate of price change, and it is an element of stability.

Stability will occur, in the phase diagram described in Figure 2, if the magnitude of the vertical v vector is greater than the magnitude of the horizontal π^* vector. This is equivalent to a negative T in equation 29a. Otherwise, instability will result. Even though the system is stable, it is unlikely that the convergence to equilibrium will be monotonic.

II

THE NOMINAL RATE OF INTEREST

AND THE RATE OF MONETARY EXPANSION

Phillip D. Cagan (1966, p. 26) concluded his empirical study of interest rates with the following statement:

Cyclical variations in monetary growth appear to be an independent contributor to interest rate movements, and, while not the only or the largest contributor, neither are they a mere reflection of those movements nor of common responses in the series to business cycles. Evidence of their contribution is a first step in tracing the path of monetary disturbances through the economy. That contribution points to effects beyond those implied by the static equilibrium conditions of traditional monetary theory and implies dynamic relationships as yet only partially understood.

A. THE PHENOMENON TO BE EXPLAINED

Cagan estimated the regression coefficients of regression equation 32a, where (using his notation) i is the interest rate, m is the monetary growth rate, M is the stock of money, W is private tangible wealth plus net debt of the government held by the public, and D is a dummy variable for reference phases of the business cycle. Operator Δ stands for changes between successive fiscal years.

(32a) $\qquad \Delta i = \alpha\, \Delta m + b\Delta \log M/W + cD + \text{constant.}$

In terms of the notation used in this book, Cagan estimated regression equation 32b, where $\Delta \rho \equiv \Delta i$, $\Delta \mu \equiv \Delta m$ and M/W is a monotonic increasing function of $v = M/pK$. Variable θ is the ratio of net private wealth to money.

(32b) $\qquad \Delta \rho = a_1 \Delta \mu + a_2 \Delta \log \dfrac{v}{1 + \theta v} + cD + \text{constant.}$

Table 1 summarizes his results. Both $\alpha(a_1)$ and $b(a_2)$ are significantly less than zero. Year-to-year changes in the nominal rate of interest are negatively related to both year-to-year changes in the rate of monetary expansion and to year-to-year changes in the ratio of money to wealth. Time deposits are included in the M/W ratio in Table 1.

The theoretical framework developed in part I can explain why

TABLE 1. REGRESSION OF INTEREST RATES ON MONETARY GROWTH RATE
AND MONEY-WEALTH RATIO HOLDING REFERENCE CYCLE PHASE CONSTANT,
CHANGES BETWEEN SUCCESSIVE FISCAL YEARS

	Partial Correlation Coefficient	
Interest Rates	*Monetary Growth Rate*	*Money-Wealth Ratio*
Commercial paper 1904–1958		
excluding war contractions and 1929–1933	−.72*	−.41*
excluding war cycles and 1929–1948	−.87*	−.49*
Treasury bills, 1920–1958		
excluding war contractions and 1929–1933	−.51*	−.38*
excluding 1929–1948	−.82*	−.40
U.S. bonds, 1920–1958		
excluding war contractions and 1929–1933	−.46*	−.57*
excluding 1929–1948	−.78*	−.59*
Corporate and municipal bonds, 1904–1958		
excluding war contractions and 1929–1933	−.56*	−.65*
excluding war cycles and 1929–1948	−.67*	−.57*

* Significant at the 5% level.   *Source:* Cagan (1966, p. 19).

Cagan obtained these results, using year-to-year changes. The negative relation between interest rates and the rate of monetary expansion reflects the movement of the economy to a short-run equilibrium position. Quite the opposite relation would occur if the two short-run equilibria were compared.

B. SHORT-RUN DYNAMICS

Suppose that the economy were in short-run equilibrium at point E in Figure 3, where real balances per worker are constant and the actual and expected rates of price change are equal to the growth of the money supply per effective worker. Suddenly, the rate of monetary expansion is raised from μ_0 to μ_1. What will happen to the nominal rate of interest?

The rise in the rate of monetary expansion will shift the VV' curve from $V(\mu_0)$ to $V(\mu_1)$ in Figure 3. This curve represents the set of (π^*, v)

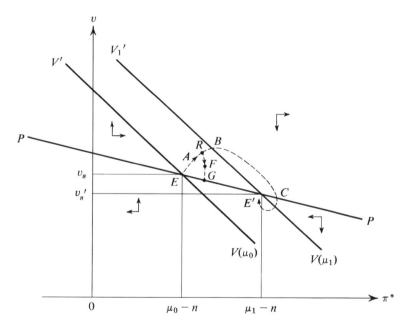

FIGURE 3. The effects of changes in the rate of monetary expansion upon real balances per unit of capital v and the expected rate of price change π^*.

such that real balances per unit of capital are constant, that is:

$$Dv/v = \mu - n - f(\pi^*, v) = 0$$

is satisfied along this curve.

Given any expected rate of price change π^*, real balances per unit of capital will only be constant if the rate of price change $\pi = f(\pi^*, v)$ rises by the same amount as the rate of monetary expansion per worker. A rise in v is required to raise π; therefore, the VV' curve shifts upward.

No change will occur in the PP' curve since it does not contain μ as an argument. It is the set of (π^*, v) such that the actual and expected rates of price change are equal:

$$D\pi^* = b[f(\pi^*, v) - \pi^*] = 0.$$

The path to the new equilibrium E' in Figure 3 will probably be cyclical, and it is indicated by the dotted path. Initially, real balances rise. Consumption will be stimulated directly, and investment will be stimulated indirectly as a result of a decline in interest rates. The actual rate of price change rises; the expected rate of price change is consequently increased. Investment is further stimulated by the increase in the expected yield on capital $r(x) + \pi^*$; and the actual rate of price change will increase further.

After a while the actual rate of price change will have caught up to the higher rate of monetary expansion: point B in Figure 3. However, the expected rate of price change will continue to rise, thereby raising the actual rate of price change. The economy will be drawn to the right of point B. Since the actual rate of price change will now exceed the rate of monetary expansion, the level of real balances per unit of capital will decline. The movement will be from B to C in Figure 3. In the dynamically stable case the real balance effect must eventually dominate the price expectations effect.

From point C the expected rate of price change will decline as it approaches the equilibrium $\pi_s^* = \mu_1 - n$. Variable π^* may converge to equilibrium E' in a cyclical manner as described in Figure 3. When the economy arrives at point E', the actual (π_s) and expected (π_s^*) rates of price change will equal the rate of monetary expansion per effective worker $\mu_1 - n$.

According to equations 24 and 25b, repeated here, the rate of interest is dependent upon π^* and v. Assume that n is constant.

(24) $dp = g_1 \, d\pi^* + g_2 \, dv$

(25b) $p = g(\pi^*, v)$,

where g_1 is assumed to be positive and g_2 is assumed to be negative.

A time profile of the nominal rate of interest can be deduced from these equations and phase diagram Figure 3. The letters in Figure 4 correspond to those in Figure 3.

Initially, the interest rate was equal to p_1 at the equilibrium level E. As the economy moves from E to B in Figure 3, there are two counterbalancing effects. The rise in real balances tends to reduce the rate of interest via liquidity preference. On the other hand, the rise in the expected rate of price change tends to raise the rate of interest by inducing a switch from bonds to capital. During the movement from E to A, the first effect dominates; and the nominal rate of interest falls. From A to B, the price expectations effect dominates, and the nominal rate of interest rises.

Interest rates rise rapidly from point B to point C. Real balances are declining and the expected rate of price change is rising. Each effect, separately, tends to raise the nominal rate of interest, and the rise in the

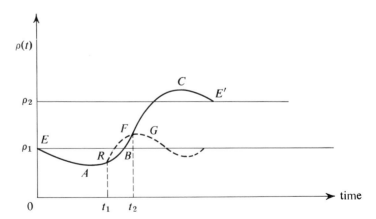

FIGURE 4. The relation between the rate of interest and the rate of monetary expansion corresponding to Figure 3.

nominal rate of interest from point B on is rapid. Overshooting occurs since at point C the level of real balances is below its equilibrium level and the expected rate of price change is above its equilibrium level. The subsequent rise in v and decline in π^* tend to reduce the nominal rate of interest to the equilibrium level.

Overshooting of the actual rate of price change is inevitable in the Synthesis model since the equilibrium level of real balances per unit of capital must be reduced[8] from v_s to v_s'. Therefore, a once and for all rise in prices relative to the trend is required. Moreover, the equilibrium trend rate of price change rises from $\mu_0 - n$ to $\mu_1 - n$. There must be a period of time when the actual rate of price change exceeds $\mu_1 - n$ in order to reduce the level of real balances per unit of capital from v_s to v_s'.

Suppose that the rate of monetary expansion reverted to its original level μ_0 at the same time $(t = t_1)$ that the economy reached point R. What would be the time profile of the nominal rate of interest? The decline in μ from μ_1 back to μ_0 would shift the VV' curve back to $V(\mu_0)$; and the economy would follow dotted path $RFG \cdots$ back to equilibrium E. Initially, real balances would decline and the nominal rate of interest would rise as described in Figure 4 in the movement from R to F.

During the interval $(0, t_1)$, the rate of monetary expansion rose from μ_0 to μ_1; the economy moved from point E to point R. The nominal rate of interest would have declined and real balances per unit of capital would have increased. At $t = t_1$ the rate of monetary expansion reverts back to μ_0. The economy moves from R to F during the interval (t_1, t_2). The nominal rate of interest would rise, and real balances per unit of capital would have declined.

If, at $t = t_1$, the rate of monetary expansion rose to $\mu_2 > \mu_1 > \mu_0$, then the nominal rate of interest would fall further. The initial impact of a rise in μ (in the stable case) is to raise real balances, which depresses the nominal rate of interest. Later, when the actual rate of price change rises, the expected rate of price change will rise. The latter effect tends to raise interest rates.

When year-to-year changes in the rate of monetary expansion are considered, then it is to be expected that there would be a negative relation between year-to-year changes in the rate of monetary expansion $\Delta\mu$ and

---

[8] This is similar to Friedman's (1969, Ch. 1) conclusion.

year-to-year changes in the nominal rate of interest $\Delta\rho$. This is precisely what Cagan observed, and it is consistent with our dynamic model. If the rate of monetary expansion remained at μ_1, then the economy would converge to point E' in Figure 3. There would be a higher rate of price change and a lower level of real balances at E' than prevailed at E. Since each effect separately tends to raise ρ, the rise in the rate of monetary expansion would have raised the nominal rate of interest from ρ_1 to ρ_2. A comparison of short-run equilibria would indicate that there was a positive relation between changes in the nominal rate of interest and changes in the rate of monetary expansion. Cagan, on the other hand, was using year-to-year changes in the variables and, for that reason, was not comparing short-run equilibria.

III

THE GIBSON PARADOX

A. WHAT IS TO BE EXPLAINED?

The well-known[9] Gibson Paradox states that there is a positive association between the price level $p(t)$ and the nominal rate of interest $\rho(t)$. Four broad swings in the wholesale price index are discernible during the past century. Prices fell until 1896 and then rose to a peak in 1920. This price index subsequently declined to 1932 and then rose until 1965. What was the relation between the price level and the nominal rate of interest during these periods? Except for the period 1933 through 1945, there was a positive relation between the nominal rate of interest and the price level. The association was very marked during the periods 1860–1896, 1897–1920, and 1946–1965, but it was very slight during the period 1921–1932. Table 2 presents the results of some sample regressions. Standard errors are noted in parentheses.

Although the standard errors are underestimated as a result of a high degree of autocorrelation of residuals, there is no doubt that ρ and p are positively associated during the periods 1860–1896, 1897–1920, and 1946–1965. If first differences are examined, $\Delta\rho$ on Δp, then no positive

[9] J. M. Keynes (1930, Vol. II, pp. 198–208); Irving Fisher (1930, Ch. 19); Cagan (1966, pp. 252–59); Meiselman (1963, pp. 112–33): Sargent (1969, pp. 127–40).

TABLE 2. RELATION BETWEEN THE NOMINAL RATE OF INTEREST AND THE PRICE LEVEL 1860–1965 BY SUBPERIOD

	Means		$\rho = a + bp$		$\rho = a + b\ln p$	
	Av. ρ	Av. p	Coefficient b	Coefficient a	Coefficient b	Coefficient a
1860–1932	4.47%	42.6	0.04 (0.01)	2.72 (0.31)	2.02 (0.30)	−3.03 (1.12)
1860–1896	4.90	41.2	0.06 (0.01)	2.43 (0.42)	2.86 (0.40)	−5.60 (1.46)
1897–1920	3.80	40.9	0.03 (0.003)	2.62 (0.13)	1.45 (0.14)	−1.49 (0.52)
1921–1932	4.50	50.5	0.007 (0.01)	4.17 (0.75)	0.26 (0.67)	3.48 (2.61)
1933–1965	3.27%	75.9	0.01 (0.004)	2.43 (0.36)	0.61 (0.31)	0.67 (1.35)
1933–1945	3.04	47.2	−0.06 (0.02)	5.72 (0.75)	−2.79 (0.72)	13.76 (2.76)
1946–1965	3.42	94.6	0.06 (0.01)	−2.27 (0.97)	5.07 (0.95)	−19.59 (4.33)

Source: United States Department of Commerce. Long-term economic growth 1860–1965. Bureau of the Census (October, 1966). Prices are wholesale prices, all commodities, Series, B69; interest rates are Series B74, B75: American railroad bond yields through 1913 and basic yields of 30-year corporate bonds thereafter. The coefficients in Table 2 have been rounded. Standard errors are in parentheses.

association is observed. Similarly, no significant positive relation exists between ρ and $\Delta \ln p = \pi$ during the periods examined.

Meiselman (1963, p. 115) obtained similar results although he used somewhat different periods. Below are the simple correlation coefficients that he derived between bond yields and the wholesale price index.

1873–1899	0.921	1931–1946	−0.764
1899–1920	0.908	1946–1960	0.793
1920–1931	0.768	1873–1960	−0.149

Why has the positive relation between the nominal rate of interest and the price level been considered paradoxical? Irving Fisher (1930), who regarded the "paradox" as an accidental consequence of more basic economic relationships, put it in a way that should be very clear to any student of Patinkin.

At any rate it seems impossible to interpret it as representing any independent relationship with any rational theoretical basis. It certainly stands to reason that *in the long run* a high level of prices due to previous monetary and credit inflation ought not to be associated with any higher rate of interest than the low level before the inflation took place. It is inconceivable that, for instance, the rate of interest in France and Italy should tend to be higher just because of the depreciation of the franc or the lira, or that a billion-fold inflation as in Germany or Russia would, after stabilization, permanently elevate interest accordingly . . . the price level as such can evidently have no permanent influence on the rate of interest except as a matter of transition from one level or plateau to another (p. 441).

Irving Fisher's well-known and widely used explanation of this phenomenon was not complete. He only considered the effect of the rate of price change upon the interest rate and failed to consider the effect of the interest rate upon the rate of price change. He was well aware of this lacuna in his theory. The Fisher (1930) explanation is as follows:

The *transition* from one price level to another may and does work havoc as we have seen, and havoc follows with a lag which is widely distributed. The result is that during a period of inflation the interest rate is raised cumulatively, so that at the end of this period when the price level is high, the interest rate is also high. It would doubtless in time revert to normal if the new high level were maintained, but this seldom happens. Usually prices reach a peak and then fall. During this fall the interest rate is subject to a cumulative downward pressure so that it becomes subnormal at or near the end of the fall of prices. Thus, at the peak of prices, interest is high, not because the price level is high, but because it has been rising and, at the valley of prices, interest is low, not because the price level is low, but because it has been falling (p. 441).

Formally, Fisher's theory can be described by two equations. The first, (F1), states that the nominal rate of interest $\rho(t)$ is the sum of the real rate of interest r_F plus the expected rate of price change $\pi^*(t)$. Second, price expectations are revised slowly. For example, an adaptive expectations equation F2 would be consistent with his theory.

(F1) $$\rho(t) = r_F + \pi^*(t)$$
(F2) $$D\pi^*(t) = b[\pi(t) - \pi^*(t)].$$

Exogenous variables are the real rate of interest r_F and the actual rate of price change π. Solve equation F2 for the expected rate of price change and derive (F3). If $\pi(t)$ is constant at π, then (F3) implies (F4).

(F3) $$\pi^*(t) = be^{-bt} \int^t \pi(\tau)e^{b\tau}\,d\tau + c(0)e^{-bt}.$$
(F4) $$\pi^*(t) = \pi + [\pi^*(0) - \pi(0)]e^{-bt}.$$

Substitute equation (F4) into (F1) to obtain equation F5, which states Fisher's explanation of the Gibson paradox.

(F5) $$\rho(t) = r_F + \pi + [\pi^*(0) - \pi(0)]e^{-bt}.$$

Figure 5a plots the exogenous price level as a function of time.

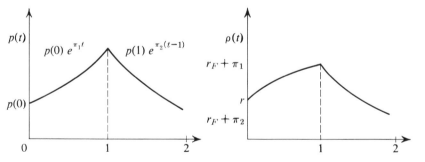

FIGURE 5A. Hypothetical profile of the price level. Inflation exists at rate π_1 from 0 to 1; deflation at rate π_2 occurs from 1 on.

FIGURE 5B. The implied profile of the nominal rate of interest in Fisher's theory.

Assume that $\pi = D \ln p$ is positive ($\pi_1 > 0$) during the interval $0 < t < 1$, and it is negative ($\pi_2 < 0$) during the interval $1 \leqq t < 2$.

The interest rate, equation F5, is plotted in Figure 5b and is based upon the profile of π implicit in Figure 5a. Initially, prices are expected to be constant. Therefore, $\pi^*(0) = 0$, and $\pi^*(0) - \pi_1$ is negative. At time $t = 1$, the expected rate of price change has (almost) caught up to the actual rate of price change π_1. When prices fall at rate π_2 from $1 \leqq t < 2$, then $\pi^*(1) - \pi_2$ is positive.

The positive association between ρ and p, the Gibson paradox is thereby generated. It represents a hunting process: that is, a disequilibrium situation, whereby the nominal rate of interest seeks the quantity $r_F + \pi$, the real rate of interest plus the exogenous actual rate of price change.

Fisher recognized a gap in his theory: there is a negative relation between the nominal rate of interest and the rate of price change, which he failed to incorporate into his explanation. He wrote:

The fact that i [the nominal rate of interest] follows P' [the rate of price change per annum], in most instances over secular and cyclical periods, is not inconsistent with the other fact that every increase or decrease in i exerts an influence upon P [the price level] in the opposite direction. Within limits, a fall in the rate of interest may and often does produce a rise in prices and in business activity almost immediately. This effect may be continued for many months until increased prices again become dominant and pull the interest rate up again. Insofar as the rate of interest is cause and the price movements are effect, the correspondence is *just the opposite* of that which occurs insofar as price movements are the cause and the interest movements effect (pp. 443–44).

Fisher concluded that: "It is outside the scope of this treatise, which has to do only with things which affect the theory of the rate of interest, to attempt to explain fully all the very complicated relations connecting interest and business" (1930, p. 444). The macro-economic (Keynes-Wicksell or Synthesis) models developed here contain the mutual interactions between the nominal rate of interest and the rate of price change that Fisher referred to. On the basis of the Synthesis model, how can the Gibson relation be explained? A similar explanation is implied by the Keynes-Wicksell model and is left to the reader.

B. AN EXPLANATION OF THE GIBSON PARADOX

The Gibson relation occurs within periods of rising and falling prices. During a period of rising (falling) prices, what causes the nominal rate of interest to rise (fall)? If a period of a price rise (fall) is considered as a transition from one short-run equilibrium to another, then the nominal rate of interest will rise (fall) if:

(a) there has been a rise (fall) in the rate of growth of the money supply per effective worker, or

(b) there has been a rise (fall) in the rate of growth of effective labor, but no change in the rate of monetary expansion per effective worker. That is, both μ and n change by the same amount.

The first effect implies Fisher's explanation, and the second effect implies Keynes' explanation, of the Gibson paradox.

These propositions can be demonstrated on the basis of SIS and SFM curves.[10] They are the IS and FM curves that would exist in short-run equilibrium. Within the dynamic model described by equations 21a–21d, short-run equilibrium prevails when, for an arbitrarily given ratio $x = x_0$, the expected rate of price change is constant at $\pi_s{}^*$ and real balances per unit of capital are constant at v_s. It follows from equations 21c and 21d that, in short-run equilibrium, the actual and expected rates of price change are equal to the growth of the money supply per effective worker.

(33a) $$\pi_s{}^* = \pi_s$$

(33b) $$\pi_s = \mu - n.$$

The SIS curve is the IS curve that would prevail in short-run equilibrium. It is equation 34a based upon (21a) and (33); it is graphed in Figure 6.

(34a) $$n + r(x_0) + \pi_s - \rho = S(x_0, \theta v_s).$$

A rise in ρ_s would lower planned investment. To preserve the equality between planned savings and investment, the value of v_s must rise. Savings would thereby be reduced to the level of investment. The SIS curve is positively sloped since ρ_s and v_s must be positively related to preserve the equality between savings and investment.

Similarly, the SFM curve is the FM curve that would prevail in short-run equilibrium. It is equation 34b, based upon (21b) and (33); it is graphed in Figure 6. Our SFM curve is the familiar liquidity preference

[10] See Chapter 4 for a discussion of these curves when $\delta = 0$ (in the Keynes-Wicksell model).

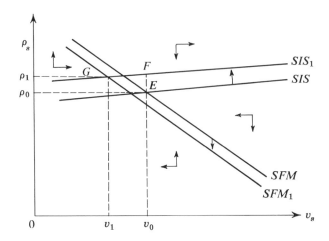

FIGURE 6. The effect of a rise in the rate of monetary expansion per effective worker upon the short-run nominal rate of interest. Equilibrium shifts from E to G.

curve, when the expected and actual rates of price change are equal to the growth of the money supply per effective worker.

$$(34b) \qquad v_s = L[y(x_0), r(x_0) + \pi_s, \rho_s, \theta v_s].$$

This curve is downward sloping. A decline in the nominal rate of interest raises the quantity demanded of real balances per unit of capital. Hence, the quantity v_s must rise when ρ_s declines.

Short-run equilibrium occurs at point E in Figure 6. Real balances per unit of capital are v_0 and the nominal rate of interest is ρ_0.

1. Changes in the Rate of Monetary Expansion per Effective Worker. Suppose that the rate of monetary expansion per effective worker increased, ceteris paribus, thereby raising the short-run equilibrium rate of price change from π_s to π_s'. What would happen?

There would be a rise in the SIS curve (equation 34a) by the amount of the rise in π_s. At a level of real balances per unit of capital v_0, the rate of savings per unit of capital is $S(x_0, \theta v_0)$. The rise in the rate of price change raises planned investment relative to planned savings. To preserve the equality between planned savings and planned investment, the nominal rate of interest must rise to offset the rise in $\pi_s^* = \pi_s$. Thereby, no change would occur in the real rate of interest $\rho_s - \pi_s^*$. The SIS curve, therefore, shifts upward to SIS_1 in Figure 6 as a result of a rise in $\mu - n$.

A downward shift would occur in the SFM curve as a result of a rise in the short-run equilibrium rate of price change. The rise in $\pi_s^* = \pi_s$ reduces the quantity demanded of real balances per unit of capital at any interest rate. To preserve equilibrium in the money market, the short-run equilibrium level of v_s would have to decline. The SFM curve shifts leftward to SFM_1.

At the new equilibrium point G, the nominal rate of interest is higher (ρ_1 relative to ρ_0); and the level of real balances per unit of capital is lower (v_1 relative to v_0).

Insofar as there is a real balance effect in the savings function ($S_2\theta < 0$), the nominal rate of interest rises by less than the rise in the rate of price change. That is:

$$\rho_0\rho_1 < EF.$$

The decline in v_s from v_0 to v_1 stimulates savings; and the rise in savings tends to reduce the rate of interest. Formally, using equation 34a, the nominal rate of interest is:

(35) $\rho_s = \pi_s + n + r(x_0) - S(x_0, \theta v_s).$

The rise in π_s raises ρ_s; and the rise in $S(x_0, \theta v_s)$ resulting from the decline in v_s tends to lower ρ_s. Figure 6 has been drawn on the assumption that the real balance effect in the savings function is relatively weak. On balance, a rise in $\pi_s = \mu - n$ raises ρ_s.

If $\pi_s = \mu - n$ is positive, then two phenomena would be observed during this period. First, the price level would be rising since $\pi_s > 0$. Second, the nominal rate of interest would rise from ρ_0 to ρ_1 during the period. The movement of the interest rate would probably not be monotonic for reasons discussed in section IIB of this chapter. If p rises (falls) when there is excess demand for (supply of) goods, then the economy would move in the direction of the horizontal vectors. If the nominal rate of interest rose (fell) when there was an excess demand for (supply of) real balances, the economy would move in the direction of the vertical vectors. A cyclical convergence to equilibrium would result.

A Gibson paradox has been generated. Both the nominal rate of interest and the absolute price level have increased during this period.

In long-run equilibrium the ratio x of effective labor per unit of capital is endogenous. What will be the relation between the nominal rate of interest ρ_e and the rate of monetary expansion per effective worker? When $\delta = 1$ in the Synthesis model, savings per unit of capital are equal to the growth of effective labor n. When this condition is taken into account, equation 35 implies equation 36. Variable ρ_e refers to the steady state nominal rate of interest.

$$(36) \qquad \rho_e = n + r(x_e) + \pi_e - S(x_e, \theta v_e) = r(x_e) + \pi_e,$$

which is equation 12. A rise in the rate of monetary expansion per effective worker will raise π_e but will lower $r(x_e)$. For that reason it is to be expected that the nominal rate of interest will rise by less than the steady state rate of price change. If π_e is positive, then the transition from one steady state to another will be characterized by: (a) a rise in the nominal rate of interest and (b) a rise in the price level. When the steady state is attained, then the nominal rate of interest will remain at ρ_e although prices will rise at rate π_e.

2. Changes in the Real Rate of Interest without Corresponding Changes in the Equilibrium Rate of Price Change. Short-run equilibrium equation 35 in our model expresses the nominal rate of interest ρ_s as the sum of two elements. The first term is $\pi_s = \pi_s{}^*$, the short-run equilibrium rate of price change. The second term:

$$\rho_s - \pi_s = n + r(x_0) - S(x_0, \theta v_s)$$

would correspond to the real rate of interest or to Wicksell's natural rate of interest. Whereas Fisher explained the Gibson paradox exclusively in terms of movements in the expected rate of price change, Keynes (1930, Vol. II, pp. 198–208) explained it on the basis of the real rate of interest. In this way it can be shown that both explanations are contained in our model.

Assume that there occurs a rise in the rate of Harrod neutral technical change but there are no changes in the growth of the money supply per effective worker, which is equal to the equilibrium rate of price change π_s. If we assumed that the growth of high-powered money rises by the rate of technical change, then no changes need occur in the deposit-reserve or the deposit-currency ratios. Under these conditions the Gibson relation will be generated.[11] The argument applies, mutatis mutandis, for declines in the rate of Harrod neutral technical change.

Figure 7 illustrates the effects of a shift in the investment-demand schedule, resulting from a rise in the rate of technical progress upon the short-run equilibrium. Underlying Figure 7 are the SIS and SFM curves described by equations 34a and 34b.

The rise in the rate of technical progress shifts the SIS curve upward to SIS'. Unless the nominal rate of interest rose by EF, when $v_s = v_0$, planned investment would exceed planned savings. To preserve equilibrium in the market for goods, either the nominal rate of interest must rise or the level of real balances per unit of capital must decline. For this reason the SIS curve shifts upward to the left.

No change occurs in the SFM curve since the short-run equilibrium rate of price change $\pi_s = \mu - n = \pi_s{}^*$ is assumed to be constant: that is, the rate of monetary expansion rises by as much as the rate of technical

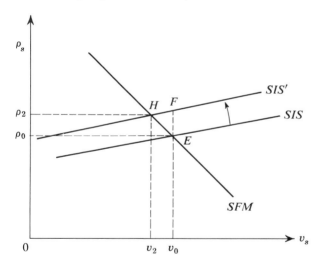

FIGURE 7. The effect of a rise in the rate of Harrod neutral technical progress upon the short-run equilibrium, given the rate of monetary expansion per effective worker.

[11] These conditions overcome Cagan's objections to the Keynes explanation. See Cagan (1966).

progress. It makes no difference whether the major component of the growth of the money supply is the growth of high-powered money or changes in the deposit-reserve and deposit-currency ratios.

Although the short-run equilibrium rate of price change is constant at $\pi_s = \mu - n$, the nominal rate of interest rises from ρ_0 to ρ_2. Such a phenomenon involves a change in the real rate of interest. The rise in the rate of interest induces a decline in real balances per unit of capital from v_0 to v_2 in Figure 7. Consequently, there is a rise (relative to trend) in the absolute price level during the transition from short-run equilibrium E to short-run equilibrium H. Even if the short-run equilibrium rate of price change $\pi_s = \mu - n = 0$, a rise in the absolute price level would accompany the rise in the nominal rate of interest from ρ_0 to ρ_2. A fortiori, if π_s were positive, then both the interest rate and the price level would rise during the transition period from one short-run equilibrium to another. The Gibson relation has been generated by a rise in the rate of technical change with no change in the rate of monetary expansion per effective worker. Such a phenomenon was not implied by Fisher's incomplete model since he treated the real rate of interest as constant.

In long-run equilibrium the effect of a rise in n is to raise the rent per unit of capital.[12] Since the rate of price change has been assumed constant at $\pi_e = \mu - n$, the steady state rate of interest:

$$\rho_e = r(x_e) + \pi_e$$

rises. Insofar as π_e is positive, the transition from one steady state to another is accompanied by rises in the nominal rate of interest and the absolute price level.

C. A HEURISTIC CONCLUSION

The model implies that interest rates will be rising (falling) if there has been a rise (decline) in the rate of monetary expansion per effective worker or a rise (decline) in the growth of effective labor.

One rough estimate of the growth of effective labor is the growth of real GNP. Although GNP and effective labor grow at the same rate n in

[12] Use equations 13 and 14b, described by Figure 1. A rise in n shifts the LX curve to the right. Since π_r is fixed at $\mu - n$, no change occurs in the LV curve. The LX curve is steeper algebraically than the LV curve when the equilibrium is stable. Therefore, a rise in n, given $\mu - n$, raises x_e.

the steady state, this will not necessarily be true at other times. Nevertheless, it is the closest index of the growth of effective labor that is readily available. Despite its short-comings, we shall use the growth of GNP per annum as an index of the growth of effective labor. Since our data concerning the growth of GNP begin in 1890, we are forced to use subperiod 1890–1896 instead of 1860–1896.

In one important respect the model is not appropriate for the analysis of historical data. A fixed unemployment rate is assumed in the model, whereas the periods covered contain recessions and depressions. Consequently, the present discussion is only heuristic and is not to be construed as a test of alternative hypotheses. Table 3 contains a summary of various periods. It should be clear that (in growth models) $\mu - n$ and n refer to pervasive movements of these variables rather than to ephemeral year-to-year changes.

During the period 1890–1896, the money supply grew at a smaller rate than output, and prices declined. A very different phenomenon occurred during the period 1897–1920. There was a substantial rise in the growth of the money supply per effective worker, from -1% p.a. to 6.1% p.a. Moreover, the growth of effective labor rose from 2.5% p.a. to 3.1% p.a. Each phenomenon by itself served to raise the short-run

TABLE 3. INTEREST RATES, GROWTH RATES, AND RATES OF MONETARY EXPANSION PER UNIT OF OUTPUT

	Interest Rates		Rate of Price Change p.a.	Growth p.a. of Money Supply per Unit of Output	Growth p.a. of Real G.N.P.
	Movement	Mean			
1890–1932			0.3%	3%	2.3%
1890–1896		3.6%	−3.1	−1	2.5
1897–1920	rising	3.8	5.3	6.1	3.1
1921–1932	falling	4.5	−3.6	−0.5	1.1
1933–1965		3.3	3.4	2.6	4.7
1933–1945	falling	3.0	2.3	4	8
1946–1965	rising	3.4	2.3	0.4	3.6
1890–1965		4.1*	1.5	2.7	3.3

Source: U.S. Department of Commerce, Long-Term Economic Growth.
* 1860–1965.

equilibrium rate of interest (see Figures 6 and 7). Therefore, this period of rising prices was also a period of rising interest rates.

Prices fell from a peak in 1921 to a trough in 1932. The growth of the money supply per effective worker was -0.5% p.a.; and the growth rate of output declined to 1.1% p.a. during this period. No wonder that prices and interest rates fell. What is surprising is that the Gibson relation was quite weak during the 1921–1932 period. Meiselman's use of the 1920–1931 period, on the other hand, yields a stronger relation.

The next period, 1933–1945, contains both a recovery from the depression and World War II. Prices rose, but interest rates were pegged during the war. The expected rise in interest rates was restrained by the monetary authorities. Once the pegs were removed, interest rates were expected to rise. However, during the 1946–1965 period, the growth of the money supply was only slightly higher than the growth of output; and the latter was lower than the rate prevailing during the recovery and war period. If interest rates had not been pegged during the war period, the level of interest rates during 1946–1965 would have declined. We must attribute the rise in interest rates to the disequilibrium that prevailed during the preceding period. A large part of the movement of interest rates during the postwar period consisted of a recovery of interest rates from unduly low-pegged levels.

IV

SUMMARY OF THE SYNTHESIS

MODEL

Two separate questions are immediately suggested by the previous chapters. First, are the Neoclassical and Keynes-Wicksell models of growth mutually exclusive? Is it possible that both views are correct? The Neoclassical model ignores the developments in aggregative economics associated with the name of Keynes; it does not appear to be a useful technique for short-run analysis. On the other hand, the Keynes-Wicksell model implies that market disequilibrium must exist in the steady state if there is secular inflation or deflation. Many economists feel uneasy with that conclusion. Is a reconciliation of the two approaches possible? A model which synthesizes these views is developed in this chapter. The resulting synthesis has the properties of a Keynes-Wicksell model outside the steady state but becomes a Neoclassical model in the steady state.

Second, how useful are the previous models in explaining observed empirical regularities? Two phenomena are not easily explainable by conventional macrostatic models. (a) Year-to-year changes in the nominal rate of interest are negatively related to year-to-year changes in the rate of monetary expansion and to year-to-year changes in the money-wealth ratio. (b) A positive association exists between the nominal rate of interest and an index of prices during periods of rising and falling prices: the Gibson paradox. Both the Keynes-Wicksell and the Synthesis models are capable of explaining these phenomena.

Only one slight change is required to transmute the Keynes-Wicksell into the Synthesis model. The former assumes that prices are changing in a competitive economy if, and only if, there is an excess demand or supply. Prices are rising if, and only if, there is an excess of buy orders over sell orders, that is, if there is a rise in unfilled orders. Expectations by themselves do not change prices; but expectations must work through excess demands to change prices. On the other hand, the Synthesis model assumes that the rate of price change is the sum of two components. First, specialists who make markets initially change prices at a rate equal to the expected rate of price change. Second, prices are changed further at a rate proportional to the excess demand per unit of capital. This important assumption is stated as:

(A) $$\pi = \delta\pi^* + \lambda\left(\frac{I}{K} - \frac{S}{K}\right),$$

where π is the actual rate of price change, π^* is the expected rate of price change, investment minus savings per unit of capital $I/K - S/K$ is the excess demand for goods per unit of capital, λ is a speed of price response, and δ is the Kronecker delta. In the Keynes-Wicksell model delta is equal to zero; but it is equal to unity in the Synthesis model.

(1) In all models the actual and expected rates of price change are always equal in the steady state. According to equation A, when $\delta = 1$ in the Synthesis model, market disequilibrium prevails only when the actual and expected rates of price change differ. A change in the rate of monetary expansion will produce temporary market disequilibrium, that is, a temporary deviation between planned savings and investment. Once

specialists fully anticipate the new rate of price change, they will change prices at this rate without any concomitant excess demand or supply. In the Keynes-Wicksell model ($\delta = 0$), on the other hand, the anticipation of price changes can only lead to actual price changes via excess demands or supplies. Inflation implies excess demand, that is, unfilled orders, even when all agents fully anticipate it. Were it not for the pressure of excess demand, prices would not be rising.

(2) The steady state growth of capital will be equal to planned savings per unit of capital in the Synthesis model. Outside the steady state, however, when the actual and expected rates of price change differ, the growth of capital will be (as it was in the Keynes-Wicksell model) a linear combination of planned savings and planned investment. The long-run capital intensity will be affected by financial variables in the Synthesis model only if they affect planned savings per unit of capital. If there is a negligible real balance effect in the savings function, then a rise in the rate of monetary expansion will only exert an ephemeral effect upon the capital intensity.

(3) A rise in the rate of monetary expansion always produces the Neoclassical result in the steady state. A rise in the steady state rate of price change will lower real balances per unit of capital. Planned savings per unit of capital will rise, and the steady state capital intensity will increase. It is assumed that the decline in real balances does not significantly reduce output produced by the fully employed resources. Since all markets are in equilibrium in the steady state, the ambiguity that was possible in the Keynes-Wicksell model does not arise in the Synthesis model.

(4) There is a greater element of instability in the Synthesis model than existed in the Keynes-Wicksell model. This instability tendency arises because price expectations tend to be self-realizing. A rise in the expected rate of price change by one unit has a direct effect upon the actual rate of price change resulting from the initial behavior of specialists who raise the rate of price change by one unit. Moreover, the rise in the expected rate of price change raises the excess demand for goods and thereby adds to the initial rise in the rate of price change. The net effect in the Synthesis model is that a rise in the rate of price change by one unit tends to raise the actual rate of price change by more than one unit.

The inflation or deflation tends to be cumulative, that is, the system tends to be dynamically unstable since a rise in the rate of price change tends to raise the actual rate of price change by a larger amount. In the presence of such an instability element, some friction must be invoked to help the real balances effect stabilize the Synthesis model. The rise in the actual rate of price change lowers real balances per unit of capital. Total spending for consumption and investment is positively related to real balances. When real balances tend to decline, excess demand for goods also declines; and the rate of price change generated by the excess demand for goods tends to decline. This real balance effect is a stabilizing force which works in a direction opposite to the expectations effect.

If the price expectations effect dominates, the system is explosive. Stability can only occur if the real balance effect dominates. A strong real balance effect and a sufficiently small adaptive expectations coefficient (which is equivalent to a sufficiently large amount of friction) are required to stabilize the system. In the Keynes-Wicksell model the instability element is not so strong. A rise in the expected rate of price change only affects the actual rate of price change indirectly through the excess demand functions. Therefore, a rise in price expectations need not raise prices by the same amount. For this reason the Keynes-Wicksell model is more likely to be dynamically stable than is the Synthesis model.

The Synthesis model and the version of the Keynes-Wicksell model, which implies that a rise in the rate of monetary expansion will lower real balances per unit of capital are consistent with the tentative findings that: (a) the rate of monetary expansion per worker is positively related to the nominal rate of interest, and (b) year-to-year variations in the rate of monetary expansion are negatively associated with year-to-year variations in the nominal rate of interest. Result (a) involves a comparison of short-run (or long-run) equilibria, whereas result (b) is based upon the path to short-run equilibrium.

Define short-run equilibrium as a situation where (i) the capital intensity is arbitrarily fixed, (ii) real balances per unit of capital are at an equilibrium, and (iii) the actual and expected rates of price change are equal. In short-run equilibrium planned savings and investment are equal in the Synthesis model. A rise in the rate of monetary expansion per worker implies a rise in the equilibrium expected rate of price change. Planned investment per unit of capital depends upon the rent per unit of capital less the real rate of interest, where the latter is equal to the nominal rate of interest less the expected rate of price change. Unless the nominal rate of interest rises, planned investment will exceed planned savings, which would violate the equilibrium condition in the Synthesis model. For this reason the short-run equilibrium nominal rate of interest would have to rise to restore the equality between savings and investment. On the other hand, in the Keynes-Wicksell model, the real rate of interest declines relative to the rent per unit of capital during inflationary periods.

The magnitude of the rise in the short-run equilibrium nominal rate of interest depends upon the magnitude of the real balance effect in the savings function.[13] When the rate of price change rises, real balances per unit of capital decline, and planned savings rise. Insofar as planned savings rise, the nominal rate of interest does not have to rise by the full amount of the rise in the rate of price change to bring savings and investment into equality again. Result (a) is explained as a comparison of equilibria.

On the other hand, result (b) is based upon a dynamic adjustment process rather than an equilibrium analysis. Suppose that the economy started at an equilibrium position where real balances per unit of capital were constant and the actual and expected rates of price change were equal to the rate of monetary expansion per worker. The rate of monetary expansion per worker then rises to a new level. What will happen in a dynamically stable system?

Initially, real balances per unit of capital rise, producing an excess supply of real balances per unit of capital. Consumption will be stimulated directly. There will also be an excess demand for securities which will lower the nominal rate of interest and stimulate investment. With the rise in excess demand, the actual rate of price change rises. Using an adaptive expectations framework, the expected rate of price change is consequently increased. Investment is further stimulated by the rise in the expected yield on capital (the rent plus the anticipated capital gain); and the actual rate of price change will increase further. Eventually, the actual rate of price change will catch up to the higher rate of monetary expansion; and the level of real balances per unit of capital is higher than it was initially. Given an adaptive expectations function, the expected rate of price change will continue to rise. Consequently, the actual rate of price change will rise further. Since the actual rate of price change now exceeds the rate of monetary expansion per worker, the level of real balances per unit of capital will decline. In a dynamically stable system, the real balance effect must eventually dominate the price expectations effect.

[13] See Robert Mundell (June, 1963, pp. 280–83).

What has been happening to the nominal rate of interest during this process? Initially, the rise in real balances tends to reduce the nominal rate of interest via the substitution of bonds for money. The subsequent rise in the expected rate of price change tends to raise the nominal rate of interest by inducing a switch from bonds to capital. The rise in the nominal rate of interest is aggravated by the reduction in the level of real balances that occurs when the rate of price change has exceeded the rate of monetary expansion per worker.

By focusing upon year-to-year changes in the rate of monetary expansion, only the initial effect is detected: that is, the major effect of the rise in the rate of monetary expansion is the use of the increment of real balances to purchase securities. The subsequent effects which tend to raise the nominal rate of interest are not detected when the year-to-year changes in the rate of monetary expansion is the independent variable.

Finally, the models developed here can explain the well-known Gibson paradox: the positive relation between the price level and the nominal rate of interest during periods of rising and falling prices. If a period of a price rise (for example, 1896–1920) or price fall (for example, 1865–1896 or 1921–1932) is considered as a transition from one short-run equilibrium to another, then the models imply the nominal rate of interest will rise (fall) if: (i) there has been a rise (fall) in the rate of monetary expansion per effective worker ($\mu - n$), or (ii) there has been a rise (fall) in the rate of growth of effective labor (n) but no change in the rate of monetary expansion per effective worker ($\mu - n$); that is, the rate of monetary expansion changes by as much as the rate of growth of effective labor.

The equilibrium nominal rate of interest depends upon (i) $\mu - n$ and (ii) n. The effect of the first variable is Irving Fisher's explanation of the Gibson paradox. A rise in $\mu - n$ raises the rate of price change and the nominal rate of interest. During inflationary periods the nominal rate of interest tends to be higher than it is during periods of deflation. Therefore, the interest rate rises during inflationary periods to a higher equilibrium, and it falls during deflationary periods to a lower equilibrium.

The second variable (n) was used by Keynes in his explanation. A rise in n, with no change in the rate of monetary expansion per effective worker, raises the desired growth of capital relative to planned savings per unit of capital. This is based upon my investment equation that: the desired growth of the capital-labor ratio is positively related to the difference between the rent per unit of capital and the real rate of interest. When the investment-demand schedule rises, the inflationary gap is increased. The rate of price change rises above the rate of monetary expansion per effective worker (which is assumed to be constant). Real balances in existence are reduced and the transactions demand for real balances increases. Both the nominal rate of interest and the rate of price change are increased. Equilibrium will be restored when the nominal rate of interest is higher and the level of real balances is lower, thereby restoring the equality between the rate of growth of capital and the rate of planned savings per unit of capital. The reduction in the level of real balances per unit of capital results from the higher than trend rate of price change. Therefore, we observe a rise in the nominal rate of interest and an above trend rise in prices. When n falls, we observe a decline in the nominal rate of interest and a below trend change in prices. If there is a zero trend over the period, which contains rising and falling prices, then the Gibson relation will be generated.

🏿🏿🏿🏿

CHAPTER SIX

Stabilization Policy in
a Growing Economy

I
THE AIMS OF STABILIZATION POLICY IN
A GROWING ECONOMY

How SHOULD stabilization policy be conducted? This question must be answered, regardless of whether one advocates the use of discretionary, countercyclical policy or an automatic policy which is not based upon forecasts of disturbances. Critics of discretionary stabilization policies claim that we may know the basic outlines of the dynamic structure of the economy, but we do not know the exact form of the structural equations, let alone the magnitudes of the coefficients. Moreover, many of the key variables are not directly measurable: for example, the rates of Harrod and Solow neutral technical change and the expected rate of price change. Given this situation, what policies should be followed? Why?

The dynamic structure of the economy could be described by differential equation 1, where X is a vector of the endogenous variables, C is a vector of exogenous variables, A and B are real matrices, and u is a vector of policy variables.

(1) $$DX = AX + Bu + C.$$

Critics of discretionary policy would claim that we only know the signs of the elements of A and B, and we are fairly ignorant of vector C.

Suppose, on the other hand, that the econometrician's dream came true. As a result of his efforts, the elements of matrices A and B are known with certainty and vector C of exogenous disturbances can confidently be predicted. How should policy vector u be selected? For example, should the authorities control the rate of change of the money supply, the nominal rate of interest, or the rate of change of the interest plus the noninterest bearing debt? Or should a compatible proper subset of these variables be controlled? What should be the time path of the policy chosen? These questions apply equally to the case where A and B are known only with respect to the signs of the elements and where we have quantitative knowledge of A, B, and C.

Usually, a performance criterion is postulated, which is a function of certain state variables and the policies undertaken. Optimum policies are those which maximize (or minimize) the performance criterion, subject to certain constraints imposed by the economic system. For example, the performance criterion could be:

$$(2) \qquad W(X_0, u) = \int^{\infty} g(x, u) \, dt,$$

where x is a subset of the state variables X and u refers to the controls used. Immediately the question arises: What should be included among the arguments of the g function? Certainly, per capita consumption of goods, c should be included. How should real balances per worker m be treated? Does it produce a direct flow of utility as was assumed in Chapter 2, or should it be treated as a productive service which raises the productivity of labor and capital? In the former case we would include m as an argument in the performance function in addition to c. If m is to be treated as a productive service, then it only has value insofar as it affects the time profiles or per capita consumption and leisure over an infinite horizon. Double counting would result if both c and m were included as arguments in the g function in that case.

How should the rate of inflation or deflation be viewed in terms of the performance function? Should inflation and deflation be treated symmetrically in terms of their effects upon the performance function? Is an inflation of π_0 better or worse than deflation at the same rate? In the Keynes-Wicksell model inflation implies unsatisfied demands; and deflation implies a greater rate of capital accumulation than firms desire.

This is true, regardless of whether the price change is or is not anticipated. Therefore, price changes should be treated as disutilities. By contrast, the Synthesis model implies that markets will be cleared (eventually) when price changes are anticipated. In that case disutility would arise from unanticipated deflation or inflation $|\pi - \pi^*|$. Should unanticipated inflation be treated in a symmetrical way with unanticipated deflation: that is, should $(\pi - \pi^*)^2$ or $|\pi - \pi^*|$ be the variables that produce disutility? Of course, the rate of price change will affect the level of real balances in all models. Insofar as real balances are productive services, inflation will affect output and thereby the level of per capita consumption. The question, however, is whether price changes enter the performance function directly or only indirectly through the effects upon per capita consumption.

Some studies include the unemployment rate (or the rate of capacity utilization) as an argument in the performance function. Others include the level of international liquidity relative to a desired level. The justification for their inclusion in the g function, which already includes per capita consumption, is not clear. Unemployment will affect output and thereby per capita consumption. Or unemployment will affect the rate of price change. If c and the rate of unanticipated price change (to take one example) are already considered as arguments in g, why should the unemployment rate be added? Is it not double counting? Similar criticisms could be made concerning the inclusion of foreign exchange reserves. If they are increased, that is, there is foreign investment, per capita consumption is affected. If they are too low to permit a steady flow of imports, then the time profile of per capita consumption will be affected. Why should the level of foreign exchange reserves be treated as an independent argument?

What are the costs of control? What social disutilities are involved in using controls u in equation 1? Variations in the rate of monetary expansion, which arise as a result of net transfer payments to or from the public, imply variations in the amount of the checks passing between the public and the private sector. What is the marginal social cost of changing the amount of the check? Another control is open-market operations: variations in the composition of the private sector's claims upon the public sector. What are the marginal social costs involved in such an operation? If the Federal Reserve System sells $500 million rather than one million dollars in securities to the private banks, what incremental disutilities arise? What additional resources are used up in the process?

It is not clear what should be the arguments, let alone their weights, in the performance criterion. The optimality question has as many answers as there are different performance functions. Policies which are optimal with one function are not necessarily optimal with a different function. In view of these unanswered questions we shall approach the control problem in a less elegant manner.

Traditionally, the moderation of price inflation or deflation has been the object of stabilization policy, especially in a full employment model. When attention is directed to a fully employed growing economy, stabilization policy must be viewed in terms of an additional criterion. What will be the effect of the policy upon the steady state ratio of effective labor per unit of capital (x) or upon its reciprocal $k \equiv 1/x$, the capital intensity? If the capital intensity diverged to plus infinity (that is, x converged to zero), then the marginal product of capital would go to zero (if the elasticity of substitution did not exceed unity). As Koopmans and Phelps have shown, where the marginal product of capital is permanently below the growth rate $n > 0$, such a situation is inefficient in a welfare sense. A consumption of capital by one generation could raise its welfare without adversely affecting the welfare of future generations, where welfare is positively related to consumption per capita. Stabilization policy, which prevents the capital intensity $(1/x)$ from diverging to plus infinity, would tend to raise some measure of economic welfare.

On the other hand, if x diverged to plus infinity (that is, the capital intensity converged to zero), the real wage of an efficiency unit of labor would go to zero (if the elasticity of substitution did not exceed unity). Social unrest or unemployment would be inevitable if the real wage of a natural unit of labor had to be decreased. A decline in the real wage of a natural unit of labor would occur if the real wage of an efficiency unit of labor declined at a faster rate than the rate of Harrod neutral technical change.[1] For these reasons assume that the object of stabilization policy is not only the moderation of inflation or deflation but also the prevention of $x \equiv 1/k$ from going to either zero or plus infinity. More precisely, suppose we want the equilibrium capital intensity to stay sufficiently close to the Golden Rule. For example, let r_e be the equilibrium rent per unit of

[1] This is the only kind of technical change considered here.

capital and $\bar{r}$ is some upper bound on r. Then, we may want to keep r_e within a range: $\bar{r} > r_e \geq n$. Stability in terms of keeping the rate of price change and the capital intensity within bounds, rather than optimality in terms of a well-defined performance function, is our goal in this exploratory study.

How can we stabilize a model of a growing economy with the following characteristics? The model (1) must be dynamic with noninstantaneous speeds of response. Balance-sheet adjustments should be sluggish in the sense that individuals and firms spread adjustments over a considerable period of time. Moreover, the effects of expenditures on prices should also be distributed overtime. These characteristics imply variable lags in policy. (2) Our knowledge of the structure of the economy described by matrix equation $DX = AX + Bu + C$ should be imprecise. State variables are denoted by vector X and controls are denoted by u. Although the signs of the elements in matrices A and B are known, we do not know their quantitative magnitudes. Vector C of exogenous disturbances is not fully known. (3) It is quite possible that the dynamic system may be unstable. Or, the convergence to equilibrium may be slow and cyclical.

Certain simplifying assumptions will be made in this exploratory study of control policy. Assume that (4) the system is deterministic rather then stochastic. For example, the direct effects of policies u, described by matrix Bu above, are unknown in magnitude but are not stochastic. Exogenous disturbances such as the growth of effective labor are unknown constants but are not stochastic variables. (5) The rate of capacity utilization and the unemployment rate are constant. Disturbances affect the price level and nominal value of national income, but no unemployment problems are produced. The object of stabilization policy is to find control laws $u(X)$, which will achieve (a) a reasonable degree of price stability and (b) bring the ratio of effective labor per unit of capital into some desired range.

The models presented in Chapters 3, 4, and 5 are consistent with such a description of an economy. They are dynamic and are driven by an unknown growth of effective labor. Adjustments to an excess supply of, or demand for, real balances per unit of capital are spread out over time. This is reflected in our formulation of Walras' law: the excess demand for goods per unit of capital is proportional to the excess stock supply of real balances per unit of capital. The factor of proportionality h, or the speed of response, is finite, and it could be quite small. Portfolio adjustments are, therefore, distributed over time.

Effects of expenditures on prices are also distributed over time. Prices do not rise or fall at such a rate as to clear markets instantly. Instead, the rate of price change (in the Keynes-Wicksell model) is proportional to the excess demand for, or supply of, goods per unit of capital. Money-market disequilibrium encounters two frictions: (a) the rate h at which stock disequilibrium is converted into a flow and (b) the rate λ at which prices change in response to excess demands or supplies of goods.

Two general controls were already encountered in the previous chapters. They were (a) the growth of the money supply μ and (b) the ratio θ of the total stock of interest plus noninterest-bearing federal debt to the total stock of money. Recall the steady state solution of the Synthesis model ($\delta = 1$) described in Chapter 5. When capital and labor grow at the same rate, then:

(3) $S(x_e, \theta v_e) = n;$

planned savings per unit of capital are equal to the growth of effective labor.[2]

When real balances per unit of capital are constant, then:

(4) $v_e = L[y(x_e), r(x_e) + \pi_e, r(x_e) + \pi_e, \theta v_e];$

money-market equilibrium prevails in the steady state.[3] When investment per unit of capital is equal to n, the nominal rate of interest $\rho_e = r(x_e) + \pi_e$. Alternatively, the real rate of interest $\rho_e - \pi_e$ is equal to the rent per unit of capital. The equilibrium rate of price change π_e is equal to the growth of the money supply per worker.

(5) $\pi_e = \mu - n.$

Figure 1 in Chapter 5 described the long-run solution of the Synthesis model. Since θ, which represents the ratio of the total interest plus noninterest-bearing federal debt A to the total stock of money M, was treated as a parameter of the system, the total debt A also grows at rate μ.

[2] Chapter 5, equation 13.
[3] Chapter 5, equation 14b.

We could have described the steady state rate of price change as being equal to the growth of the total federal debt per effective worker.

(6) $$\pi_e = DA/A - n.$$

It was shown how a rise in $DA/A = \mu$ raised the steady state capital intensity (lowered x_e) and lowered the steady state value of real balances per unit of capital v_e. Since θ was treated as a constant, the rise in the growth of the total debt also lowers the steady state value of the real federal debt per unit of capital $A/pK = \theta v$.

Monetary authorities could also use θ, the ratio of A to M, as a control variable. Variations in ratio θ will affect the steady state solution. A rise in θ will raise the steady state rent per unit of capital,[4] $r(x_e)$, and also the steady state real balances per unit of capital v_e. A simple graphic proof of this proposition follows.

Figure 1, based upon equations 3, 4, and 5, can be used to demonstrate the effect of a change in θ upon x_e and v_e in the Synthesis ($\delta = 1$) model. It is the same as Figure 1 in Chapter 5. The LX curve is based

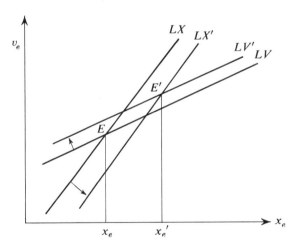

FIGURE 1. The effect of raising the ratio $\theta = A/M$ upon the steady state solution in the Synthesis model.

[4] This was proved, for the Keynes-Wicksell ($\delta = 0$) case, in J. L. Stein's study (1966, pp. 463–64).

upon equation 3, and the LV curve is based upon equations 4 and 5. Equilibrium was initially at point E. What will be the effect of a rise in θ, the ratio of total federal interest plus noninterest-bearing debt to the stock of money? When θ rises to a higher level, then both A and M continue to grow at the same rate μ (except at the point of discontinuity). Therefore, no change will occur in the steady state rate of price change.

The LV curve will shift upward. Given the value of x, the rise in θ raises real private financial wealth. Since real balances are complementary in demand with real private financial wealth (that is, $L_4 > 0$), the quantity of real balances demanded increases. Money-market equilibrium requires that the quantity of real balances in existence also rise. Therefore, the LV curve shifts upward to LV'.

Similarly, a rise in θ will shift the LX curve to the right. Why? Given v, a rise in θ will raise real private financial wealth per unit of capital. Planned savings per unit of capital would decline below the growth rate of effective labor. To preserve the equality $S(x, \theta v) = n$, described by equation 3, there must be a rise in output per unit of capital $y(x)$. This would offset the decline in planned savings resulting from the operation of the real balance effect. Since output per unit of capital is positively related to x, the ratio of effective labor per unit of capital, the LX curve would shift to the right.

In the new steady state x_e and v_e will be higher than before. The rise in A/M will permanently increase the rent per unit of capital, output per unit of capital, and real balances per unit of capital. Since the steady state nominal rate of interest is:

$$(7) \qquad\qquad \rho_e = r_e + \pi_e,$$

the rise in θ will raise the steady state nominal rate of interest.

We have seen that the dynamic system responds to (a) changes in the growth of the total debt when the A/M ratio is constant and to (b) changes in the ratio $\theta = A/M$ when the growth of A and M is constant, except at the point of discontinuity. For this reason we shall consider the effects of two control laws. First, let the proportionate rate of change of A, denoted by α, be negatively related to the current rate of price change:

$$(8) \qquad\qquad \alpha = DA/A = \alpha_0 - \alpha_1\pi.$$

Second, change the ratio A/M via open-market operations and debt-management policies in such a way as to produce a desired nominal rate of interest:

(9) $$\rho = \rho_0 + q_1\pi,$$

where the desired nominal rate of interest is positively related to the rate of price change.

Our analysis of control laws proceeds in two stages. First, a short-run model is considered where the capital intensity is approximately constant. This model is almost identical to the dynamic model examined in Chapter 5, Section IB. How effective are different control laws or stabilization policies in producing a reasonable degree of price stability (within the context of that model)? An advantage of starting with a short-run model, where the capital intensity is fixed, is that the instability elements are quite apparent; and the ways in which control policies operate are easily explained. Second, a long-run dynamic growth model is considered, where the capital intensity is an endogenous variable. Our aim is to discover the effects of different control laws upon the time profiles of the capital intensity and the rate of price change. Which control laws will simultaneously achieve a reasonable degree of price stability and bring the capital intensity into a desired range?[5]

The main conclusions are that our control laws will:

(i)   stabilize the dynamic growth model used in this chapter.
(ii) achieve a reasonable degree of price stability.
(iii) produce the desired real rate of interest.

No quantitative knowledge of the structural equations (described by matrices A and B) is required.

A brief heuristic explanation of these conclusions can be given. In the steady state (denoted by subscript e), capital and effective labor grow at rate n. Moreover, the rent per unit of capital r_e will be equal to the real rate of interest i_e, where i_e is equal to the nominal rate of interest ρ_e less the rate of price change. Long-run equilibrium implies that the actual rate of price change π_e is equal to the expected rate of price change $\pi_e{}^*$.

(10) $$r_e = i_e = \rho_e - \pi_e.$$

[5] This chapter is a development of J. L. Stein and K. Nagatani's study (April, 1969, pp. 165–83).

Control law (9) produces a nominal rate of interest which is a linear function of the rate of price change. The steady state rent per unit of capital is, therefore, a linear function of the rate of price change.

(11) $r_e = i_e = \rho_0 + (q_1 - 1)\pi_e.$

Insofar as the monetary authorities can control the rate of price change π_e, they can control the real rate of interest and the steady state rent per unit of capital r_e.

Control law (8) enables them to determine the steady state rate of price change. When real federal debt per unit of capital is constant, the proportionate rate of change of real federal debt $D \ln (A/p) = \alpha_e - \pi_e$ is equal to the growth of capital. Since capital and effective labor grow at rate n, the steady state rate of price change is:

(12) $\pi_e = \alpha_e - n.$

But the growth of total federal debt α is given by control law (8). Therefore, the steady state rate of price change:

(13) $\pi_e = \dfrac{\alpha_0 - n}{1 + \alpha_1}.$

If the monetary authorities desire a stable level of prices, they could set α_0 equal to their estimate of n and also select a large value of α_1. They can raise or lower the steady state rate of price change by raising or lowering α_0.

Equations 11 and 13 show how the control laws enable the monetary authorities to achieve a desired rent per unit of capital. No detailed quantitative knowledge of the economic system is required.

A value of q_1 greater than unity stabilizes the economy. The usual source of instability results from the volatility of price expectations. If the rate of price change is expected to rise, it is tantamount to a decline in the real rate of interest. Goods are substituted for money, and the price expectations may be self-realizing. If control law (9) is followed with $q_1 > 1$, then the nominal rate of interest is raised by more than the rate of price change. Therefore, the real rate of interest is raised and excess demand is lowered. The destabilizing effects of volatile price expectations are negated.

II

A SHORT RUN DYNAMIC

MODEL

Assume that the ratio of effective labor per unit of capital $x \equiv 1/k$ is approximately constant at x_0. Select for our model a slight variation of the one developed in Chapter 5, Section IB. A very brief review of this model is in order.

The price determination equation 14 could be either of the Keynes-Wicksell ($\delta = 0$) or the Synthesis ($\delta = 1$) type.

$$(14) \qquad \pi = \delta\pi^* + \lambda\left(\frac{I}{K} - \frac{S}{K}\right),$$

where π is the actual rate of price change, π^* is the expected rate of price change, and λ represents the speed at which prices change in response to market disequilibrium.

A slight change will be introduced into the investment equation. The speed of response, of the desired rate of change of the capital-labor ratio with respect to changes in the net expected rate of return, will no longer be standardized at unity. It will be a positive constant ξ, which is a component of the elasticity of the investment-demand schedule.

$$(15) \qquad \frac{I}{K} - n = \xi[r(x) + \pi^* - \rho] = \xi[r(x) - i],$$

where I/K is the desired growth of capital, n is the growth of effective labor, $r(x) + \pi^*$ is the marginal efficiency of investment, and ρ is the nominal interest rate. Alternatively, $r + \pi^* - \rho$ can be written as $r - i$, where the real rate of interest i is $\rho - \pi^*$.

Savings per unit of capital will depend upon output per unit of capital $y(x)$, the rent per unit of capital $r(x)$, and real net claims of the private sector upon the public sector per unit of capital A/pK. Variable A is the nominal value of the interest plus noninterest-bearing net claims of the private sector upon the public sector. Variable A/pK is the same as θv in the previous chapters. Denote this measure of wealth by z.

$$(16) \qquad S/K = S(x, z); \qquad S_1 > 0, \, S_2 < 0.$$

Price expectations are assumed to be formulated on the basis of "adaptive expectations":

(17) $D\pi^* = b(\pi - \pi^*),$

where b is nonnegative.

Walras' law states that the excess flow demand for bonds is equal to the excess flow supply of money plus the excess flow supply of goods. Assume that the bond market is always in equilibrium. Then the excess demand for goods is equal to the excess flow supply of real balances.[6]

(18) $$\frac{\pi - \delta\pi^*}{\lambda} = h\left\{v - L\left[y(x) + \frac{(\pi - \delta\pi^*)}{\lambda}, r(x) + \pi^*, \rho, z\right]\right\}.$$

In the previous chapters it was assumed that the ratio of the total federal debt (interest plus noninterest bearing) to the total stock of money was constant at θ: that is, $z = \theta v$. When the money supply grew at exogenous rate μ, then the quantities of interest-bearing debt, noninterest-bearing federal debt, and inside money all grew at the same rate μ. This assumption is no longer made.

The reader will recall that the system will not possess a saddle point. Either it is stable or it is unstable at all points in a neighborhood of the equilibrium.

Two countervailing forces are operative in the Synthesis ($\delta = 1$) model. On the one hand, the real balance effect is a stabilizing force. A rise in the rate of price change above the equilibrium value lowers real balances per unit of capital. Consumption per unit of capital is reduced directly since consumption is positively related to $z = A/pK = \theta v$. Furthermore, when the stock of real balances per unit of capital is reduced, the bond market will be affected by the reduction in liquidity. As bonds are offered for sale in an attempt to restore real balances to their previous level, the nominal rate of interest will rise. Investment will be adversely affected, and the aggregate demand for goods will decline. Since the rate of price change is positively related to the excess demand for goods, the rate of price change will tend to revert to the equilibrium level.

[6] See Chapter 5, equation 21b. Variable z replaces θv.

Operating against the stabilizing real balance effect, particularly in the Synthesis ($\delta = 1$) model, are the effects of price expectations. Suppose that prices are expected to rise at 4 per cent per year rather than at 3 per cent per year. Will this expectation be realized? Were it not for the real balance effect the answer is yes. Specialists who make markets immediately raise the rate of price change to 4 per cent per annum. Moreover, the anticipated yield on capital has increased as a result of the rise in the expected capital gain. Investment per unit of capital is directly affected by the expected rate of price change. A direct shift can occur from money to real capital. When the expected rate of price change rises by one percentage point, planned investment rises by ξ percentage points (equation 15). Thereby the excess demand for goods is raised. Prices rise at a higher rate than 4 per cent per annum since both π^* and $\lambda(I/K - S/K)$ in equation 14 have increased. Expectations are certainly self-justifying in the absence of a strong real balance effect. The Keynes-Wicksell ($\delta = 0$) model is less subject to dynamic instability than is the Synthesis model. When π^* rises, the actual rate of price change rises only insofar as the excess demand for goods rises. As a rule we shall use the less stable Synthesis model in devising control laws. All arguments will apply a fortiori to the Keynes-Wicksell model, which differs from the Synthesis model only insofar as $\delta = 0$, rather than $\delta = 1$.

Stability will only occur if the real balance effect exceeds the price expectations effect. The magnitude of the constant rate of monetary expansion μ plays no role in determining the stability of the system. Furthermore, the system may be dynamically stable in the sense that (π^*, v) will eventually converge to ($\mu - n, v_s$). However, as Figure 3 of Chapter 5 indicates, the approach to equilibrium may be cyclic and slow. In the "tug of war" between the real balance effect and the price expectations effect, the former may eventually win. But the latter may cause a considerable (that is, undesirable) amount of overshooting.

The question is whether we can devise a set of control laws which will achieve the following objectives.

(1) It will not destabilize an otherwise stable system.

(2) It will stabilize an otherwise unstable system.

(3) It will produce a reasonable amount of price stability.

(4) It will decrease the degree of overshooting of the equilibrium. This is independent of the stability questions (1) and (2).

III
CONTROLLING THE SHORT RUN
SYSTEM

A. A HEURISTIC DISCUSSION OF THE CONTROL LAWS

If there is instability, it can be expected to arise from the price expectations equation. A control law which is designed to stabilize the system must, therefore, prevent price changes from feeding upon themselves. Consider equation 19, which is the *IS* equation in the ($\delta = 1$) Synthesis model. It is based upon equations 14–16.

(19) $\pi = \pi^* + \lambda\{n - S(x, z) + \xi[r(x) + \pi^* - \rho]\}$.

It describes the effect of changes in price expectations upon the actual rate of price change. Suppose, for expositional simplicity at this point, that the expected and actual rates of price change are always equal. Then Figure 2a describes equation 19. *RHS* (*LHS*) refers to the right (left)-hand side of equation 19.

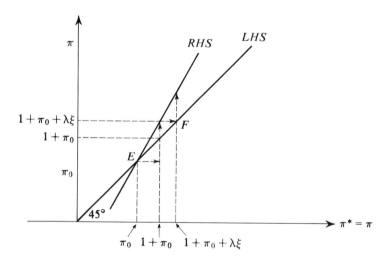

FIGURE 2A. How price expectations are self-justifying. A rise in the expected rate of price change from π_0 to $\pi_0 + 1$ raises the actual rate of price change to $\pi_0 + 1 + \lambda\xi$.

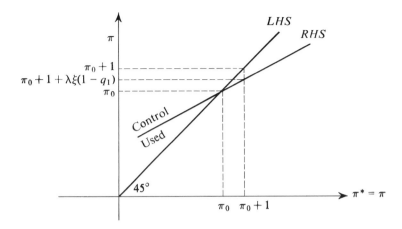

FIGURE 2B. When $q_1 > 1$, the control law on the nominal rate of interest prevents price expectations from being self-justifying.

If the actual rate of price change rose by one unit from the equilibrium E, are there forces tending to restore the equilibrium? The expected rate of price change will rise by one unit. Specialists who make markets raise the rate of price change by one unit. Moreover, the marginal efficiency of investment $r(x) + \pi^*$ rises by one unit. Investment per unit of capital is raised by ξ units; and the actual rate of price change rises by an additional $\lambda\xi$ units. From an initial rise in the rate of price change by one unit, the subsequent rate of price change rises by $1 + \lambda\xi$ units. A dynamically unstable situation tends to develop, as is indicated by the direction of the arrows in Figure 2a.

An adjustment of the nominal rate of interest ρ would seem to be the logical candidate for a stabilizing control. If $\Delta\rho$ were always a multiple q_1 of $\Delta\pi^*$, then the changes in price expectations would not be self-justifying. A rise in $\pi^* - \rho$ tends to raise planned investment. However, if a rise in π^* were accompanied by a rise in ρ by $q_1\Delta\pi$, where $q_1 > 1$, then the opportunity cost of funds would rise by more than the expected capital gain. Investment per unit of capital would be reduced as a result of a rise in the real rate of interest.

Figure 2b describes equation 19 when $\pi^* = \pi$ and

(20) $$\rho = \rho_0 + q_1\pi.$$

In that case equation 19 becomes equation 19a.

(19a) $\pi = \pi^* + \lambda\{n - S(x, z) + \xi[r(x) + \pi^* - \rho_0 - q_1\pi^*]\}.$

A rise in the actual rate of price change by one unit is assumed to raise the expected rate of price change by the same amount. Specialists raise the rate of price change from π_0 to $\pi_0 + 1$ immediately in the Synthesis model.

Firms realize that prices are rising at $\pi_0 + 1$ instead of at π_0 per cent per year; and expect a unit rise in the capital gain. By itself this would raise the rate of investment demanded per unit of capital. According to our control law (20), the monetary authorities immediately raise the nominal rate of interest by $q_1 > 1$ percentage points. As a result the profitability of investment is reduced. The rate of planned investment changes by $\xi(1 - q_1) < 0$ percentage points. A smaller excess demand for goods, or a larger excess supply of goods, develops. Therefore, the realized rate of price change will be $1 + \lambda\xi(1 - q_1) < 1$. The initial rise in the rate of price change will not be self-justifying as it was in the previous case.

A feedback control was devised. A rise in $\pi^* = \pi$ will call for a rise in ρ. The rise in the nominal rate of interest will counterbalance the rise in π^* and serve to reduce the rise in $\pi^* = \pi$. The control law on ρ is a stabilizing force. In its absence the rise in π^* will also tend to raise ρ (as was seen in Chapter 5). But the induced rise may be insufficient to stabilize the system. A control law $\Delta\rho = q_1 \Delta\pi$ with $q_1 > 1$ would provide the extra braking power necessary for dynamic stability.

An intuitive argument has been given for the stabilizing characteristics of the control law on the nominal rate of interest. A basic question concerns the method of achieving the desired change in the rate of interest and the implications of this control law for the rest of the system. This question will be discussed in part B of this section.

If the interest rate is used as a control variable, then the monetary authorities abdicate control over the money supply! How can a reasonable degree of price stability be achieved when (i) the monetary authorities refrain from controlling the rate of monetary expansion and (ii) the rate of growth of effective labor is unknown? The second control law is designed to achieve this end by operating on the total federal debt A.

In the usual models of money and growth, all money is outside money and there is no interest-bearing federal debt. The stock of money changes as a result of net transfer payments to and from the public. These transfers correspond to budget deficits and surpluses. There is no reason to restrict the analysis to the case where $A \equiv M$. Let there be outside money, government bonds, and inside money. Net transfer payments consist of changes in A, the stocks of outside money (currency plus unborrowed reserves), and government bonds.

The second control law concerns the growth of A, the total federal debt. Devise a tax and expenditure policy such that the total federal debt A will tend to grow at proportionate rate α_0 in periods of price stability, where α_0 is an estimate of the unknown rate of growth of effective labor n. However, if there is inflation, then A should grow at a slower rate than α_0; and if there is deflation, A should grow at a faster rate than α_0. If N^* represents the estimate of the quantity of effective labor, then the second control law states that:

$$(21a) \qquad D \ln (A/N^*) = -\alpha_1 \pi$$

or

$$(21b) \qquad D \ln A = \alpha_0 - \alpha_1 \pi.$$

The desired growth of the total debt per effective worker should be negatively related to the actual rate of price change. The total debt in all forms would be:

$$(21c) \qquad A(t) = N^*(0)e^{\alpha_0 t} \cdot \exp \left[-\alpha_1 \int^t \pi(\tau) \, d\tau \right].$$

Control law (21) determines the government budget deficits or surpluses in terms of (a) the estimated growth of effective labor and (b) the current rate of price change.

In the steady state real debt per unit of capital $z \equiv A/pK$ will stabilize at some value. This means that eventually:

$$(22a) \qquad \frac{Dz}{z} = D \ln \frac{A}{pK} = \alpha_s - \pi_s - n + \frac{Dx}{x} = 0.$$

The steady state rate of price change π_s will converge to the growth of the total federal debt per effective worker ($\alpha_s - n$). Relation $\pi_s = \alpha_s - n$ is graphed in Figure 3. Suppose that out second control law varied α, the proportionate rate of change of A, in a direction opposite to the rate of

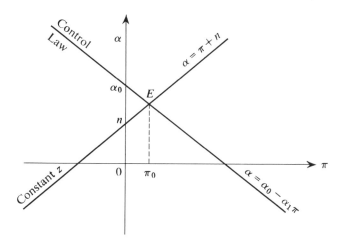

FIGURE 3. The magnitude of the feedback control α_1 affects the absolute value of the equilibrium rate of price change.

change of the price level: equation 21b. Then there is a feedback control on α. A high initial value of α will imply a high value of π_s. In turn, a high π_s will induce a lower value of α. As a result of the feedback control in a dynamically stable system, control law (21b) will reduce the steady state value of π_s.

Control law (21b) is also graphed in Figure 3, describing the feedback effect of π on α. Equilibrium E is obtained.[7]

Algebraically, equilibrium E (in Figure 3) implies that:

(22b) $$\alpha_s - n = \pi_s.$$

Substitute control law (21b) into (22b) and derive:

(22c) $$\alpha_0 - \alpha_1 \pi_s - n = \pi_s.$$

Solving for π_s, we find that:

(22d) $$\pi_s = \frac{(\alpha_0 - n)}{(1 + \alpha_1)}.$$

[7] Subscript s refers to short-run equilibrium.

Regardless of our knowledge of n, the steady state rate of price change is inversely related to α_1. Raising α_1 is equivalent to rotating the control law line clockwise. The equilibrium π_s will move down the curve $\pi_s = \alpha - n$ toward zero.

It seems that the use of two control laws, one on the nominal rate of interest and the other on the growth of the total federal interest plus noninterest-bearing debt, are what we are looking for. The first control is concerned with the stability of the system; and the second is concerned with the steady state rate of price change. Although the second law is reminiscent of Friedman's 1948 stabilization proposal (pp. 245–64), the package of controls proposed here differs fundamentally from his proposals in three respects.

(a) The monetary authorities engage actively in open-market operations to determine the nominal rate of interest.

(b) They pay no direct attention to the money supply per se but focus upon the interest rate.

(c) The monetary-fiscal authorities vary the rate of growth of the total public interest plus noninterest-bearing debt, not the stock of money to achieve control law (21).

B. A FORMAL ANALYSIS OF THE CONTROL LAWS IN THE SHORT-RUN MODEL

Our short-run model consists of six equations: (a) the IS curve (equation 23), (b) the FM curve (equation 24), (c) the adaptive expectations equation 25, (d) a differential equation describing the change in $z \equiv A/pK$ (equation 26), (e) a control law on the interest rate (equation 27), and (f) a control law (equation 28) on the growth of the total federal interest plus noninterest-bearing debt A. The value of x, that is, the ratio of effective labor per unit of capital, is held constant in the short-run model but not in the long-run model.

Unknowns are six in number. (i) The rate of price change π, (ii) the expected rate or price change π^*, (iii) the nominal rate of interest ρ, (iv) the ratio of real balances per unit of capital v, (v) the ratio of real debt per unit of capital z, and (vi) the growth of the nominal federal debt α. Variable θ, which was used in previous chapters, is no longer exogenous but is the endogenous ratio of z to v, when control law (27) is followed.

Equations 23–28 describe the six equations mentioned above, respectively.

(23) $\dfrac{\pi - \delta\pi^*}{\lambda} = n - S(x, z) + \xi[r(x) + \pi^* - \rho].$

(24) $\dfrac{\pi - \delta\pi^*}{\lambda h} = v - L\left[y(x) + \dfrac{(\pi - \delta\pi^*)}{\lambda}, r(x) + \pi^*, \rho, z \right].$

(25) $D\pi^* = b(\pi - \pi^*),$

(26) $\dfrac{Dz}{z} = \alpha - \pi - n + \dfrac{Dx}{x} = \alpha - \pi - n,$

where α is the growth of the total debt A and $Dx_0 = 0$ in the short run.

(27) $\rho = \rho_0 + q_1\pi.$

(28) $\alpha = \alpha_0 - \alpha_1\pi.$

A graphic examination of the FM curve (24) and control law (27) shows that the stock of money is not a control but must adjust to achieve the desired interest rate. Suppose that the rates of price change π, π^*, and real debt per unit of capital z were given at the moment. Then the FM curve implies that the nominal rate of interest is negatively related to real balances per worker. A given rate of inflation (in the $\delta = 0$ model), or unanticipated inflation (in the $\delta = 1$ model), implies a given excess supply of real balances per unit of capital. A lower ρ induces a rise in the quantity demanded of real balances per unit of capital. To keep π constant, there must be a rise in $v \equiv M/pK$ real balances per unit of capital. Therefore, the liquidity preference relation is generated. Control law (27) is graphed in the left-hand side of Figure 4; and the liquidity preference relation between ρ and v, implied by the FM curve equation 24, is graphed in the right-hand side of that figure.

If the rate of price change were π_1, then the monetary authorities try to achieve a nominal rate of interest ρ_1. They do so by engaging in open-market operations. The composition of the total interest plus noninterest-bearing debt (A) changes, as a result of open-market operations, until the market rate of interest ρ_1 emerges. This implies that the ratio of money to the value of capital M/pK must settle at v_1. The monetary authorities do not directly concern themselves with the stock of money. It has to adjust

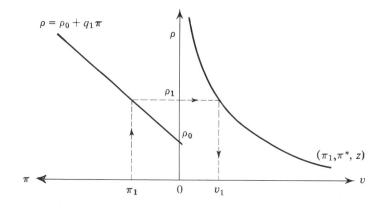

FIGURE 4. The relation between the interest rate control law and the stock of real balances per unit of capital.

to produce the desired market rate of interest; and open-market operations are the means to this end. Variable $z/v \equiv \theta$ adjusts to produce the desired nominal rate of interest.

Substitute control law (27) into the *IS* curve (23) and derive equation 29.

$$(29) \quad \frac{\pi - \delta\pi^*}{\lambda} = n - S(x, z) + \xi[r(x) + \pi^* - \rho_0 - q_1\pi].$$

Therefore, the rate of price change π is a function of π^* and z (given the values of x_0 and n). Equations 29a and 29b describe this relation when $\delta = 1$ in the Synthesis model.[8]

$$(29a) \quad \pi = f(\pi^*, z)$$

$$(29b) \quad d\pi = \frac{(1/\lambda + \xi)}{(1/\lambda + \xi q_1)} d\pi^* - \frac{S_2}{(1/\lambda + \xi q_1)} dz = f_1 \, d\pi^* + f_2 \, dz.$$

Given z, expectations tend to be self-justifying if the control law raises the nominal rate of interest by less than the rise in the rate of price change ($q_1 < 1$). Of course, if the interest rate is pegged, then $q_1 = 0 < 1$. On the other hand, the expectations will not be self-justifying if $q_1 > 1$. The reason for this was discussed earlier and revolves around the answer to the question: Does a rise in π^* lower or raise the real rate of interest $\rho - \pi^*$? If the real rate of interest is lowered, then aggregate demand rises

[8] A similar relation can be derived in the case of the $\delta = 0$ model.

and (in the Synthesis model) justifies the specialists' decision to raise π. On the other hand, if the real rate of interest were raised as a result of the control law ($q_1 > 1$), then aggregate demand would decline. The decision of the specialists would not be justified.

The growth of the total debt DA/A would be given by equation 30, based upon 28 and 29a.

(30) $$DA/A = \alpha = \alpha_0 - \alpha_1 f(\pi^*, z).$$

Substitute (30) into (26) and derive a differential equation for the growth of real debt per unit of capital (when $Dx = 0$ in the short-run model).

(31) $$Dz/z = \alpha_0 - n - (1 + \alpha_1)f(\pi^*, z).$$

Substitute (29a) into the adaptive expectations equation 25 and derive the differential equation for price expectations.

(32) $$D\pi^* = b[f(\pi^*, z) - \pi^*].$$

The values of partial derivatives f_1 and f_2 are given by equation 29b above.

System 31–32 is to be examined in terms of its stability and steady state properties. In the steady state these equations are equal to zero. Therefore, from 32, the actual and expected rates of price change are equal.

(33a) $$\pi_s^* = f(\pi_s^*, z_s).$$

Moreover, the actual rate of price change will be given by (33b) based upon (31).

(33b) $$f(\pi_s^*, z_s) = \frac{\alpha_0 - n}{1 + \alpha_1}.$$

As Figure 3 indicates, the higher the values of α_1, the lower will be the absolute value of the steady state rate of price change. The line $\alpha = \alpha_0 - \alpha_1 \pi$, representing the control law, would rotate clockwise through α_0 when α_1 is increased. A lower absolute value of π_s would be produced.

If system (31)–(32) is linearized around the equilibrium point (π_s^*, z_s), given by (33a)–(33b), then differential equations 34a and 34b are obtained. Variable $x_1 \equiv \pi^* - \pi_s^*$ is the deviation of the expected rate of price change from its short-run equilibrium value $(\alpha_0 - n)/(1 + \alpha_1)$. Variable $x_2 \equiv z - z_s$ represents the deviation of $A/pK \equiv z$ from its short-run equilibrium value z_s.

(34a) $Dx_1 = b(f_1 - 1) \cdot x_1 + bf_2 \cdot x_2.$

(34b) $Dx_2 = -z_s(1 + \alpha_1)f_1 \cdot x_1 - z_s(1 + \alpha_1)f_2 \cdot x_2.$

Necessary and sufficient conditions for stability are that the sum of the characteristic roots of system (34a)–(34b) be negative and that their product be positive. We know that the product of the roots, equation 36, will always be positive. Therefore, necessary and sufficient conditions for local stability are that inequality (35) describing the sum of the roots be satisfied.

(35) $T = b(f_1 - 1) - z_s(1 + \alpha_1)f_2 < 0,$

or

$$T = \frac{b\xi(1 - q_1)}{\dfrac{1}{\lambda} + \xi q_1} + z_s\frac{(1 + \alpha_1)S_2}{\dfrac{1}{\lambda} + \xi q_1} < 0.$$

(36) $(\det) = bz_s(1 + \alpha_1)f_2 > 0$

or

$$(\det) = bz_s\frac{(1 + \alpha_1)(-S_2)}{\dfrac{1}{\lambda} + \xi q_1} > 0.$$

Control laws (27) and (28) can guarantee stability. If $q_1 > 1$, that is, the interest rate is changed by more than the rate of price change, then $T < 0$, and the system is locally stable. No quantitative knowledge of the economic system is required; and any value of $q_1 > 1$ will stabilize such a system. A heuristic explanation of this result was given in part A of this section.

Moreover, the real balance effect is always a stabilizing force. If A grew at rate α_0, that is, $\alpha_1 = 0$, then a rise in the rate of price change would lower real balances per unit of capital. Spending would be adversely affected; and the rate of price inflation would be mitigated. Such a stabilizing effect would be magnified if the growth of A declined when π rose. A more powerful negative real balance effect would then occur; and the rate of price change would be reduced. Equilibrium would occur at a rate of price change equal to $(\alpha_0 - n)/(1 + \alpha_1)$.

A very strong interest rate adjustment policy, that is, a large value of

q_1, can prevent cyclical fluctuations; and the economy would converge monotonically to the equilibrium. Suppose that q_1 grew infinitely large. Then (from 29b) both f_1 and f_2 would go to zero from above. The sum of the roots would converge to:

(a) $$\lim_{q_1 \to \infty} T = -b;$$

and the product would converge to zero from above:

(b) $$\lim_{q_1 \to \infty} (\det) \downarrow 0.$$

The characteristic roots are derived from the equation:

(37) $$\lambda^2 - T\lambda + (\det) = 0.$$

Cyclical fluctuations would occur only if $T^2 - 4(\det) < 0$. When q_1 is very large, this inequality cannot occur. Therefore, a large value of q_1 is both a stabilizing force and one that prevents cyclical fluctuations.

An intuitive explanation can be given for this result. The cyclical forces in the economy stem from the adaptive expectations function. Prices rise and further inflation is expected. Only when this inflation has reduced real balances to a sufficiently large degree do prices tend to decline. The stronger the price expectations effect, the greater the overshooting of the equilibrium. A vigorous interest rate adjustment policy neutralizes the effect of price expectations. The interest rate is adjusted to prevent the real rate of interest $\rho - \pi^*$ from changing. Any time $\rho - \pi^*$ declines, aggregate demand rises and price inflation is increased. But if q_1 is large, the slightest price inflation induces a substantial rise in the nominal rate of interest. Thereby, the inflation is "nipped in the bud." Policies which effectively restrain movements in π will succeed in neutralizing the destabilizing or cyclical effects of price expectations.

IV

EFFECTS OF THE CONTROL LAWS

UPON LONG-TERM GROWTH

A. THE GROWTH MODEL

The long-run model differs from the short-run model insofar as x, the ratio of effective labor per unit of capital, is endogenous. A differential equation in x is added to the system. If the adaptive expectations equation 17 were retained, then the system would contain three differential equations in x, π^*, and z. To reduce the level of complexity, without changing the model in any substantive way, assume that the expected rate of price change is equal to the current rate. Substitute equation 38.6 for equation 17. The former is a special case of the latter; and it is a destabilizing element that must be brought under control. For the reader's convenience, the growth model is summarized.

$$(38.1) \qquad Dx/x = n - DK/K$$

is the rate of change of the ratio of effective labor per unit of capital.

$$(38.2) \qquad Dz/z = \alpha - \pi - DK/K$$

is the rate of change of the total interest plus noninterest-bearing federal debt per dollar of capital.

$$(38.3) \qquad \pi = \delta\pi^* + \lambda\left(\frac{I}{K} - \frac{S}{K}\right)$$

is price determination equation 14 above.

$$(38.4) \qquad I/K = n + \xi[r(x) + \pi^* - \rho]$$

is investment equation 15 above.

$$(38.5) \qquad S/K = S(x, z)$$

is savings equation 16 above.

$$(38.6) \qquad \pi^* = \pi$$

is the price expectations equation.

$$(38.7) \quad \frac{\pi - \delta\pi^*}{\lambda} = h\left\{v - L\left[y(x) + \frac{(\pi - \delta\pi^*)}{\lambda}, r(x) + \pi^*, \rho, z\right]\right\}$$

is Walras' law when the bond market is in equilibrium: equation 18 above.

$$(38.8) \quad \frac{DK}{K} = a\frac{I}{K} + (1 - a)\frac{S}{K}, \qquad 1 > a > 0 \quad \text{when} \quad \pi > 0$$
$$a = 0 \quad \text{otherwise}$$

is the rule for determining the rate of capital formation. During inflationary periods planned investment exceeds capital formation which exceeds planned savings.

(38.9) $$\rho = \rho_0 + q_1\pi$$

is the control law for open-market operations.

(38.10) $$\alpha = \alpha_0 - \alpha_1\pi$$

is the control law for the rate of change of the total debt A.

Ten endogenous variables: x, z, v; DK/K, I/K, S/K; ρ, π, π^*; α are determined in terms of exogenous variable n and control variables α_0, α_1; ρ_0, q_1.

Substitute (38.3) into (38.8) and derive equation 39 describing the growth of capital. When $\delta = 0$, the Keynes-Wicksell model is derived; when $\delta = 1$, the Synthesis model is derived:

(39) $$\frac{DK}{K} = S(x, z) + \frac{a}{\lambda}(\pi - \delta\pi^*).$$

Substitute (39) into (38.1) to derive equation 40a. Similarly, substitute (39) and (38.10) into (38.2) to derive equation 40b. These are the fundamental equations of the growth model.

(40a) $$\frac{Dx}{x} = n - S(x, z) - \frac{a}{\lambda}(1 - \delta)\pi$$

(40b) $$\frac{Dz}{z} = \alpha_0 - S(x, z) - (1 + \alpha_1)\pi - \frac{a}{\lambda}(1 - \delta)\pi.$$

Once the rate of price change π is expressed in terms of state variables x and z, yielding $\pi = \pi(x, z)$, then the time paths of $x(t)$ and $z(t)$ can be determined. Substitute equations 38.4, 38.5, 38.6, and control law (38.9) into price determination equation 38.3 and derive equation 41.

(41) $$\pi\frac{(1 - \delta)}{\lambda} = n - S(x, z) + \xi[r(x) + \pi - \rho_0 - q_1\pi].$$

Variable π can be written compactly as a function of x and z, which is equation 41a.

(41a) $$\pi = \pi(x, z).$$

Equation 42 is derived by taking differentials of equation 41.

(42) $d\pi = \pi_x \, dx + \pi_z \, dz,$

where

(42a) $\pi_x = \dfrac{\xi r' - S_x}{\xi(q_1 - 1) + \dfrac{1}{\lambda}(1 - \delta)},$

(42b) $\pi_z = \dfrac{-S_z}{\xi(q_1 - 1) + \dfrac{1}{\lambda}(1 - \delta)}$

A graph will facilitate the interpretation of equations 42a and 42b. Two equations were used to derive equation 41, which implies (42a)–(42b). First, control law (38.9) states that open-market operations or debt-management policies are used to achieve a desired interest rate. The latter is positively related to the rate of price change and is graphed in Figure 5, given the assumption that $q_1 > 1$. Second, the price change equation 38.3 states that:

$$\pi \frac{(1 - \delta)}{\lambda} = n - S(x, z) + \xi[r(x) + \pi - \rho],$$

when the expected rate of price change π^* is equal to π the rate currently

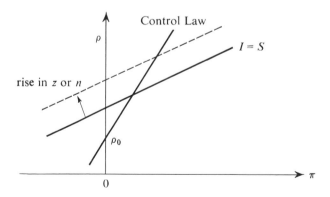

FIGURE 5. A rise in z or n raises π and ρ when $q_1 > 1$.

experienced. In the Synthesis model,[9] it follows that savings and investment are equal: equation 43.

(43) $$S(x, z) = n + \xi[r(x) + \pi - \rho].$$

A unit rise in $\pi^* = \pi$ must be offset by a unit rise in ρ if planned savings
and investment are to be equal. Therefore, equation 43 is drawn as the
positively sloped curve labeled $I = S$ in Figure 5. Only if $q_1 > 1$ will the
control law curve be steeper than the $I = S$ curve.

Shifts in the $I = S$ curve, equation 43, occur as a result of changes in
x, z, or n. If real federal debt per unit of capital rose, then planned savings
per unit of capital would decline. To equate savings and investment, the
nominal rate of interest would have to rise. This means that the $I = S$
curve will have to shift upward. Both the nominal rate of interest and the
rate of price change will increase as a result of this shift. The magnitude
of the rise in π will be related to q_1, the magnitude of the interest rate
control policy. With a higher value of q_1, the control law curve would be
steeper: that is, it would rotate in a counterclockwise direction through ρ_0.
Therefore, a rise in excess demand would induce a significant open-market
sale which would tend to offset the initial rise in excess demand. For this
reason the algebraic values of π_x and π_z in equation 42 are negatively
related to q_1, the magnitude of the interest rate control policy.

Substitute equation 41a into equations 40a and 40b to derive
equations 44 and 45. Control parameters α_0 and α_1 are explicit in these
equations; but control parameters ρ_0 and ρ_1 are implicit in the π function
(41a). Linearize (44) and (45) around the steady state x_e, z_e; and define
$x_1 \equiv x - x_e$, $x_2 \equiv z - z_e$. Equations 44a and 45a are obtained.

(44) $$\frac{Dx}{x} = n - S(x, z) - \frac{a}{\lambda}(1 - \delta)\pi(x, z) = F(x, z).$$

(45) $$\frac{Dz}{z} = \alpha_0 - S(x, z) - \left(1 + \alpha_1 + \frac{a}{\lambda}(1 - \delta)\right)\pi(x, z) = G(x, z).$$

The linear system is written compactly as:

(44a) $$Dx_1 = x_e F_1 \cdot x_1 + x_e F_2 \cdot x_2$$

(44b) $$Dx_2 = z_e G_1 \cdot x_1 + z_e G_2 \cdot x_2,$$

---

[9] The graphic interpretation of the Keynes-Wicksell ($\delta = 0$) model is left to the reader.

where:

$$\begin{pmatrix} F_1 & F_2 \\ G_1 & G_2 \end{pmatrix}$$

$$\equiv (-1) \begin{bmatrix} \dfrac{a}{\lambda}(1 - \delta)\pi_x + S_x & \dfrac{a}{\lambda}(1 - \delta)\pi_z + S_z \\[2ex] \left[1 + \alpha_1 + \dfrac{a}{\lambda}(1 - \delta)\right]\pi_x + S_x & \left[1 + \alpha_1 + \dfrac{a}{\lambda}(1 - \delta)\right]\pi_z + S_z \end{bmatrix}$$

B. STABILITY CONDITIONS

Necessary and sufficient conditions for stability in the neighborhood of a steady state are that inequalities (45a) and (45b) be satisfied.

(45a) $T = -x_e\left[\dfrac{a}{\lambda}(1 - \delta)\pi_x + S_x\right]$

$$- z_e\left[\left(1 + \alpha_1 + \dfrac{a}{\lambda}(1 - \delta)\right)\pi_z + S_z\right] < 0$$

(45b) $(\det) = -x_e z_e(1 + \alpha_1)[\pi_x S_z - S_x \pi_z] > 0$

or

$$(\det) = \dfrac{x_e z_e(1 + \alpha_1)\xi r'(-S_z)}{\left(\dfrac{1}{\lambda}(1 - \delta) + \xi(q_1 - 1)\right)} > 0.$$

If the nominal rate of interest is changed by more than the rate of price change, then $(q_1 - 1)$ is positive. The real parts of the two roots will have the same signs. If their sum T is negative, then the system will be stable.

The elements of stability and instability, which determine the sign of T, can be understood by examining the linear system (44). The value of:

$$T = x_e F_1 + z_e G_2.$$

Suppose that the economy were displaced from the steady state as a result of a rise in the ratio of effective labor per unit of capital: that is, $x_1 > 0$. Would the economy tend to return to the steady state? That will depend (partially) upon F_1, where:

$$F_1 = -\dfrac{a}{\lambda}(1 - \delta)\pi_x - S_x.$$

The rise in x_1 exerts two effects in the Keynes-Wicksell ($\delta = 0$) model and one effect in the Synthesis ($\delta = 1$) model. A rise in x will raise output per unit of capital and thereby increase savings per unit of capital ($S_x > 0$). As a result capital grows more rapidly than before; and x tends to revert to its initial level.

In the Keynes-Wicksell model there can be forced savings. If the rise in x_1 raises the rate of price change, the rate of growth of capital:

$$DK/K = \frac{a}{\lambda} \pi + S(x, z)$$

will rise. The convergence of x_1 to its original level of zero would be accelerated. However, if the rise in x_1 exerted a deflationary effect upon the economy, by raising planned savings by more than it raised planned investment, the growth of capital would be reduced. Stability in the x_1 direction would depend upon which effect were stronger: the rise in planned savings or the decline in forced savings.

The effect of a rise in x upon the rate of price change π_x is given by (42a). The rise in labor per unit of capital raises the rent per unit of capital by r' and stimulates investment by $\xi r'$. On the other hand, it raises savings by S_x. It is not clear which effect dominates. However, if the interest rate adjustment coefficient q_1 is large, then π_x will be small in absolute value. This can be seen in Figure 5. Shifts in the $I = S$ curve do not change π by much. Therefore, the main component of the growth of capital will be planned savings. Under these conditions F_1 would be negative; and deviations of x from x_e tend to be corrected.

What happens if the equilibrium were displaced in the $z \equiv A/pK$ direction? For example, suppose that $x_2 \equiv z - z_e$ became positive as a result of a rise in real federal debt per unit of capital. Are there forces to stabilize this system? The rise in x_2 lowers planned savings per unit of capital since $S_z < 0$. This effect tends to raise the growth of real debt per unit of capital and therefore is a destabilizing force. On the other hand, the rise in z will raise the rate of price change $\pi_z > 0$. Real debt will be reduced because not only does the rate of price change rise but also the growth of A is negatively related to the rate of price change through control law (38.10). Stability in the x_e direction would only occur if:

$$G_2 = -\left[1 + \alpha_1 + \frac{a}{\lambda}(1 - \delta)\right]\pi_z - S_z < 0,$$

that is, if the reduction in the growth of A/p exceeded the reduction in the growth of K. If a very strong interest adjustment policy were followed, then π_z would be small, and an element of stability would be attenuated. Theoretically, the response to this danger is that α_1, the debt adjustment coefficient, should be large to offset this. Since:

$$(42b) \qquad \pi_z = \frac{(-S_z)}{\xi(q_1 - 1) + \dfrac{1}{\lambda}(1 - \delta)} \, ,$$

let α_1 be a multiple of the denominator in (42b). Then G_2 will be negative.

Local stability will occur if T, the sum of the roots, is negative. If the (positive) value of the elasticity of savings with respect to x is greater than the (absolute) value of the (negative) elasticity of savings with respect to z, then the system can be expected to be stable. This is a sufficient condition for stability in the Synthesis ($\delta = 1$) model where $q_1 > 1$.

Write the elasticities as:
(i) $\eta_x \equiv S_x \cdot x_e/S > 0$.
(ii) $\eta_z \equiv S_z \cdot z_e/S < 0$.
Substitute these definitions into (45a) and derive (45c).

$$(45c) \quad T = -(\eta_x + \eta_z)S_e - (1 - \delta)\frac{\alpha}{\lambda}(\pi_x \cdot x_e + \pi_z \cdot z_e) - z_e(1 + \alpha_1)\pi_z.$$

The first term is negative by assumption, and the third term will be negative if $q_1 > 1$. The middle term is zero in the Synthesis ($\delta = 1$) model. In the Keynes-Wicksell ($\delta = 0$) model, a high value of q_1 will make that term small in absolute value. Therefore, the system will be stable if $(\eta_x + \eta_z) < 0$.

C. THE EFFECTS OF THE CONTROL LAWS UPON THE STEADY STATE SOLUTION

In the steady state x is equal to $x_e \equiv 1/k_e$ and z is equal to z_e. Therefore, equations (40a) and (40b) are equal to zero. Specifically:

$$(46) \qquad \frac{Dx}{x} = 0 = n - S(x_e, z_e) - \frac{a}{\lambda}(1 - \delta)\pi_e.$$

$$(47) \qquad \frac{Dz}{z} = 0 = \alpha_0 - S(x_e, z_e) - (1 + \alpha_1)\pi_e - \frac{a}{\lambda}(1 - \delta)\pi_e.$$

It follows that the proportionate rate of change of the price level is equal to:

$$(48) \qquad \pi_e = \frac{\alpha_0 - n}{1 + \alpha_1},$$

regardless of whether δ is equal to zero or unity. If the monetary authorities set $\alpha_0 = n$, then price stability will occur in the steady state. Otherwise, the absolute value of the rate of price change will be inversely related to $(1 + \alpha_1)$, as illustrated in Figure 3 above.

The nominal rate of interest can be determined from equation 48 and control law (38.9). It is equal to:

$$(49) \qquad \rho = \rho_0 + q_1 \frac{(\alpha_0 - n)}{(1 + \alpha_1)}.$$

By selecting the appropriate parameters, the monetary authorities can determine the steady state nominal rate of interest. Only the growth of effective labor n is beyond the control of the monetary authorities. The latter can form some estimate of n, but it is unknown outside of the steady state.

Define the real rate of interest i as the nominal rate of interest less the rate of price change. In the steady state the actual and expected rates of price change are equal. Equation 50 determines the steady state real rate of interest i_e.

$$(50) \quad i_e \equiv \rho_e - \pi_e = \rho_0 + (q_1 - 1)\pi_e = \rho_0 + (q_1 - 1)\frac{(\alpha_0 - n)}{(1 + \alpha_1)},$$

using equations 48 and 49. The monetary authorities can determine the steady state real rate of interest by selecting the appropriate parameters in control laws (38.9) and (38.10). For example, if they want the real rate of interest to be equal to the growth rate n, they should:

(a) set ρ_0 equal to their estimate of n;
(b) set α_0 equal to their estimate of n;
(c) select a value of q_1 greater than unity;
(d) select a high value of α_1.

If their estimate of n is correct, then there will be price stability ($\pi_e = 0$) and a real rate of interest equal to the growth rate. If their estimate is incorrect, a high value of α_1 will produce a low absolute value of the rate of price change.

Control laws (38.9) and (38.10) enable the monetary authorities to determine the steady state values of the real variables. Consider two cases: the Synthesis model and the Keynes-Wicksell model.

1. *The Synthesis Model.* In the steady state ($Dx = 0$), savings per unit of capital are equal to the growth rate n (from equation 46). Whenever the actual and expected rates of price change are equal (and $\delta = 1$), then planned savings and planned investment are equal. This statement is based upon equation 38.3. Consequently, planned investment per unit of capital is equal to the growth rate n. This is described by equation 51, based upon (38.4) and the previous conclusions.

(51) $$\left(\frac{I}{K}\right)_e = n = n + \xi(r_e + \pi_e{}^* - \rho_e),$$

which implies that:

(51a) $$r_e = \rho_e - \pi_e = i_e.$$

The steady state rent per unit of capital r_e will be equal to the steady state real rate of interest i_e. The rent per unit of capital is a function of x_e, and the real rate of interest i_e is given by equation 50. This equality can be written as:

(51b) $$r(x_e) = \rho_0 + (q_1 - 1)\pi_e = \rho_0 + (q_1 - 1)\frac{(\alpha_0 - n)}{(1 + \alpha_1)}.$$

The relation between changes in the steady state rate of price change π_e and changes in the steady state capital intensity $k_e \equiv 1/x_e$ depends upon the magnitude of the interest rate adjustment coefficient. In the steady state the real rate of interest i will be equal to the rent per unit of capital $r(x_e)$. Since the nominal rate of interest is a linear function of the rate of price change, the real rate of interest is a linear function of the rate of price change: equation 51b. If the steady state rate of price change were raised, what would happen to the real rate of interest? It would depend upon the value of q_1, that is, upon whether the nominal rate of interest is raised by more or by less than the rate of price change. Were the value of q_1 greater than unity, the real rate of interest would rise. As a result, the rent per unit of capital $r(x_e)$ must also rise. This can only occur if the capital intensity ($k_e \equiv 1/x_e$) fell. Therefore, a rise in the rate of price change would be associated with a decline in the steady state capital intensity—the reverse of the usual result.

On the other hand, if q_1 were less than unity, then a rise in the rate of price change will lower the real rate of interest. The rent per unit of capital will fall to the lower value of the real rate of interest. Since the capital intensity k_e is negatively related to the real rate of interest i_e, the former will rise as a result of the rise in the rate of price change. This is the conventional result.

Since the monetary authorities can control the real rate of interest by controlling the nominal rate of interest and the rate of price change, they determine the steady state values of the real variables: the rent per unit of capital $r(x_e)$, output per unit of capital $y(x_e)$, and the real wage per unit of effective labor $y'(x_e)$. The steady state value of real debt per unit of capital is derived from the equation:

$$n = S(x_e, z_e).$$

Given x_e and n, the value of z_e follows. Since x_e and z_e are positively related for any given n, there will be a positive relation between the real rate of interest i_e and real federal debt per unit of capital z_e. These controls do not presuppose any quantitative knowledge of the parameters of the structural equations of the economic system. To compensate for their ignorance of n, a high value of α_1 is called for.

2. *The Keynes-Wicksell Model.* Similar results occur in the Keynes-Wicksell model. The difference between the Synthesis ($\delta = 1$) and the Keynes-Wicksell ($\delta = 0$) model concerns the relation between price inflation and the excess demand for goods per unit of capital. The $\delta = 0$ model drives a wedge between investment and savings during periods of price change. With secular inflation at a constant rate, the ratio of unfilled orders per unit of capital will be a positive constant. On the other hand, there is no change in unfilled orders in the Synthesis model; hence, the ratio of unfilled orders per unit of capital will go to zero asymptotically.

Three equations are needed to describe the steady state characteristics of the Keynes-Wicksell model. Equation 52a is investment equation 38.4; and equation 52b states that capital and effective labor grow at the same rate n in the steady state.

(52a) $$\frac{I}{K} = n + \xi[r + \pi^* - \rho] = n + \xi(r - i).$$

(52b) $$\frac{DK}{K} = n.$$

Equation 52c is based upon equation 38.3 when $\delta = 0$ and equation 38.8. During inflationary periods when there is excess demand per unit of capital, neither consumers nor investors will be able to purchase their desired quantitites. Everyone will be partially frustrated. Equation 52c states that the difference between the desired I/K and the actual DK/K is proportional to the excess demand for goods per unit of capital:

(52c)
$$\frac{DK}{K} = \frac{I}{K} - (1 - a)\frac{\pi}{\lambda},$$

where π/λ is equal to $I/K - S/K$, the excess demand for goods per unit of capital.

Combining these equations we derive equation 53. The rate of price change is positively related to the difference between the rent per unit of capital r_e and the real rate of interest $i_e = \rho_e - \pi_e = \rho_e - \pi_e{}^*$.

(53)
$$r_e - i_e = \frac{(1 - a)}{\xi}\frac{\pi_e}{\lambda}.$$

(53a)
$$r_e = i_e + \frac{(1 - a)}{\xi}\frac{\pi_e}{\lambda}.$$

The real rate of interest, the reader will recall, is a linear function of the rate of price change π_e. It is repeated here as equation 53b.

(53b)
$$i_e = \rho_0 + (q_1 - 1)\pi_e.$$

If $q_1 > 1$, then a rise in the rate of price change will raise the real rate of interest. Moreover, a higher rate of inflation must also raise the gap between the rent per unit of capital and the real rate of interest. This gap is the driving force behind inflation in the Keynes-Wicksell model. Therefore, the rent per unit of capital described by equation 53a must rise. As in the Synthesis model, when $q_1 > 1$, a rise in π_e raises the rent per unit of capital and lowers the steady state capital intensity k_e. The only difference between the models is that the gap between the rent per unit of capital and the real rate of interest is positively related to the rate of price change in the Keynes-Wicksell model.[10]

3. A Paradox Explained. The apparent paradox that, if $q_1 > 1$, a rise in the rate of price change π_e will lower the steady state capital intensity is easily explained. When the rate of price change rises, open-market sales are conducted to raise the nominal rate of interest by more than the

[10] The case where $q_1 < 1$ is left to the reader.

rise in π_e. Therefore, $\theta \equiv z/v$ is raised: that is, the ratio of federal debt to money is increased. According to Figure 1, the rise in θ lowers the capital intensity k_e and raises the real rate of interest. The paradox is explained by the fact that control law (38.9) changes θ and produces the results described in Figure 1.

D. STABILIZATION POLICY IN A GROWING ECONOMY: SUMMARY

How can we stabilize a model of a growing economy with the following characteristics? The model must be dynamic with noninstantaneous speeds of response. Balance-sheet adjustments should be sluggish, in the sense that individuals and firms spread adjustments over a considerable period of time, and the effects of expenditures on prices should also be distributed overtime. These characteristics imply variable lags in policy. Our knowledge of the structure of the economy should be imprecise. It is quite possible that the dynamic system may be unstable or the convergence to equilibrium may be slow and cyclical.

Certain simplifying assumptions are made in this exploratory study of control policy. Assume that the system is deterministic rather than stochastic. Moreover, assume that the rate of capacity utilization and the unemployment rate are constant. Disturbances affect the price level and nominal value of national income, but no unemployment problems are produced.

The object is to derive control laws which will (1) achieve a reasonable degree of price stability and (2) produce a desired real rate of interest and rent per unit of capital in the model of an economy described above. Two control laws are sufficient to achieve these goals. First, the monetary authorities engage in open-market operations or use debt-management policies to achieve a nominal market rate of interest ρ, which is positively related to the rate of price change π. Formally, they vary the composition of the federal interest plus non-interest bearing debt to produce a rate of interest ρ described by equation 54.

$$(54) \qquad\qquad \rho = \rho_0 + q_1\pi,$$

where ρ_0 and q_1 are constants. A unit rise in the rate of price change π induces the monetary authorities to raise the nominal rate of interest by q_1 units. Insofar as the nominal rate of interest is used as a control variable, the monetary authorities abdicate control over the money supply.

Second, they control the proportionate rate of change of the total federal interest plus non-interest bearing debt. This quantity is the net claims of the private sector upon the public sector and is net private financial wealth. Denote the proportionate rate of change of this quantity by α. The second control law states that:

$$(55) \qquad \alpha = \alpha_0 - \alpha_1 \pi.$$

During periods of price stability net private financial wealth grows at proportionate rate α_0. If there is inflation, then α is reduced below α_0; if there is deflation, then α is raised above α_0. Ideally, a tax and expenditure policy should be devised to implement control law (55) automatically.

How do these control laws achieve their intended objectives? Assume that the economy is described by the Synthesis model (for expositional simplicity). In the steady state (denoted by subscript e), capital and effective labor grow at proportionate rate n, and the rent per unit of capital r_e will equal the real rate of interest i_e. The real rate of interest is equal to the nominal rate of interest ρ_e less the expected rate of price change π_e^*; hence i_e measures the real yield that could be obtained from holding bonds rather than capital in portfolios. Long-run equilibrium in the Synthesis model requires that:

$$(56) \qquad r_e = i_e = \rho_e - \pi_e^* = \rho_e - \pi_e,$$

since the actual and expected rates of price change must be equal in the steady state.

Control law (54) produces a nominal rate of interest which is a linear function of the rate of price change. The steady state real rate of interest i_e is therefore also a linear function of the rate of price change. Since the rent per unit of capital will equal the real rate of interest, in long-run equilibrium the rent per unit of capital will be a linear function of the rate of price change as described by:

$$(57) \qquad r_e = i_e = \rho_0 + (q_1 - 1)\pi_e.$$

Insofar as the monetary authorities can control the rate of price change π_e, they can control the steady state rent per unit of capital r_e and the values of the other real variables.

Control law (55) enables the monetary authorities to determine the steady state rate of price change. In the steady state real federal debt A/p per unit of capital (K) is constant. Therefore, the steady state rate of price change π_e is equal to the growth of the nominal value of the federal debt less the growth of capital. But the growth of capital is equal to the growth of effective labor n. It follows that the equilibrium rate of price change is equal to the growth of the federal debt per unit of effective labor.

$$\text{(58)} \qquad\qquad \pi_e = \alpha_e - n.$$

A feedback control exists relating the growth of the federal debt α and the rate of price change π. An increase in α raises the rate of price change (equation 58); but a rise in π lowers the growth in the federal debt (equation 55). Therefore, the steady state rate of price change is:

$$\text{(59)} \qquad\qquad \pi_e = (\alpha_0 - \alpha_1\pi_e) - n = \frac{\alpha_0 - n}{1 + \alpha_1} .$$

If the monetary and fiscal authorities desire a stable level of prices, they could set α_0 equal to their estimate of the growth of effective labor n and also select a large value of α_1. They can raise or lower the steady state rate of price change by raising or lowering parameter α_0.

Equations 57 and 59 indicate how the two control laws enable the monetary authority to achieve a desired rent per unit of capital. For example, if they want (a) the rent per unit of capital to equal the growth rate of effective labor and (b) prices to be stable, they should:

(i)   set parameter ρ_0 equal to their estimate of n;
(ii) set parameter α_0 equal to their estimate of n;
(iii) select a high value of α_1;
(iv) select a value of q_1 greater than unity.

If their estimate of n is correct, then according to equation 59, there will be price stability ($\pi_e = 0$). Moreover, the real rate of interest according to (57) will be equal to the growth rate. If their estimate of the growth rate n is incorrect, then a high value of α_1 will produce a low absolute value of the rate of price change. Therefore, the equilibrium real rate of interest will be close to the growth rate. It has been shown how control laws (54) and (55) enable the monetary and fiscal authorities to guide the economy close to a desired point, *without quantitative knowledge* of the parameters of the economic system, within the framework of the model described in this chapter.

A value of q_1 greater than unity stabilizes the economy. If the monetary authority wishes to avoid cycles of inflation and deflation, it should change the nominal rate of interest (via open-market operations) by more than the rate of price change π. The usual source of instability in monetary growth models results from the volatility of price expectations. If the rate of price change is expected to rise, it is equivalent to a decline in the real rate of interest. Goods are substituted for money and the price expectations may be self-realizing. If control law (54) is followed with $q_1 > 1$, then the nominal rate of interest is raised by more than the rate of price change. Inflation activates a control law, which raises the real rate of interest. Excess demand is lowered and the price expectations are not realized. The destabilizing effects of (even the most) volatile price expectations are negated.

An interesting and unusual conclusion emerges. If $q_1 > 1$, then not only is the economy made more stable but also a rise in the rate of price change raises the rent per unit of capital (that is, lowers the capital intensity). This can be seen from equation 57. The reason is that a rise in the rate of price change leads to a rise in the real rate of interest when control law (54) is used with a value of q_1 greater than unity. The rent per unit of capital will equal the real rate of interest. Therefore, the rent per unit of capital will rise and the capital intensity will decline when the rate of price change rises. There is another way of viewing this phenomenon. A rise in π induces open-market sales to raise the nominal rate of interest. These sales reduce the ratio of money to net private financial wealth. A decline in this ratio raises the real rate of interest.

Even though the monetary and fiscal authority has only qualitative knowledge of the economic system, it can guide it to a desired point without any danger of economic instability.

CHAPTER SEVEN

*Competitive Markets
and Optimal Growth*

AN OPTIMAL GROWTH PATH is derived from three functions and an initial condition. The first function is an optimality criterion which states what we wish to maximize, and it is an explicit value judgment. Second, there is an assumption concerning the rate of population growth. Third, an aggregative production function is specified. Two major questions are discussed in this chapter. (1) Will competitive markets lead the economy to the optimal growth path if there are no externalities? (2) If there is a deviation between the market-generated growth path and the optimal growth path, how can this deviation be corrected? When the questions are posed in this way, it is apparent that the optimality criterion must be based to some extent upon the utility functions of households. Otherwise, the issue would be prejudged: the market growth path generated by households could not be expected to coincide with the optimal growth path except under very peculiar conditions.

There are two main classes of growth models based upon the rational behavior of households. First, there are the infinite horizon models where an immortal family is assumed to select the time path of consumption which will maximize a utility functional subject to a constraint. I prove that in a purely competitive economy with no externalities, the market-generated growth path in a Neoclassical economy will converge to the optimal stationary point. Second, there are the intergeneration models where the economy consists of a vicissitude of generations, each of which has a finite life. There is no presumption at all that the market-generated growth path in a Neoclassical econo ny will be efficient or optimal in the intergeneration model of economic growth. However, there are certain institutions whose mere existence will ensure that the market-generated equilibrium solution will coincide with the stationary point on the optimal growth path.

I

SOCIETY AS AN IMMORTAL FAMILY

A. THE MARKET-GENERATED GROWTH PATH

The accumulation process, as described by Frank Knight (1921, Ch. XI), can be described schematically in the diagram below.

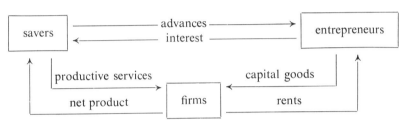

As a result of the division of labor, certain persons devote their efforts to the production of capital goods rather than to the production of consumer goods. Savers advance claims on consumer goods to entrepreneurs who are engaged in the production of capital goods. Those advances are used by those engaged in the production of capital goods to purchase consumer goods. The entrepreneurs promise to pay the savers interest for the advances of consumer goods. When completed, the capital goods will be rented to firms producing consumer goods. As a result of competition, the rent per unit of capital good paid by the firms to the entrepreneurs will be equal to the marginal product of the capital good. In turn, the firms will sell the output of consumer goods to the suppliers of productive services who are the ultimate savers.

The entrepreneurs use a dollar of advances to produce a capital good which has a net marginal product of y_k dollars per unit of time.

These capital goods will command a rent of y_k dollars per unit of time if firms are able to bid competitively for the use of these capital goods. The value of the capital goods will be the capitalized value of the rents, where the capitalization factor is the real rate of interest i paid to savers. Therefore, the value of the capital goods produced by one dollar of advances is y_k/i. Entrepreneurial profits will be made if y_k exceeds i, that is, if the capitalized value of the capital good exceeds its supply price. Certainly, in the steady state, competition will eliminate profits, and the interest payments to savers will equal the rents received by the producers of capital goods. Outside the steady state, when technology is changing in an unpredictable manner, there may be profits to the entrepreneurial firms. Uncertainty concerning the marginal product of new types of capital goods may result in a situation where the rents received for the use of new capital goods exceed the interest paid to savers. However, once the marginal product of the capital good can be estimated fairly accurately, competition will eliminate entrepreneurial profits and lead to the equality of y_k and i.

Savers consist of families, in this set of models, who attempt to maximize utility over infinite horizons.[1] But what is the optimality criterion that they attempt to maximize? Any hypothetical optimality criterion will not do; it must be one which has a maximum. Otherwise, it would be meaningless to discuss a maximization procedure.

1. Consumer Utility Maximization. Suppose that the immortal family attempts to maximize a weighted sum W_1 of utilities of per capita consumption. Assume that $u(c)$ is a concave utility function, such that the marginal utility of a zero level of per capita consumption is infinite and there is no satiation. Consumption is assumed to occur at the end of the period in this discrete model. Assume that future utilities are discounted at rate $\delta > 0$, such that the utility per capita enjoyed at time $t = 0, 1, \ldots$ is $[u(c_t)/1 + \delta](1 + \delta)^{-t}$, since consumption is assumed to occur at the end of the period. The arbitrariness of this discounting assumption in an infinite horizon model is exceeded only by its mathematical convenience in describing a maximization procedure. Suppose that population grows exogenously at constant rate $n \geqq 0$, such that

[1] The model is based upon my unpublished paper "The Optimality of Competitive Growth" (May, 1967) and N. Liviatan's (1968) extension of it: "Competitive Growth under Alternative Expectations Models" (unpublished, 1968).

$N_t = (1 + n)^t$ is the population at time t. Despite the exogenous nature of the population growth, assume that the growth is anticipated and that the members of our immortal family believe that "the more souls, the more joy." These assumptions can be summarized by stating that the family selects as its optimality criterion:

(1)
$$W_1 = \sum_{t=0}^{\infty} \frac{u(c_t)}{1 + \delta} N_t(1 + \delta)^{-t},$$

a discounted sum of total utility over an infinite horizon. The weighted sum of utilities (1a), which is based upon (1) and the assumption concerning population growth, will only exist if the discount rate δ exceeds the exogenous rate of population growth.

(1a)
$$W_1 = \sum_{t=0}^{\infty} \frac{u(c_t)}{1 + \delta} \left(\frac{1 + n}{1 + \delta}\right)^t.$$

Optimality criterion (1), expressing certain value judgments, is arbitrary as should be clear from the chain of assumptions stated above. What mitigates the arbitrary assumption concerning the optimality criterion is that we shall use the exact same criterion in deriving the optimal growth path and in comparing the optimal growth path with the market-generated growth path. Since the constraints facing the immortal family will differ from those used in determining the optimal growth path, there could conceivably be a divergence between the two paths.

For the budget constraint facing the immortal family, assume equation 2: the present value of total consumption should equal the family's wealth. To be a meaningful constraint, the family's wealth must be finite. Initially, the family owns capital k_0. During any period the family earns a real wage of v_t per member, and the consumption is c_t per family member. Therefore, total savings out of human income are $(v_t - c_t)N_t$ per unit of time, where both the wage and consumption are assumed to occur at the end of the period. If the interest rate earned on a dollar of savings is assumed to be constant at $r > 0$, then the budget constraint is equation 2.

(2)
$$\frac{1}{1 + r} \sum_{t=0}^{\infty} \frac{(v_t - c_t)N_t}{(1 + r)^t} + k_0 \cdot 1 = 0.$$

Assume that the agents in the economy have static expectations concerning the wage rate v_t and the interest rate r_t, such that they are expected to remain at their current levels $v_t = v_0$ and $r_t = r_0$. Each immortal family at time $t = 0$ selects that time profile of per capita consumption $(c_0, c_1, c_2, \ldots)$ which would maximize optimality criterion (1) or (1a), subject to budget constraint (2) and their static expectations.

Along an optimal consumption path it must not be possible to raise total utility W_1 via an intertemporal shift of consumption. If a unit of per capita consumption is given up at time t, then total utility declines by $(u'(c_t)/1 + \delta)N_t(1 + \delta)^{-t}$, which is equal to the marginal utility of per capita consumption multiplied by the size of the population. The arbitrary discounting operation converts utility received in time t into units of utility received at $t = 0$.

A unit of per capita savings at time t will become $(1 + r)/(1 + n)$ units of per capita consumption in the subsequent period. The gain in interest is partially offset by the larger population. The marginal utility of per capita consumption in the subsequent period is

$$\frac{u'(c_{t+1})}{1 + \delta}(1 + \delta)^{-(t+1)},$$

which would be multiplied by the population N_{t+1}. The gain in utility in period $t + 1$ is equal to

$$\left(\frac{1 + r}{1 + n}\right)\frac{u'(c_{t+1})}{(1 + \delta)}(1 + \delta)^{-(1+t)}N_{t+1}.$$

Along an optimal consumption path, equation 3a must be satisfied. It must not be possible to raise total utility via a reallocation of consumption per capita among periods.[2] Equation 3b follows directly from equation 3a.

(3a) $-\dfrac{u'(c_t)}{1 + \delta}(1 + \delta)^{-t}N_t + \dfrac{(1 + r)}{(1 + n)}\dfrac{u'(c_{t+1})}{1 + \delta}(1 + \delta)^{-(t+1)}N_{t+1} = 0,$

or

(3b) $-u'(c_t) + \dfrac{(1 + r)}{(1 + \delta)}u'(c_{t+1}) = 0.$

Alternatively, equation 3b may be written as equation 3c. The marginal rate of substitution between c_t and c_{t+1} must be equal to $(1 + r)/(1 + \delta)$.

(3c) $\dfrac{u'(c_t)}{u'(c_{t+1})} = \dfrac{1 + r}{1 + \delta}.$

[2] These conditions for $t = 0, 1, \ldots$ are derived by maximizing (1a) subject to constraint (2). By assuming that $u'(0)$ is infinite, consumption will occur during each period.

This is an important equation, for it states that if planned per capita consumption is constant $c_t = c_{t+1} = c$, then the interest rate will be equal to the arbitrary discount rate. If the interest rate exceeds (is less than) the discount rate, then per capita consumption must be rising (falling). These conclusions follow from the assumption that the utility function u is smooth and concave and that there will be consumption in each period.

If the utility function is such that the ratio of the marginal utilities is equal to c_{t+1}/c_t, that is, if:

(4)
$$\frac{u'(c_t)}{u'(c_{t+1})} = \frac{c_{t+1}}{c_t},$$

then equation 3c implies equations 4a and 4b.

(4a)
$$c_{t+1} = \left(\frac{1+r}{1+\delta}\right)c_t$$

or

(4b)
$$c_t = c_0\left(\frac{1+r}{1+\delta}\right)^t.$$

A formulation of the problem in terms of discrete time periods is very useful in bringing out the simple and direct economic logic of the optimizing procedure. It is often convenient to formulate and solve the optimizing problem in terms of continuous time, although a heavier reliance must then be placed upon mathematical techniques whose economic interpretation is not transparent. If the problem is posed in terms of continuous time, then the object of the immortal family would be to maximize integral (5a) instead of sum (1a).

(5a)
$$W_2 = \int_0^\infty e^{-(\delta-n)t}u(c)\,dt.$$

Consumption per capita will be related to human income per capita v, which the family assumes will remain constant, and nonhuman wealth $k \equiv K/N$ according to equation 5b.

(5b)
$$c = v + rk - nk - Dk,$$

where $Dk \equiv DK/N - nk$ is the time rate of change of nonhuman wealth per capita.

Our problem is to select a feasible time profile of wealth per capita k which would maximize total utility W_2 in equation 5c.

(5c) $\text{Max } W_2 = \underset{k}{\text{Max}} \int_0^\infty e^{-(\delta-n)t} u(v + rk - nk - Dk) \, dt.$

The necessary Euler-Lagrange condition for an optimizing extremal to (5c) is equation 5d. Ratio $-u''/u'$ is the percentage decline in per capita consumption. If the utility function is $u = \ln c$, then equation 5d becomes equation 5e.

(5d) $r - \delta = (-u''/u')Dc,$

(5e) $Dc/c = r - \delta,$

which is the continuous version of equation 4a. As long as the rate of return exceeds the discount rate, then per capita consumption must rise along an optimal growth path. Integrate equation 5e and obtain (5f).

(5f) $c_t = c_0 \exp (r - \delta)t,$

which is the continuous version of equation 4b.

The profile of the optimum level of c_t, relative to the per capita level of consumption at the planning date $t = 0$, is given by equation 4b in the case of discrete time and equation 5f in the case of continuous time. What will be the optimum level of c_0, the first period's level of per capita consumption? It can be found in the discrete case by substituting (4b) into the budget constraint (2) that is assumed to be relevant at period $t = 0$. The optimum level of c_0 is described by equation 6a or 6b in the case of discrete time.

(6a) $\dfrac{v_0}{r-n} + k_0 = c_0 \dfrac{(1+\delta)}{(\delta-n)} \dfrac{1}{1+r}.$

(6b) $c_0 = (1 + r) \dfrac{(\delta - n)}{(1 + \delta)} w_0,$ where

(6c) $w_0 = \dfrac{v_0}{r-n} + k_0.$

Utility maximization is only meaningful if wealth per capita at $t = 0$, denoted by w_0, is finite. Therefore, we require that $(r - n)$ and $(\delta - n)$ be positive. Consumption per capita will be proportional to wealth per capita in the manner described by equation 6b.

Assume[3] that this utility maximization procedure is carried out in every period, that is, plans are completely reformulated in each period based upon the current values of v and r. History is disregarded: the only thing that men learn from history is that men do not learn from history. What has been called period zero is always defined as the present. Consequently equation 6b is the current period consumption function where $c_0 = c_t$ and $w_0 = w_t$.

In the continuous case the budget constraint is equation 7a, which is analogous to equation 2. Since population grows according to $N_t = 1 \cdot e^{nt}$, the budget constraint can be written as (7b).

(7a)
$$\int_0^\infty (v - c)Ne^{-rt}\,dt + k_0 = 0.$$

(7b)
$$\int_0^\infty (v - c)^{-(r-n)t}\,dt + k_0 = 0.$$

Along an optimal path of accumulation, the time profile of consumption per capita is given by equation 5f. Therefore, substitute (5f) into budget constraint (7b) and derive the optimal value of the current level of per capita consumption c_0. This is described by equation 7c and is analogous to equation 6b.

(7c)
$$c_0 = (\delta - n)w,$$

where $w = (v_0/r - n) + k_0$ as in equation 6c. Therefore, per capita consumption is proportional to wealth. The factor of proportionality $(\delta - n)$ must be positive to make economic sense. Similarly, $r - n$ must be positive if wealth is to be finite; otherwise, integrals (7a) or (7b) would not exist.[4]

We have derived the consumption function (7c) or (6b) for a rational immortal family. Before we can solve for the growth path in a competitive market, we must discuss the determination of the real interest rate r and the role of a competitive banking system.

2. Real Balances and a Competitive Banking System. Output is assumed to be produced by competitive firms using the services of capital, labor, and real balances as inputs. The use of real balances serves several

[3] This assumption was borrowed from Liviatan (1968).
[4] The case where $r - n < 0$ is discussed below.

purposes. (a) It permits a separation of the act of sale from the act of purchase of goods and services, and (b) it provides a readily marketable store of value. If there were no medium of exchange in a multicommodity world, then the sellers of goods and services would have to be paid in kind. A search would have to be made for parties with different marginal rates of substitution, such that trade would be mutually advantageous. Brokerage firms can be expected to develop to reduce the costs of search by bringing potential buyers and sellers together. Marginal rates of substitution between goods would be more uniform as a result of these brokerage activities, and welfare would be increased. The cost of this intermediation consists of the opportunity cost of the resources used in the brokerage business. If there were an explicit medium of exchange which is costless to produce, then the scale of the brokerage industry could be reduced without a reduction in economic efficiency. Trading via the medium of exchange is simpler and more efficient than trading goods and services directly for goods and services. If there are n goods and services plus the medium of exchange, then n exchange ratios are relevant. On the other hand, in a world where people are paid in kind, there are $\binom{n}{2}$ ratios that people are concerned about. The effort involved in effecting trades is greatly reduced, and information can be disseminated more efficiently by the introduction of an explicit medium of exchange which is relatively costless to produce. Labor and capital services would be available for the production of goods (and leisure) when they are released from the brokerage function of distribution. For this reason real balances can be considered productive services in a multicommodity world.[5] Although the rationale for the use of a medium of exchange arises from the existence of many goods, we have focused attention upon aggregative variables in this book and have ignored problems of aggregation. The output of society is assumed to be described by aggregate production function (8), where y is output per worker, k is capital per worker, and m is real balances per worker. Function y is concave, and marginal products are nonnegative. Assume that inputs k and m are independent or complementary, $y_{km} \geqq 0$.

(8) $$y = y(k, m).$$

---

[5] In this chapter the role of real balances as a consumer's good is ignored.

Assume that there are two types of money. Fiat money is issued by the government. Bank deposit money is produced by a competitive, but regulated, banking industry. To limit the total stock of money the government imposes a minimum reserve requirement on banks. Their holdings of fiat money relative to deposits must at least equal some fraction h between zero and unity. No legal barriers to entry are assumed to exist; and the government antitrust policy attempts to maintain competition. Assume that the required reserve ratio is equal to the actual ratio.

Banks purchase the equities or bonds of firms which promise to pay profits or interest, in exchange for deposit money. The latter enables firms to bid for goods and services. With a required reserve ratio of h, the bank can lend to firms $1 - h$ dollars for each dollar of fiat (or claims on other banks convertible into fiat) deposited with it. The nominal interest rate on securities ρ tends to equal the rent plus the anticipated capital gain π^*, which can be derived from a dollar of savings invested in capital goods. If reserves do not earn interest, banks can earn $i_D = \rho(1 - h)$ dollars on each dollar deposited with them, less the marginal operating costs which I shall disregard for the sake of simplicity. On the other hand, if required reserves bear the market rate of interest, then banks earn ρ dollars for each dollar of deposits. In that case deposit rate i_D will be equal to marginal loan rate ρ. The banks are not only fulfilling the brokerage function of providing a medium of exchange but they tend to act as intermediaries between the savers and the entrepreneurs. Competition among banks will lead to an interest rate on deposits equal to i_D (less the marginal operating costs which we disregard). When reserves bear no interest, the difference between the loan rate and the deposit rate would be equal to ρh, which is the opportunity cost of holding deposit money rather than securities issued by entrepreneurs. If required reserves bear interest, the difference would be zero. The opportunity cost of holding fiat money on the part of the nonbank public is equal to the yield that could have been earned on deposit money i_D. If the nonbank public does not think that the advantages of using fiat money justify this cost, then the entire stock of fiat money would be held as bank reserves. On the other hand, those who hold fiat money will hold such a quantity that its marginal convenience yield is at least equal to the sacrificed yield on deposit money.

The private sector is assumed to allocate its wealth among several assets: capital, bonds, deposit money, and fiat money. In equilibrium, the marginal net yields from each type of wealth will be equal. Compare the marginal yields on capital with those on deposit money. The anticipated return on capital is its expected rent, which is assumed to be equal to its current marginal product $y_k(k, m)$. The anticipated return on real balances has three components. First, there is the anticipated marginal product of real balances, which is assumed to be equal to its current level $y_m(k, m)$. This return arises because the quantity of real balances facilitates the exchange of goods and services and thereby liberates labor and capital for the production of goods and services, including leisure. Second, there is the anticipated appreciation $-\pi^*$ in terms of its command over goods. Third, there is the explicit interest paid on deposit money i_D.

Equilibrium between the holding of real capital and real deposit balances requires that equation 9 be satisfied. On the margin the net yields of the two assets must be equal.

(9) $$y_k(k, m) = y_m(k, m) + i_D - \pi^*,$$

or

(9a) $$y_k(k, m) + \pi^* - i_D = y_m(k, m).$$

Competition will force the interest rate on deposits i_D to equal the marginal loan rate $\rho(1 - h)$ when no interest is paid on reserves; but i_D will be equal to ρ when the market rate of interest is paid on required reserves. When savings and investment are equal in long-run equilibrium, then the interest rate on bonds will be equal to the expected marginal yield on capital $y_k + \pi^*$ (as was shown in the Synthesis model in Chapter 5). Under these conditions the portfolio balance equation 9 implies (10a), when reserves bear no interest, and (10b), when the market rate of interest is paid on required reserves.

(10a) $$\rho_e h = y_m(k, m),$$
(10b) $$0 = y_m(k, m).$$

The long-run interest rate on bonds is ρ_e. If the convenience yield to the nonbank public of using fiat money rather than deposit money is less than the interest rate paid on bank deposits, then only banks would hold fiat money. Real balances, in that case, would refer to the deposit money held by the public.

3. The Growth Path and the Steady State Solution. Savers can advance consumer goods directly to entrepreneurs, or indirectly by purchasing the liabilities of the banks which are intermediaries between the savers and the entrepreneurs. Assume that fiat money is only held by banks as reserves and that the market rate of interest is paid on required reserves. The nonhuman wealth held by savers is equal to the capital stock; and the yield paid by entrepreneurs to savers will equal the yield that the banks pay to savers. The real yield r earned by savers, which is $\rho - \pi^*$, is equal to y_k. The consumption function relating per capita consumption c to the capital intensity k is equation 11, based upon equation 7c and the assumption that competition leads to $r = y_k$. I shall work with the continuous rather than with the discrete case in the remainder of this section.

$$(11) \qquad c = (\delta - n)\left(\frac{v}{r - n} + k\right) = \frac{(\delta - n)}{(r - n)}(y - nk),$$

since the real wage plus the rent per worker $v + rk$ equals y output per worker in the current period. The present analysis is only valid for capital intensities below the Golden Rule value (such that $r = y_k > n$).

Consider the ratio of consumption per worker to net output per worker $c/(y - nk)$ in equation 12.

$$(12) \qquad \frac{c}{y - nk} = \frac{\delta - n}{y_k - n}, \, y_k > n.$$

Three aspects of consumption function (11) or (12) must be noted. First, if both capital and labor are essential for the production of output, then $k = 0$ implies that $y = 0$ and $c = 0$. There would be neither human nor nonhuman national income; output and wealth would be zero. Second, if the marginal product of capital $r = y_k$ were equal to the discount rate δ, then consumption per worker c would be equal to $y - nk$ net output per worker. Third, the ratio of consumption per worker to net output per worker is monotonic increasing in the relevant range; and it goes to plus infinity as the capital intensity approaches the Golden Rule value k_G. This feature stems from the usual assumption that the marginal product of capital y_k diminishes as the capital intensity rises.

Figure 1, which is familiar from Chapter 1, relates the consumption function c (based upon equation 11) to net output per worker (defined as)

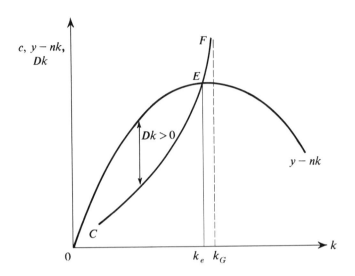

FIGURE 1. The market-generated growth path in a
model of an economy with rational immortal
families. Convergence of capital intensity $k(t)$,
where $0 < k_t < k_G$, to k_e is monotonic. At k_e
the rent per unit of capital is equal to the discount rate.

$y - nk$. The general growth equation, it will be recalled from Chapter 1,
is equation 13.

(13) $Dk = (y - nk) - c,$

which is graphed in Figure 1 for an economy with rational immortal
families. It is seen that the capital intensity k will converge monotonically
from below to the stationary solution k_e, where the marginal product of
capital y_k will equal the discount rate δ.

(14) $y_k = \delta$

occurs in the steady state.

If the initial capital intensity were between zero and k_e, then both
consumption per capita and the capital intensity would rise steadily to
equilibrium point E. If the initial capital intensity were between the Golden
Rule value and k_e, then both consumption per capita and the capital

intensity would decline steadily to the equilibrium point E. This is the monotonicity aspect of the convergence process.

What would happen if the capital stock exceeded its Golden Rule value k_G? There are two replies to this question in a model based upon immortal families. First, given our assumption of static expectations, people would think that their wealth is infinite when the interest rate is below the growth rate. Effectively, there would be no budget constraint; and consumption per worker would exceed the finite output per worker of the economy. Capital decumulation would take place. As long as $k \geqq k_G$, the capital intensity would decline. Once the capital intensity were brought below the Golden Rule value k_G, consumption function FEC would be relevant, and the economy would converge to k_e. Second, this question is similar to the problem of finding the optimal growth path of consumption of a family of fixed size ($n = 0$) when the interest rate is negative: that is, $r - n < 0$. Consumption today would exceed consumption tomorrow in such a case. But how large will present consumption be? Would there be dissaving? If we simply assume that the representative family would dissave at a negative interest rate (that is, when $r - n < 0$), then the capital stock would decline. Eventually, either the interest rate will become positive, or the capital stock will vanish. There is an economic mechanism in the immortal family model which would drive the economy out of the region where $k \geqq k_G$. What is not clear is the exact path that will be taken out of that region in the case of the rational immortal family.

A significant question has been left unanswered: What will be the net production function $y - nk$? We know that equilibrium will occur when equation 14 is satisfied. But that equation, per se, does not determine the capital intensity when real balances are productive services. Equation 14 should be written explicitly as:

(14) $$y_k(k_e, m_e) = \delta.$$

Unless we know the equilibrium value of real balances per worker m_e, we do not know which net product curve $y - nk$ we are operating with. Alternatively point E (Figure 1), where the marginal product of capital is equal to the discount rate δ, is not unique. The equilibrium k_e will depend upon the discount rate δ and upon m_e—the equilibrium level of real balances per worker.

If the market rate of interest is paid upon required reserves, then portfolio balance equation 10b is valid. That means that the economy is operating upon the highest possible net output curve $y - nk$. Why? At each capital intensity, a rise in m will raise $y(k, m) - nk$ as long as the marginal product of real balances is positive. When $y_m = 0$, then output per worker can only be increased by raising the capital intensity; and the economy is operating on the maximum net output curve. Alternatively, if no interest were paid on required reserves, then (from 10a) the marginal product of real balances would be equal to the opportunity cost of holding the required reserves $\rho_e h$. If, however, the nominal interest rate were zero, then the opportunity cost would be zero; and equation 10b would again result.

When equation 10b is satisfied, then the value of m, which is associated with a zero marginal product of real balances, is given by equation 15.

$$(15) \qquad\qquad m = A(k),$$

where $A' = y_{km}/(-y_{mm}) > 0$. Substitution of (15) into the net output curve yields:

$$(16) \qquad\qquad y[k, A(k)] \geqq y(k, m).$$

When the market rate of interest is paid on required reserves and the banking system is competitive (or the nominal rate of interest is zero), the economy will operate on the maximum net output curve.

B. THE OPTIMAL GROWTH PATH

Suppose that the optimality criterion used in defining the optimal growth path were based upon the preferences of the immortal family, equations 1 or 1a. The constraint facing society is that consumption per worker be equal to output per worker y less investment per worker $I/N = nk + Dk$, where the capital intensity k and consumption per worker c must be nonnegative.

$$(17) \qquad\qquad c = y(k, m) - nk - Dk.$$

From the point of view of the economy as a whole, no resources are required to produce real balances. With a given stock of nominal balances, a lower absolute price level will raise real balances at no social cost. To maximize output per worker, given the capital intensity k, the value of the marginal product of real balances per worker should be driven to zero as described by equation 18a.

(18a) $y_m(k, m) = 0$.

Corresponding to any capital intensity, the quantity of real balances per worker along the optimal growth path must be:

(18b) $m = A(k)$,

where $A' = y_{mk}/(-y_{mm}) > 0$. The socially optimal net output curve at every moment of time must be:

(18c) $y[k, A(k)] - nk \geqq y(k, m) - nk$

such that the marginal product of real balances is equal to zero.

It is apparent that the competitive economy will be operating on the optimal net output curve $y[k, A(k)] - nk$ if equation 10b is satisfied. If required reserves yield the market rate of interest, or if the nominal rate of interest is zero, the competitive economy will be operating on the optimal net output curve. If, however, m differed from $A(k)$, that is, if the economy were economizing on real balances which are costless to produce (from the point of view of the economy as a whole), then $y - nk$ would be less than the maximal net output curve.

The optimal growth path of the economy can be determined from equation 19, once we specify the optimal consumption function.

(19) $Dk = y[k, A(k)] - nk - c$; $k \geqq 0$, $c \geqq 0$.

The question is whether the optimal consumption function will be the same as the market-generated consumption function, equation 11 or CEF in Figure 1.

Along an optimal path it must be impossible to raise the value of optimality criterion W_1 (equation 1 or 1a) or W_2 (equation 5a) by changing the time path of consumption per worker, subject to constraint (19). A literary explanation of the optimality conditions can be given by using a period analysis. This is followed by the Euler-Lagrange equation for a maximum when continuous time is used.

If an extra unit of per capita consumption is saved at time t, then total utility W_1 declines by the marginal utility of per capita consumption multiplied by the population N_t. During the subsequent period the output of society will have increased by the marginal product of capital $dy/dk = y_k$ (since $y_m = 0$). Therefore, per capita consumption could be increased during period $t + 1$ by consuming the extra savings plus the marginal product of these savings. Since population is growing at proportionate rate n, a unit decline in per capita consumption in period t will permit a rise in per capita consumption of $(1 + y_k)/(1 + n)$ units in period $t + 1$. Total utility will rise by the total increment of consumption $(1 + y_k)N_{t+1}/(1 + n)$ multiplied by the marginal utility of per capita consumption as a result of the postponement of consumption. A unit of utility in period $t + 1$ is worth $1/(1 + \delta)$ units of utility enjoyed in period t, according to optimality criterion (1). The net change in total utility would be given by equation 20. The $1/(1 + \delta)^{t+1}$ term outside the brackets arises because consumption is assumed to occur at the end of the period.

$$(20) \qquad \Delta W_1 = \left[-u'(c_t)N_t + \frac{(1 + y_k)}{(1 + n)} \frac{u'(c_{t+1})}{(1 + \delta)} N_{t+1} \right] \frac{1}{(1 + \delta)^{t+1}}.$$

Along an optimal growth path ΔW_1 should be zero. It must not be possible to raise total welfare through an intertemporal reallocation of per capita consumption. Equation 21 must be satisfied along an optimal growth path. It is based upon $\Delta W_1 = 0$ and $N_{t+1} = N_t(1 + n)$.

$$(21) \qquad \frac{u'(c_t)}{u'(c_{t+1})} = \frac{1 + y_k}{1 + \delta}.$$

In the continuous case the optimal growth path maximizes W_2 (in equation 5a) subject to constraint (19). Then the Euler extremal conditions for a maximum of W_2 are that:

$$(22) \qquad Dc = \frac{u'}{-u''} (y_k - \delta).$$

In particular, if $u = \ln c$ is the instantaneous utility function, then the necessary conditions for optimal growth are that:

$$(22a) \qquad \frac{Dc}{c} = y_k - \delta.$$

Regardless of whether the continuous or the discrete approach is taken (equation 22 or 21), the stationary point on the optimal growth path satisfies the condition:

$$(23) \qquad y_k[k^*, A(k^*)] = \delta,$$

the marginal product of capital must equal the discount rate. Equation

23, which defines the capital intensity k^*, follows from (21) or (22), because consumption per capita c^* and the capital intensity k^* are constant at the stationary point.

The laws of motion describing the optimal growth path are derived from equations 22 and 19. According to equation 22, consumption per capita is rising when y_k exceeds δ, is falling when y_k is less than δ, and is constant when they are equal. We also know that integral W_2 exists if $\delta > n$. The equilibrium capital intensity k^* must be below the Golden Rule value. In Figure 2 we draw a vertical line at k^* where the marginal product of capital is equal to the discount rate. For values of k less than k^*, $y_k > \delta$, and consumption per capita must rise. When the capital intensity k exceeds k^*, then $y_k < \delta$, and consumption per capita must fall. The vertical vectors (Figure 2) describe the movement of per capita consumption along the optimal growth path.

Equation 19 implies the motion of the capital intensity. When the capital intensity is constant, $Dk = 0$, then consumption per capita is given by the maximal net output curve as described in equation 24. The familiar maximal net output curve is drawn in Figure 2.

(24) $c \mid_{Dk=0} = y[k, A(k)] - nk.$

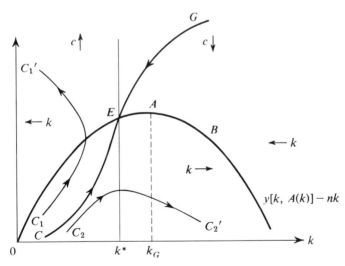

FIGURE 2. The optimal growth path. Convergence of $k(t)$ to k^* is monotonic.

It is obvious from equation 19 that when c exceeds the net output curve, Dk is negative, and when c is below the net output curve, Dk is positive. Horizontal vectors (in Figure 2) describe the movement of the capital intensity along the optimal growth path.

There is only one path (CEG) which satisfies equations 19 and 22 and the constraints that c and k be nonnegative. If the economy traveled on another path, for example, $C_1 C_1'$, then the necessary conditions for optimal growth would be satisfied; but k would eventually become negative, which is nonsensical. Or, if the economy traveled along path $C_2 C_2'$, then the necessary conditions for optimal growth would be satisfied, but c would become negative.

C. THE FREE MARKET AND THE OPTIMUM SOLUTION

We have assumed that the economy is described by a set of rational immortal families. If required reserves yield the market rate of interest (or, if the nominal rate of interest is zero), then the free market growth path for $k \leq k^*$ will be quantitatively optimal. Optimal growth path CE in Figure 2 coincides with the market-generated path CE in Figure 1. Both paths have the same optimal stationary solution where (14), (23) $y_k[k^*, A(k^*)] = \delta$, which is equation 14 and also equation 23.

When the capital intensity k is below the equilibrium value k^*, then per capita consumption is rising toward equilibrium E at rate:

$$(5d) \qquad Dc = \frac{r - \delta}{(-u''/u')}.$$

Along the optimal growth path, when $k < k^*$, the level of per capita consumption is rising toward the equilibrium E at rate:

$$(22) \qquad Dc = \frac{y_k - \delta}{(-u''/u')}.$$

In a competitive economy of the type described above, the real interest rate paid to savers r will be equal to the marginal product of capital y_k. Moreover, when the banking system earns the market rate of interest on its required reserves, y_k is equal to dy/dk, that is, the economy operates on its maximal net output curve. Therefore:

$$(25) \qquad r = y_k = \frac{dy}{dk};$$

and equations 5d and 22 are identical. Therefore, the section of the free market-consumption function CE in Figure 1 coincides with the section of the optimal consumption function CE in Figure 2.

There are, however, quantitative but not qualitative differences between the free market and the optimal growth path for values of the capital intensity above the equilibrium k^*. In either case the capital intensity will decline if k exceeds the equilibrium value; and it will converge to the equilibrium monotonically. However, the free market solution implies that the ratio of consumption per worker to net output per worker goes to plus infinity as k approaches the Golden Rule value k_G. This is described be section EF of the consumption function in Figure 1. The reason for this asymptotic behavior is that, with static expectations, people think that their wealth is infinite when $r = n$. Such a situation does not occur along optimal growth path EG in Figure 2 when k approaches the Golden Rule value from below. The capital intensity $k > k^*$ declines towards k^* at a slower rate in Figure 2 than it does in Figure 1.

The price level will grow at the rate of monetary expansion per worker. Since banks are assumed to be fully loaned up, the growth of the money supply will be equal to the growth of fiat reserves. In the long run the growth of the price level will be equal to the growth of fiat reserves per worker. The monetary authorities could, therefore, set the growth of reserves equal to n and produce price stability in the long run.

II

SOCIETY AS A VICISSITUDE
OF FINITELY LIVED GENERATIONS[6]

A much more interesting and fruitful Neoclassical growth model is the intergeneration model[7] developed by P. A. Samuelson and P. Diamond. Decisions are not made by immortal families with infinite horizons, but by a vicissitude of ephemeral generations flitting across the infinite span of time. Even if we assume perfect competition, perfect foresight, and no external economies or diseconomies, laissez-faire cannot be counted upon

[6] This part is based upon my article "A Minimal Role of Government in Achieving Optimal Growth," *Economica* (May, 1969), pp. 139–50.
[7] See reference section and P. A. Samuelson (1968, pp. 85–89).

to produce efficient, let alone optimal growth. The main purpose of this section is to show how the introduction of government institutions, which may have little foresight and which will not engage in central planning or use direct controls, can guarantee that the equilibrium solution of the growth process in a free market economy will be optimal. I am interested in determining a minimal amount of government which is sufficient to produce long-run optimality. It is unrealistic to expect the government to obtain the requisite empirical information for optimal planning, for it would have to know the production function and the utility functions of the economic agents. The slightest error would force the economy to follow an errant trajectory to either $k = 0$ or $c = 0$. Quantitative economics has not been developed to such a high degree that we can have faith in such a control policy.

My concern is with a variant of the intergenerational model that was discussed in Chapter 2. Whereas the services of real balances were treated there as a consumer good which yields utility directly, in the present chapter real balances are treated as a producer's good. Assume in part C of this section that there exists a public debt (government bonds) which serves as the medium of exchange and also promises the same real yield as can be earned on real capital. Therefore, society does not economize on real balances and operates on its maximal production function. The role of real balances will be ignored in part A of this section, where the emphasis is entirely upon real variables.

A brief review of the intergeneration model we wish to consider is in order. Two generations are alive at any time: a younger generation which works and a retired generation. Population born at time t is $(1 + n)^t$; and the participation rate is 100 per cent of the younger generation. There are $(1 + n)^{t-1}$ retired people who were born during the preceding period. These periods are of equal, but arbitrary, length. Savings of a worker are designed to maximize his finite lifetime utility; and his decision involves the substitution between future and present consumption, subject to a constraint. Let $c_1(t)$ be consumption of a worker during his youth and $c_2(t + 1)$ be his consumption during retirement one period later. Utility depends upon $[c_1(t), c_2(t + 1)]$, the pattern of lifetime consumption. As an example Diamond selected a utility function for the individual family:

(26) $U[c_1(t), c_2(t + 1)] = \beta \log c_1(t) + (1 - \beta) \log c_2(t + 1),$

where $1 > \beta > 0$. Ratio $\beta/(1 - \beta)$ reflects the value of present relative to future utility.

There is no satiation with this function; and zero consumption would imply that U is minus infinity. Each family seeks to maximize U subject to the constraint that he (that is, the head of the family and the family are regarded synonymously) end his life with a zero net worth. Consumption during retirement is equal to one's savings plus interest. Let $w'(t)$ be the net real income received during one's youth. For the present, assume that it is his real wage. Assume that all forms of saving promise a real rate of interest $r(t + 1)$. Then his savings $s_1(t) = w'(t) - c_1(t)$ will command, or be convertible into, $s_1(t)[1 + r(t + 1)]$ of goods during his retirement. His consumption during retirement will be:

(27) $$c_2(t + 1) = [w'(t) - c_1(t)][1 + r(t + 1)].$$

Maximize (26) subject to (27) and derive the optimum savings of a worker, equation 28.

(28) $$s_1(t) = (1 - \beta)w'(t).$$

A constant fraction $(1 - \beta)$ of the real wage, which is his wealth, will be saved.

Production is assumed to be carried out subject to constant returns to scale along the maximal production function, where the marginal product of real balances is zero in the relevant range. Production function (29) relates output per worker y to capital per worker k.

(29) $$y = f(k).$$

Samuelson and Diamond show that, in such an economy, there is no "invisible hand." Unlike the previous model of rational immortal families, the attempt by each agent to optimize is not likely to lead to an optimal situation. Suitable government intervention could raise the welfare of each generation.

A. THE MARKET-GENERATED GROWTH PATH UNDER LAISSEZ-FAIRE

Pure competition, perfect foresight, and no externalities are assumed to exist in the economy. Competition will ensure that the real wage paid by firms will equal the marginal product of labor; and the rent per unit of capital will be equal to the marginal product of the capital goods

Competition among entrepreneurs will ensure that the interest paid to savers will be equal to the rents yielded by the capital goods produced with the aid of their savings.

The real wage $w'(t)$ is equal to the marginal product of labor as described by equation 30a; and the rent per unit of capital is equal to the marginal product of capital 30b.

(30a) $w'(t) = f(k_t) - k_t f'(k_t) = W[k(t)]$.

(30b) $r(t) = f'(k_t) = R(k_t)$.

The capital stock prevailing at the beginning of period $t + 1$ denoted by $K(t + 1)$ is the savings, that is, unconsumed output, of the workers in the previous period denoted by $S(t)$. Equation 31b relates the capital intensity prevailing at the beginning of period $t + 1$, denoted by $k(t + 1)$, to the savings per worker $s_1(t)$ made at the end of period t. The older people in period t consume their capital plus interest; hence, the capital in period $t + 1$ can only come from the unconsumed wages received at the end of period t.

(31a) $K(t + 1) = S(t)$.

(31b) $\dfrac{K(t + 1)}{N(t + 1)} = k(t + 1) = \dfrac{S(t)}{N(t)} \dfrac{N(t)}{N(t + 1)} = \dfrac{s_1(t)}{1 + n}$.

(31c) $\dfrac{K(t + 1)}{N(t)} = w'(t) - c_1(t)$.

Substitute (28) and (30) into the right-hand side of (31b) and derive the growth equation 32.

(32) $k(t + 1) = F[k(t)]$,   where

(32a) $F[k(t)] = \dfrac{(1 - \beta)}{(1 + n)} W[k(t)]$.

We know that $F' > 0$. Assume that W is sufficiently concave such that:

(32b) $F'(0) = \dfrac{(1 - \beta)}{(1 + n)} W'(0) > 1$,

(32c) $F(k) = k$,   for a sufficiently large value of k.

Then $F[k(t)]$ will have the shape described in Figure 3; and the existence of a strictly positive stable equilibrium value of $k = k_e$ is assured.

The dynamics of difference equation 32 are as follows. For any $k(t)$,

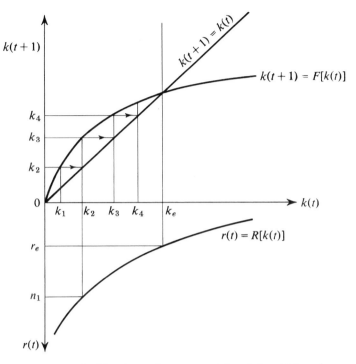

FIGURE 3. The dynamic process determining $k(t)$ and $r(t)$ in the absence of government. Inefficiency results: $r_e < n_1$.

the curve $F[k(t)]$ indicates what the value of $k(t + 1)$ will be. If we start with $k(1) = k_1$, then the real wage will be $w_1 = W[k_1]$ and savings per worker will be $(1 - \beta)w_1$. The ratio of capital to the labor force in the subsequent period will be $F(k_1) = [(1 - \beta)/1 + n]w_1 = k(2) = k_2$. With $k(2) = k_2$, the subsequent period's ratio of capital to labor will be $F(k_2) = k(3) = k_3$. In this manner the value of $k(t)$ will rise to k_e. At the equilibrium $k_e = F(k_e)$. As we have drawn Figure 3, the equilibrium k_e is stable.

A negative relation exists between the marginal product of capital $r(t)$ and the ratio of capital to labor $k(t)$, described in equation 33 and graphed in the lower half of Figure 3.

(33) $r(t) = f'(k_t) = R[k(t)], \qquad R' < 0.$

At $k = k_e$, the marginal product of capital is given by:

(34) $r_e = R(k_e)$.

There is no reason why r_e cannot be less than the growth of the economy n_1. Diamond has shown that, if the production function is:

(35a) $y = k^\alpha$,

then the equilibrium rent per unit of capital r_e is given by (35b).

(35b) $r_e = \dfrac{\alpha}{1-\alpha}\dfrac{1+n}{1-\beta} \gtreqless n$.

The more families value future utilities (that is, the larger the value $1 - \beta$) the greater will be the rate of savings and the lower will be the real rate of interest r_e. Also, the more rapid the rate of population growth n, the lower will be the capital intensity and the higher will be the value of r_e. It is apparent that r_e could be greater than or less than the growth rate.

In equilibrium the real wage is constant at $w_e = W(k_e)$. Each generation of workers consumes $c_1 = \beta w$, and each retired person consumes $c_2 = (1 + r)(1 - \beta)w$, where $w = w_e$. Total consumption per worker:

$$c = c_1 + \frac{c_2}{1 + n}$$

will remain constant, regardless of whether r_e is greater than or less than the growth rate. Such a result could not occur in the model based upon immortal families.

B. WHAT IS AN OPTIMAL GROWTH PATH?

If the equilibrium r_e is less than the growth rate n, then the capital intensity would be permanently above the Golden Rule value k_G (where $R(k_G) = n$). As Koopmans (1965) and Phelps have shown, such a condition is inefficient. The welfare of some generations can be improved without adversely affecting the welfare of any subsequent generation. A graphic description of this well-known result can be given with the aid of Figure 2.

Suppose that $R(k_e)$, the equilibrium solution of the intergeneration model, implies that the economy is at point B in Figure 2. Total consumption per worker c_e is not maximal. A consumption of capital which would bring the economy to point A (the Golden Rule point) would raise the welfare of the present population by increasing their consumption. If the capital intensity were kept constant at k_G, then consumption per worker for each subsequent generation would be higher than it would have been at equilibrium point B. Point A dominates point B, that is, it is inefficient to have a capital intensity permanently in excess of the Golden Rule value k_G.

What is the optimum stationary solution in the intergeneration model? The stationary solution is characterized by constant values of c_1, c_2, c, and k. Each generation would have the same life cycle of consumption (c_1, c_2) and hence the same lifetime utility $u(c_1, c_2)$ for all time. For this reason Samuelson (1967, p. 237) conceived of the optimal stationary solution in the following way.

What common rule or configuration would, if it were to be established for every representative man by universal (self-imposed) fiat, lead each man to the highest point on his preference field.

The optimal stationary solution is the consumption profile $c_1(t)$, $c_2(t + 1)$ over a lifetime that an economic unit would prefer over any other one available to him and everyone else. The optimum stationary consumption pattern must satisfy the constraint $c_1(t) = c_1$ and $c_2(t + 1) = c_2$ for each individual and for all t. Such a concept of an optimum does not involve a summation of utilities (as does Lerner's[8]). Instead, it reflects a social compact that economic units would enter into given a knowledge of production conditions. There are three aspects to this concept of an optimum.

First, the economy should be operating on its maximal net output curve $f(k) - nk$. The satiety level of real balances, which are treated here as productive services, should be held.

Second, given the total consumption per worker available in the economy, no intergeneration transfer should be able to raise total utility. If a unit of consumption is taken from each younger worker, his total utility declines by $\dfrac{\partial U}{\partial c_1}(c_1, c_2) = u_1 = \beta/c_1$. Since there are $(1 + n)$ workers per retired person at all times, this transfer will be able to increase each retired person's consumption by $(1 + n)$ units. Since everyone is assumed to have the same lifetime consumption profile (c_1, c_2), each worker would

[8] See A. P. Lerner (1959, pp. 512–18) and P. A. Samuelson (1959, pp. 518–22).

receive an extra $(1 + n)$ units of consumption when he is retired. His total utility would rise by $(1 + n)\dfrac{\partial U}{\partial c_2}(c_1, c_2) = (1 + n)u_2 = \dfrac{(1 - \beta)}{c_2}(1 + n)$. If no intergeneration transfer can raise an economic unit's total utility given the total consumption per worker in the economy, then equation 36 must be satisfied.

(36) $u_1 = (1 + n)u_2,$ or

(36a) $\dfrac{\beta}{c_1} = (1 + n)\dfrac{(1 - \beta)}{c_2}$.

We know that c_1 and c_2 must be positive. A value of c_1 or c_2 of zero implies that (with the utility function chosen as an example) U is minus infinity. Equation 36 is a necessary condition for a maximum.

Third, no change in the amount of capital per worker should be able to raise his total utility. If a worker increases his savings (that is, decreases his consumption) by one unit, his utility declines by u_1. One unit of saving is convertible into $1 + r$ units of goods during the next period which he consumes during his retirement, where $r = f'(k)$ is the marginal product of capital along the maximal production function. Utility during retirement rises by $(1 + r)$ multiplied by the marginal utility of consumption u_2. At an optimum no change in the stock of capital should be able to raise an individual's total utility. Equation 37 is a condition for a maximum.

(37) $u_1 = (1 + r)u_2,$ or

(37a) $\dfrac{\beta_1}{c_1} = (1 + r)\dfrac{(1 - \beta)}{c_2}$.

Combining (36) and (37), the Samuelson "Two-Part Golden Rule" is deduced.

(38) $1 + r = 1 + n,$ that is,

                        $r = n.$

The well-known Golden Rule should prevail at the stationary point on the optimal growth path. Utility during retirement can be produced from a sacrifice in current consumption in two ways. First, there can be an intergenerational transfer from the young to the old. The marginal rate of transformation of c_1 into c_2 is $(1 + n)$, reflecting the fact that there are

$(1 + n)$ workers per retired person. At an optimum the marginal rate of substitution derived from the utility function between c_1 and c_2 should be equal to the marginal rate of transformation. People should adjust their life cycle of consumption as if the real rate of interest were n.

Second, people could provide for their retirement consumption by saving in the form of capital. The marginal rate of transformation of c_1 into c_2 is $(1 + r)$. If people are saving in the form of investment in capital goods, the marginal rate of transformation $1 + r$ should be equal to the marginal rate of substitution based on the utility function. Therefore, if people seek to maximize total utility $u(c_1, c_2)$ over their lifetimes, then the marginal rate of transformation should be equal to the marginal rate of substitution: that is, $r = n$.

Competitive markets only reflect the marginal rate of transformation $r = f'(k)$, the rent per unit of capital, in this intergeneration model. If r is less than n, then people will save in the form of capital to provide for their retirement consumption. A higher return $n > r$ could be obtained via a scheme whereby the young generation advances consumer goods to the older generation in exchange for claims upon the next generation of workers. In the absence of a social compact or government, such a scheme is not feasible. For this reason inefficient capital intensity k_e (Figure 3) could be a competitive equilibrium.

The optimal growth path should converge to the point where $r_e = n$, that is, where $k_e = k_G$. The resulting life cycle of consumption for every generation to the infinite end of time would be $(c_1{}^*, c_2{}^*)$, where:

(39a) $\qquad\qquad c_1{}^* = \beta W(k_G)$

(39b) $\qquad\qquad c_2{}^* = (1 - \beta)(1 + n)W(k_G).$

Samuelson has examined the dynamic aspects of the optimal growth path terminating at $(c_1{}^*, c_2{}^*, k_G)$, and it will not be repeated here. What we do seek is a sufficient set of social institutions which would lead the economy to the stationary optimum point and which do not entail the use of direct controls or central planning.

C. SOCIAL CAPITAL (AN INHERITANCE RULE) AND A SUFFICIENTLY LARGE INTERNAL DEBT GUARANTEE LONG-RUN OPTIMALITY

1. Institutional Arrangements and the Growth Equilibrium. There are several devices which are sufficient to ensure that the equilibrium solution of a competitive economy will be optimal. These devices or institutions are sufficient, but not necessary, to produce the desired optimal stationary solution. The choice of institution to achieve this end will depend upon the model, the state of our quantitative knowledge of the economic system, and one's political predilections. It is very doubtful that we can obtain sufficiently precise quantitative knowledge of the present state of the economy, and a sufficiently high ability to forecast quantitative changes in the economy, to justify direct controls or central planning. For this reason we introduce two instruments into the above model which do not entail direct controls or government foresight, such that the equilibrium solution will be optimal. Both instruments must exist simultaneously.

The first device is social capital, and the second is an internal debt floated by the government. Let there exist an initial stock of social capital. A social rule exists which restricts an individual to consume no more than the present value of his human income. That is, we impose the same consumption constraint as existed in the laissez-faire model but introduce social capital. This implies that the stock of social capital which is rented to firms and its imputed rent cannot be consumed, although it is used along with private capital. Every generation leaves a legacy for the future and provides for intergeneration continuity.

Define $a(t)$ as social capital per worker. Since its rents are reinvested:

$$(40) \qquad a(t + 1) = \frac{[1 + r(t)]}{[1 + n]} \, a(t).$$

The social capital grows at rate $r(t)$ during period t, while the labor force grows at rate n. As long as $r(t)$ exceeds n, then social capital per worker rises. Social capital per worker will be constant if either $r(t) = n$ or if $a(t) = 0$. This can also be seen by solving (13) and writing the solution as:

$$(40a) \qquad a(t) = \prod_{i=0}^{t-1} \left[\frac{1 + r(i)}{1 + n} \right] a(0).$$

The second device, which must be used along with social capital, is an internal debt.[9] Let the government ensure that a constant (g_2) amount of internal debt per worker will be maintained such that:

$$(41) \qquad g_2 = G(t - 1)/L(t),$$

[9] P. Diamond (1965). All variables are real unless otherwise specified.

where $G(t-1)$ is the real debt issued in $(t-1)$ and $L(t)$ is the current labor force. This debt is sold to workers and will be redeemed by them during their retirement. The government promises to pay the same interest rate on the debt as could be earned on the purchase of real capital.

The government levies a tax on, or grants a subsidy to, each worker such that its receipts from new sales of debt plus taxes (or minus subsidies) are equal to debt redemptions plus interest. At time t, the government must redeem $G(t-1)$ of debt plus interest $r(t)G(t-1)$. Receipts from the sale of debt are $G(t)$. Hence, taxes $(+)$ or subsidy $(-)$ per worker are:

(42)
$$\frac{G(t-1)[1 + r(t)] - G(t)}{(1 + n)^t} = g_2[r(t) - n].$$

Net real income earned by each worker $w'(t)$ is now defined by (43) using (30). It is real disposable income: wage income minus taxes or plus transfers.

(43)
$$w'(t) = W[k(t)] - g_2[r(t) - n].$$

Savings per worker are (44), based upon (43) and (28).

(44)
$$s_1(t) = (1 - \beta)\{W[k(t)] - g_2[r(t) - n]\}.$$

These savings will be divided between the acquisition of real capital and the purchase of internal debt. Therefore, the purchase of private capital by the younger generation will be:

(45)
$$s_1(t) - g_2(1 + n).$$

Total savings are $s_1(t)N(t)$ and total debt purchases are $g_2N(t + 1)$. Private capital is $N(t)[s_1(t) - g_2(1 + n)]$, and private capital per worker is defined by (45).

The younger generation has command over $w[k(t)]$ of output. It gives up $g_2[r(t) - n]$ of this output to the government in the form of taxes and an additional $g_2(1 + n)$ in the form of the purchase of government debt. The older generation consumes this transferred output in addition to its capital plus rents. Therefore:

$$W[k(t)] - g_2[r(t) - n] - g_2(1 + n) - c_1(t)$$

per worker is available for private capital formation. Table 1 describes the sources and uses of output per worker and the resulting capital intensity in the next period.

232 COMPETITIVE MARKETS AND OPTIMAL GROWTH

TABLE 1. YOUNGER GENERATION (PER WORKER)

Sources	Uses
1. real wage $w(t)$	2. net taxes $g_2[r(t) - n]$
	3. consumption $c_1(t)$
	4. debt $(1 + n)g_2$
	5. capital $(1 + n)k(t + 1)$

Items (2) plus (4) represent real transfers of output to the older generation which consumes it. If item (2) is negative, then in effect some of (4) is returned to the workers in the form of subsidies.

Total capital per worker in period $t + 1$ is the sum of private capital per worker, equation 45, and social capital per worker $a(t + 1)$. Hence, the ratio of capital to labor at time $(t + 1)$ is given by (46). It is $a(t + 1)$ plus $\dfrac{s_1(t)}{1 + n} - g_2$.

$$(46) \quad k(t + 1) = a(t + 1) + \frac{(1 - \beta)}{1 + n)} \{W[k(t)] - g_2[r(t) - n]\} - g_2, \quad \text{or}$$

$$(46a) \quad k(t + 1) = G[a(t + 1), k(t), g_2].$$

Equations 40 and 46a, constitute a pair of difference equations in $k(t)$ and $a(t)$. Notice that it is different from the Samuelson-Diamond laissez-faire model. Inspection of (40) reveals that there are two possibilities. Either $a(t)$ converges to a positive constant or it converges to zero in a dynamically stable system. If $a(t)$ converges to a positive constant a^*, then (40) shows that $r(t) = n$, that is, the Golden Rule will be attained. This means that the long-run equilibrium will coincide with the stationary point along the optimal growth path: see equation 38. On the other hand, if $a(t)$ converges to zero, then r can converge to any value above or below the Golden Rule.

2. *The Convergence to the Golden Rule.* Figure 4 is similar to Figure 3 and describes the dynamics of difference equation 46 or 46a. For any $k(t)$ and $a(t + 1)$, the G function tells us what will be $k(t + 1)$. The complete model consists of equations 46, 40, 30a, and 30b.

The G function is positively sloped;[10] Assume that it is sufficiently

[10] $\dfrac{\partial G}{\partial k(t)} = \dfrac{(1 - \beta)}{(1 + n)} (W' - g_2 r') > 0.$

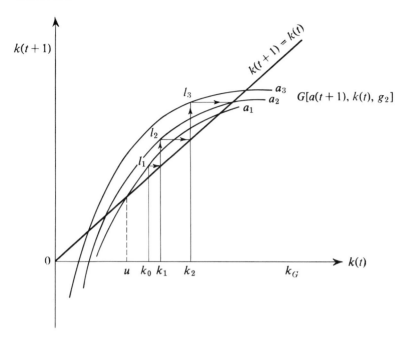

FIGURE 4. The dynamics of $k(t)$ when k_0 is below the Golden Rule value k_G. Social capital per worker $a_1 < a_2 < a_3$.

concave such that a stable (strictly positive) equilibrium exists. For any value of $k(t)$, the G curve shifts upward as $a(t + 1)$ rises. The curve a_3 represents a higher $a(t + 1)$ than does curve a_2 in Figure 4. For any value of $k(t)$, a rise in g_2 lowers the G function. This is seen by differentiating (46) partially with respect to g_2.

(47)
$$\frac{\partial G}{\partial g_2}\bigg|_{k(t)} = -\left\{\frac{(1 - \beta)}{(1 + n)} [r(k(t)) - n] + 1\right\} < 0.$$

The minimum value of r is zero; and expression (47) is negative even in that case.

Suppose that $k(0) = k_0$ and social capital per worker is a_0. Assume that k_0 is below the Golden Rule value of k_G such that $r(k_0) > n$. Then, according to (40), social capital per worker rises to $a_1 > a_0$. Total capital per worker in period $t = 1$ is given by the G function: $k(1) = l_1 = G[a_1, k_0, g_2]$. As long as $k(t)$ is below the Golden Rule value, social

capital per worker $a(t)$ continues to rise. Let it rise to $a_2 > a_1$ since $r(k_1) >$
n. Then the total ratio of capital to labor in period $t = 2$ is given by the
G function: $k(2) = l_2 = G[a_2, k_1, g_2]$. It is seen that, if $k(t)$ is less than k_G,
then $k(t)$ will tend to rise toward the Golden Rule. (We may only consider
points to the right of unstable equilibrium $k(t) = u$ in Figure 4.) We have,
therefore, proved that the existence of social capital implies that the
equilibrium $k = k_e$ will not be less than the Golden Rule k_G. The movement
of $k(t)$ need not be monotonic.

What happens if $k(0) = k_0$ exceeds the Golden Rule value? The
previous argument is applied in reverse, up to a point. As long as $r(k_t) < n$,
the G curves decline since social capital per worker $a(t)$ declines according
to equation 40. Thereby, $k(t)$ eventually declines toward the Golden Rule.
The movement need not be monotonic. A circumstance may occur which
could prevent $k(t)$ from reaching the Golden Rule. Suppose that $a(t)$
declines to zero as $k(t)$ declines toward k_G. Equilibrium could occur at k_i
in Figure 5 where $a = 0$. Although k_i exceeds the Golden Rule k_G, the
G curve does not shift since:

$$a(t + 1) = \left[\frac{1 + r(t)}{1 + n}\right] \cdot 0 = 0.$$

Competitive equilibrium would occur at a dynamically inefficient point
where the marginal product of capital $r(k_i)$ is permanently below the
growth rate n.

A sufficiently large internal debt per worker (g_2) could prevent this
situation from occurring. According to (47), a rise in g_2 lowers the G
function for all values of $k(t)$. Suppose that g_2 were sufficiently large such
that:

(48) $G[0, k^*, g_2^*] = k^* < k_G,$

as described in Figure 5.

If there were no social capital per worker (that is, $a = 0$) then equilibrium would be at k^*. At this point $r(k^*) > n$. Hence, when $g_2 \geq g_2^*$,
it is impossible for equilibrium to occur at $k = k_i$, where $r(k_i) < n$. The
case discussed above, where $k(t)$ converges to k_i and $a(t)$ converges to
zero, cannot occur if g_2 is sufficiently large.

There is a simple economic explanation of why a rise in g_2 shifts the
G function downward. Suppose we evaluate the G function at k_G. Then

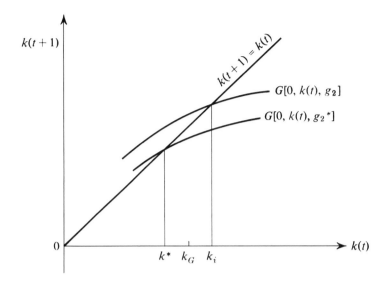

FIGURE 5. If g_2 is sufficiently large, then the equilibrium k cannot yield a marginal product of capital less than the growth rate (only part of the G function has been drawn).

there would be neither taxes nor subsidies: item (2) in Table 1 would be zero. A rise in the real debt per worker means that the younger generation holds a larger fraction of its unconsumed output in the form of government debt. But the proceeds of the government debt sales are transferred to the older generation which consumes it. Total output less total consumption declines. A smaller quantity of output is available for capital formation. Therefore, the capital intensity declines. By selecting a sufficiently large g_2 (internal debt), the government can ensure a capital intensity k_e below the Golden Rule. In this way they can guarantee that r_e exceeds n.

What may be concluded? First, if r_e exceeds $n > 0$ in Diamond's model, then the existence of social capital in our model will ensure that $r = n$ is the equilibrium solution. Second, if Diamond's solution is inefficient such that $0 < r_e < n$, a sufficiently large value of internal debt per worker (for example, $g_2 \geqq g_2{}^*$) is required to establish equilibrium at the Golden Rule in our model. The equilibrium a will be positive when $r = n$ in these cases. Q.E.D.

The previous argument may be summarized tersely. If there exists an initial stock of social capital per worker $a(0) > 0$ which, together with its imputed rent, cannot be consumed but is used in current production, then the equilibrium r cannot exceed n. Moreover, if there exists a sufficiently large amount of internal debt per worker, then, in the absence of social capital, the equilibrium r can be made to exceed n. The simultaneous existence of both social capital and a sufficiently large internal debt per worker ensures that competitive equilibrium will occur at the Golden Rule value of k.

3. Conclusion. Diamond's long-run ratio of capital to labor k_e (in Figure 3) could yield an interest rate above or below the growth rate. Capital at time $t + 1$ is equal to current savings of workers, which depend upon the current wage $W[k(t)]$. This wage was determined by the savings of the previous generation of workers and the size of the current labor force. No saver has an influence on his wage, which determines the present value of his consumption, since he has no effect upon the current stock of capital. His saving decision affects both his retirement income and the next generation's stock of capital. Only the retirement income, however, concerns him. He has no interest in the real wage of the next generation of workers. If we values current consumption highly, he will save little and the resulting interest rate next period will be high. On the other hand, if he values future consumption highly, he will save a lot and the resulting interest rate will be low in the next period. There is no reason why the equilibrium interest rate should equal the growth rate.

A different situation prevails when there is an initial stock of social capital, and there is a social rule that a generation may neither consume the imputed rent nor the social capital itself. Alternatively, we could require that each person bequeath to his children the accumulated value of the capital which he has inherited from his parents. Like any other capital, social capital commands a rent per unit of time of $r(t)$ per physical unit. All units of capital in use, private and social, are identical. Consequently, they must all yield the same rent, and they are all characterized by the same ratio of capital per worker. If the rent per unit of capital initially exceeded the growth rate, then social capital will grow at a faster rate than the labor force. As long as $r(t)$ exceeds n, the ratio of social capital to the total labor force rises. Eventually, the total stock of capital per worker will rise. A consequence of this rise is that the rent per unit of capital will decline toward the growth rate of the labor force. When rent per unit of capital equals the growth rate, then social capital and the labor force grow at the same rate.

When the initial rent per unit of capital is less than the growth rate, the stock of social capital per worker grows less rapidly than the labor force. It is possible that social capital per worker will diminish to zero before the rent per unit of capital rises to the growth rate. Equilibrium in such a situation would occur at Diamond's solution where all capital arises from savings of the previous generation of workers; and the competitive solution would be inefficient. A large value of internal debt per worker can prevent such a situation from occurring. People may save in a way that does not build up the stock of capital. They may acquire claims on the government rather than claims on physical capital. The "savings" invested in government bonds are transferred to the older generation which consumes these savings. A large internal debt per worker keeps the stock of capital low and the rent high. But the existence of social capital prevents the equilibrium marginal product of capital from exceeding the growth rate. Consequently, the combination of a high ratio of internal debt per worker and social capital ensure that the stable competitive equilibrium occur at the Golden Rule, which we proved was optimal.

Unlike the immortal generation model, total consumption per worker can be constant in a laissez-faire system regardless of whether the capital intensity is above or below its stationary optimal point. In the inter-generation model the optimum stationary capital intensity occurs when the marginal product of capital is equal to the growth rate.

CHAPTER EIGHT

𝄞𝄞𝄞

Anticipated Price Deflation
and Optimal Growth

MILTON FRIEDMAN'S ESSAY "The Optimum Quantity of Money" (1969, Ch. 1) reflects his style. Invariably, he focuses upon a significant economic problem rather than upon a minor technical point. Original ideas are always presented which stimulate economists either to reexamine their own thinking or to respond with a critical article. The subtleties and nuances are almost always recognized either in the text or in footnotes. Moreover, this essay reflects the esthetic unity of his monetary theory:

It professes to be about a very special problem; it is on a highly abstract and simplified level. Yet I believe that it provides a fairly comprehensive summary of the most important propositions of monetary theory.

A critique of Friedman's essay will indicate some of the differences between his theory and the approaches taken in Chapters 6 and 7 of this book. Friedman assumes that "The society, though stationary, is not static. Aggregates are constant, but individuals are subject to uncertainty and change. Even the aggregates may change in a stochastic way, provided that the mean values do not." (P. 2.)

Real balances are viewed by him and others as goods which produce utility directly by providing the household and firm with a relatively safe

This chapter is based upon my article "The Optimum Quantity of Money," *Journal of Money, Credit and Banking*, Vol. 2 (Nov., 1970). Copyright 1970 by the Ohio State University Press. All rights reserved.

reserve for future contingencies and as productive services which yield a marginal product in terms of output that can be produced. For example,[1] insofar as there are financial assets which promise a higher yield to the economic unit than does the medium of exchange, surplus economic units may choose to invest their working balances in these financial assets. As a result they must make frequent transactions into and out of the medium of exchange. Resources of labor and capital will be involved in the handling of these in- and out-transactions whereby economic units economize on the medium of exchange. On the other hand, if all working balances were entirely invested in the medium of exchange, then these brokerage transactions could be eliminated and resources would be free for other uses. Real balances are productive services insofar as they can liberate resources from the brokerage function which can then be used to produce output.

The first aspect of real balances implies that the instantaneous utility function of the household can be written as equation 1.

(1) $u = U(c, m),$

where c is per capita consumption, $m \equiv M/pN$ is real balances per capita,[2] M is the stock of money, p is the price level, and N is population. Function u is assumed to have the usual shape: smooth and concave.

The second characteristic of real balances implies that the aggregate production function can be written as equation 2. Output per worker is y, capital per worker is k, and real balances per worker is γm, where γ is the ratio of population to the labor force. It is convenient to assume that $\gamma = 1$ so that per capita and per worker magnitudes can be used synonymously.

(2) $y = y(k, m)$

is assumed to be smooth and concave.

Define the maximal production function as the production function that exists when the marginal product of real balances y_m has been driven to zero. Similarly, define the maximal (instantaneous) utility function as

---

[1] This example was taken from Tobin. It is not clear to me if Johnson (1970, p. 442) disagrees with this view. Also see Meltzer (1970, p. 452).

[2] Utility function (1) implicitly assumes that real balances are the only form of wealth which may yield marginal nonpecuniary services direct to the consumer. This simplification differs somewhat from Friedman's approach (discussed below) but does not alter the basic argument.

the utility function that exists when the marginal utility of the services of real balances U_2 is zero.

There are three aspects of an optimal growth path in a monetary economy. First, the economy should operate on its maximal production and utility functions. The services of the medium of exchange, which are related to the stock of real balances, may be produced at a negligible social cost if price declines can be brought about at a negligible social cost. Society will not be using its resources efficiently, that is, will not be on the boundary of its production possibility set, unless the marginal product of real balances has been driven down to this negligible social cost. Second, the capital intensity k should converge to its optimal stationary value of k^*. Third, the monetary and fiscal system should be stable enough to withstand shocks. Friedman concentrates upon the first aspect of an optimal growth path in a monetary economy: How can the economy be induced to operate on its maximal production and utility functions? He does not satisfactorily relate his theoretical proposal, concerning the optimum rate of monetary expansion, to the other two aspects of an optimal growth path. Hence: (a) he does not have any way of determining the optimum constant rate of monetary expansion, and (b) he does not indicate that his proposal would lead to hyperinflation even in his idealized economy. The object of this chapter is to develop this theme.

I

THE "OPTIMUM" RATE OF
ANTICIPATED DEFLATION

On a purely theoretical level Milton Friedman has advocated the use of a policy of anticipated deflation to induce the economy to operate on its maximal production and utility function. Specifically, his optimum rate of price deflation is equal to the discount rate δ which relates present and future utilities. He does not advocate that this policy be implemented, for it is based upon assumptions which are not consistent with experience. It is primarily[3] an essay in pure theory, not in economic policy. He wrote:

". . . this paper is mostly about *anticipated* inflations or deflations. Anticipated inflations or deflations produce no transfers from debtors to creditors which

―――――――――
[3] The exceptions to this statement are noted below.

raise questions of equity; the interest rate on claims valued in nominal terms adjusts to allow for the anticipated rate of inflation. Anticipated inflations or deflations need involve no frictions in adjusting to changing prices. Every individual can take the anticipated change in the price level into account in setting prices for future trades. Finally, anticipated inflations or deflations involve no trade-offs between inflation and employment. Hence, these considerations do not enter the analysis. . . .

Another extremely important practical consideration is that the optimum rate of price decline will change from time to time. . . .

These practical considerations, I believe, make it unwise to recommend as a policy objective a policy of deflation of final-product prices sufficient to yield a full optimum in the sense of this paper (pp. 45–46).

Assume that all price changes are anticipated and that all prices and wages are perfectly flexible such that full employment always prevails. Would Friedman's theoretical solution be optimal? My answer is decidedly in the negative. It must be stressed that we are both concerned with a hypothetical economy which is remote from reality; and that his optimal solution is criticized only on theoretical grounds within the framework of such an idealized economy.

The essence of his argument will be developed within the framework of optimal growth theory. Society is viewed as an immortal family with a nonnegative rate of time preference $\delta \geqq 0$; and attention is confined to the stationary point along the optimal growth path. All other points are ignored. The representative family derives utility from consumption of goods per capita $c(t)$, and the consumption of the services of real balances per worker which is measured by the stock $m(t)$. The object of policy is to maximize a weighted sum[4] of utilities over an infinite horizon as described by equation 3.

$$(3) \qquad W = \sum_{t=0}^{\infty} u(c_t, m_t)(1 + \delta)^{-t} N(t),$$

where $u(c_t, m_t)$ is utility per capita, $N(t)$ is the size of the population, and $\delta \geqq 0$ is the rate at which future utilities are discounted. Some models do not weight the utilities by $N(t)$, but, for the sake of generality, it will be included here.

Each family (denoted by subscript i) will have its own instantaneous utility function and discount rate $\delta_i \geqq 0$; and it will determine its savings

---

[4] A discrete, rather than a continuous, approach enables one to present the economics simply. Logically, a continuous analysis is preferable. The reader will have no difficulty in converting the relations into their continuous counterparts. See Chapter 7.

pattern such that W_i is maximized. If all families are identical, then the subscript can be dropped. For the moment assume that $\delta_i = \delta \geqq 0$ and growth rates[5] $DN_i/N_i = n_i = n$ for all families. How does the family determine its optimal savings pattern and its optimal portfolio?

The family can save by: (a) acquiring real capital which has a marginal physical product of $r(t)$ per unit of time, (b) purchasing bonds with a nominal yield of $\rho(t)$, or (c) investing in real balances which, it is assumed, pays no interest. The actual rate of price change $Dp/p = \pi(t)$ is assumed to be perfectly anticipated, such that the anticipated rate of price change $\pi^*(t) = \pi(t)$, the actual rate. The anticipated purchasing power of a dollar invested in bonds will be $(1 + \rho)/(1 + \pi)$ at the end of a unit of time;[6] and the anticipated purchasing power of a dollar invested in real balances will be[7] $1/(1 + \pi)$. Suppose that the representative family holds positive quantities of each asset in the steady state. Then the marginal utility derived from each form of wealth should be the same, and it should equal the marginal utility of the consumption sacrificed initially. The steady state is characterized by constant values of c and m; therefore, $u(c, m)$ is constant.

If the family attempts to maximize the sum $W(t)$ in equation 3, then the conditions for an optimum can be described as follows. If a dollar of consumption per capita is sacrificed, then the family's utility declines by the marginal utility of consumption $u_1(c, m)$, denoted by u_1 in the steady state. If the dollar is invested in bonds, then $(1 + \rho)$ dollars will be received at the end of the period which have a purchasing power of $(1 + \rho)/(1 + \pi)$. The marginal utility from the subsequent consumption is equal to $\dfrac{(1 + \rho)}{(1 + \pi)} \dfrac{u_1}{(1 + \delta)}$, where future utilities are discounted at rate $\delta \geqq 0$. Equilibrium at a positive value of bonds requires that equation 4 be satisfied.[8]

$$(4) \qquad -u_1 + \frac{(1 + \rho)}{(1 + \pi)} \frac{u_1}{(1 + \delta)} = 0.$$

[5] $D \equiv d/dt$.
[6] In the continuous case, the value is $\exp (\rho - \pi)t$.
[7] In the continuous case, the value is $\exp (-\pi)t$.
[8] The growth of the population cancels out since the utility per capita $u(\cdot)(1 + \delta)^{-t}$ is multiplied by the size of the family N_t. A dollar of savings per capita will yield $\dfrac{1 + \rho}{1 + n}$ dollars per capita in the subsequent period. But since the population is higher in the ratio of $(1 + n) : 1$, the $1 + n$ term cancels.

Instead of acquiring bonds, the representative family can acquire claims on real capital. The anticipated purchasing power of a dollar invested in real capital is $1 + r$, where r is the correctly anticipated marginal product of capital. Price changes will not affect the purchasing power of this investment since the value of capital in a single good economy will change in the same proportion as the price of consumption goods. Equilibrium with a positive stock of capital requires that equation 5 be satisfied.

$$(5) \qquad -u_1 + (1 + r) \frac{u_1}{(1 + \delta)} = 0.$$

Investment in real balances produces two yields: a utility yield derived from the consumption of the services of real balances $u_2(c, m)$, denoted by u_2 plus the utility of consumption purchased from the sale of real balances. A dollar invested in real balances will be able to command $1/(1 + \pi)$ of consumer goods at the end of the period. Therefore, equation 6 must be satisfied when the family is holding real balances.

$$(6) \qquad -u_1 + u_2 + \frac{1}{(1 + \pi)} \frac{u_1}{(1 + \delta)} = 0.$$

Firms may hold either capital or real balances as assets, and real balances may be productive services. Using the familiar arguments, the firm will allocate its investment between capital and real balances to equalize their marginal yields. A dollar invested in capital will yield a marginal product of y_k (say) at the beginning of the period, and the value of capital at the end of the period will be $1 \cdot (1 + \pi)$ dollars. On the other hand, a dollar invested in real balances will yield a marginal product of y_m and will be worth one dollar at the end of the period. When both assets are held by the firm, marginal condition (7) must be satisfied.

$$(7) \qquad y_k + \pi = y_m.$$

Since the marginal product of capital y_k will be equal to the rent r per unit of capital, portfolio equilibrium for the firm may be written as (7a).

$$(7a) \qquad r + \pi = y_m.$$

Friedman notes that real balances can be produced at a zero opportunity cost in a society which satisfies the ideal conditions mentioned earlier. The absolute price level can vary in a frictionless and costless manner to convert a given quantity of nominal balances into any quantity of real balances. Society will operate along its maximal production function if the marginal product of real balances y_m is driven down to its zero marginal social cost. Equation 8 must be satisfied at the optimal stationary point.

$$(8) \qquad\qquad y_m = r + \pi = 0.$$

Similarly, if the utility yield of real balances u_2 is positive, then society is not at an optimum. At no social cost the services of real balances to households can be increased. Therefore, u_2 in equation 6 should be zero: that is, equation 9 should be satisfied at the stationary optimum for households.

$$(9) \qquad 1 = (1 + \delta)(1 + \pi), \quad \text{or}$$

$\pi + \delta = 0$ when the cross product term $\pi\delta$ is ignored.

Equations 8 and 9 represent the conditions for the optimum quantity of real balances. Equation 10 represents the condition for the stationary optimum capital intensity: the marginal product of capital along the maximal production function should be equal to the discount rate. This is described by equation 10.

$$(10) \qquad\qquad r = \delta;$$

and it describes the destination of the optimal growth path.[9]

The optimum rate of price change $\pi = \pi^*$ is seen immediately from equation 9 to be minus the discount rate: that is,

$$(11) \qquad\qquad -\pi^* = -\pi = \delta.$$

Since the optimum rent per unit of capital r must equal δ, it follows from (10) and (11) that the marginal yield of capital $r + \pi^*$ must be equal to zero.

$$(12) \qquad\qquad r + \pi = 0.$$

[9] A theoretical problem exists when families have different discount rates δ. Then, as he notes, the savings will be done by those with the lowest discount rates. In a competitive economy the steady state will be characterized by $r = \delta_i$ for the families which hold capital, and $r < \delta_j$ for the families which do not. However, if the discount rates differ, what is the correct δ to use in the utility functional W (equation 3) which should be maximized? Whose δ_i should be used in evaluating public policy: Silas Marner's or the great Gatsby's? This problem was not fully recognized by Friedman.

When equations 10 and 12 are satisfied, then firms will not economize on real balances. The opportunity cost of holding real balances $r + \pi$ will be zero; hence, $y_m = 0$ from equation 7a. Society will be operating on its maximal production function.

Alternatively, we could say that the optimum stationary point can be characterized in two ways. (1) The rent per unit of capital r should be equal to the discount rate δ, and (2) the nominal rate of interest $\rho = r + \pi^*$ should be equal to zero. Then equations 10, 11, and 12 would follow: y_m and u_2 would be equal to zero.

To achieve the optimum rate of deflation, given by equation 11, the growth of the money supply[10] per worker $\mu - n$ would have to be equal to the negative of the discount rate δ. Since the equilibrium rate of price change is equal to the rate of monetary expansion per worker:

(13a) $$\pi_e = \mu - n,$$

it follows that the optimum rate of monetary expansion per worker $\mu^* - n$ is equal to:

(13b) $$\mu^* - n = -\delta.$$

This is the essence of Friedman's theoretical analysis of an ideal economy.

To be sure, Friedman does not advocate a rate of deflation equal to the discount rate for the practical reasons cited above. His policy recommendations consist of some intuitive leaps from the theory developed over forty-four pages concerning an ideal economy to the American economy as we know it. A few passages will convey the nature of this discontinuous transition.

A more limited policy objective might be to stabilize the price of factor services. If the demand for cash balances had a unitary income elasticity, this would require for the U.S. a rise in the quantity of money of about one per cent per year, to match the growth in population and labor force. If the elasticity exceeds unity as much as it has during the past century, this would require a rise in the quantity of money at the rate of about two per cent per year. . . .

The reader who knows something about my earlier work will recognize that the policy with respect to the quantity of money outlined in the preceding section is different from the policy I have long advocated. I have favored increasing the quantity of money at a steady rate designed to keep final product prices constant, a rate that I have estimated to be something like four to five per cent per year

[10] $\mu \equiv DM/M$.

for the U.S. for a monetary total defined to include currency outside of banks and all deposits of commercial banks, demand and time.

I do not want to gloss over the real contradiction between these two policies, between what for simplicity I shall call the five per cent and the two per cent rules. There are two reasons for this contradiction. One is that the five per cent rule was constructed with an eye primarily to short-run considerations, whereas the two per cent rule puts more emphasis on long-run considerations. The more basic reason is that I had not worked out in full the analysis presented in this paper when I came out for the five per cent rule. (pp. 46, 47–48.)

How does Friedman resolve the contradiction? The long-run theoretical analysis, which was careful and sensitive to fine points, is left far behind when his policy is stated.

... I have always emphasized that a *steady* and known rate of increase in the quantity of money is more important than the precise numerical value of the rate of increase. ... Either a five per cent rule or a two per cent rule would be far superior to the monetary policy we have actually followed. The gain from shifting to the five per cent rule would, I believe, dwarf the further gain from going to the two per cent rule, even though that gain may well be substantial enough to be worth pursuing. Hence, I shall continue to support the five per cent rule as an intermediate objective greatly superior to present practice (p. 48).

The remainder of this chapter will be devoted exclusively to his essay in pure theory: the optimum rate of monetary expansion in an ideal world. In Section II of this chapter I claim that Friedman cannot determine and justify the optimum rate of monetary expansion. In Section III of this chapter it is shown that his proposal will destabilize even his ideal economy. If disturbed in one direction, the economy will fly to hyperinflation.

II

THE CONSTANT RATE
OF MONETARY EXPANSION PER WORKER
IS UNKNOWN

One objection to his proposal is that Freidman cannot determine the optimal constant rate of monetary expansion per worker from an inspection of historical data. The optimal constant rate of monetary expansion per worker should be equal to the negative of the optimal steady state rent per unit of capital. He must therefore know the latter in order to determine the former. But he cannot infer the optimal steady state rent per unit of capital from empirical data. One reason is that the observed steady state rent per unit of capital is not necessarily (or even likely to be) the optimal steady state solution. Second, the discount rate δ, which is the optimal steady state solution in some models, cannot be inferred from historical data. This line of reasoning will now be developed.

A. THE OPTIMUM CONSTANT RATE OF MONETARY EXPANSION PER WORKER

The goal of Friedman's proposal is to satisfy equation 12: to produce a rate of price deflation equal to the rent per unit of capital. He would therefore select a rate of monetary expansion per worker equal to the negative of the rent per unit of capital. Thereby society would always operate on the maximal utility and production functions, regardless of the value of the rent per unit of capital.

(13c) $$\mu - n = -r.$$

Several questions arise immediately. Would Friedman vary the rate of monetary expansion per worker such that it is always equal to the changing rent per unit of capital? From the previous quotation (p. 48), it is unreasonable to believe that he would advocate a variable rate of monetary expansion per worker. He must therefore select a constant rate of monetary expansion per worker. Moreover, this constant rate of monetary expansion per worker should be equal to the negative of the optimal steady state rent per unit of capital. Equation 13b describes the optimum steady state rate of monetary expansion per worker: it is equal to the negative of the discount rate. Unless the discount rate is known, one does not know which constant rate of monetary expansion per worker to select such that equation 13b is satisfied. His proposal cannot be implemented without first finding the discount rate.

In his hypothetical economy (a) the consumption stream c is constant, and (b) individuals are immortal and unchangeable. There is no reason why, under these conditions, present utilities should be considered more valuable than future utilities. Rational behavior would imply that $\delta = 0$ instead of $\delta > 0$. If there were no population growth ($n = 0$), then the optimum rate of monetary expansion is zero when δ is zero. Friedman does not feel comfortable with this conclusion.

If one accepts this line of reasoning and supposes that the individuals in our society behave rationally, the solution to our problem is immediate. The optimum situation is reached with a constant quantity of money and an ultimately stable price level. . . .

However, I find it hard to accept this conclusion. Generalized to a world in which other forms of capital exist, it implies that a stationary equilibrium is possible only with . . . a zero marginal yield of real capital . . . . This seems to me inconsistent with experience. Much, if not most, of human experience has consisted of a roughly stationary state—Europe in part of the Middle Ages, for example, and surely Japan for centuries prior to the nineteenth. Was the marginal yield on capital zero in those communities?

If it was positive, the present analysis would have to explain the lack of growth by either a lesser regard for one's heirs than for oneself, or by irrational behavior by selfishness or short-sightedness. Neither approach appeals to me strongly as a satisfactory explanation. Yet I must confess that I have found no others.

Nonetheless, it seems worth examining the effect of . . . [δ] not equal to zero for every individual . . . leaving open whether such a situation is to be explained by selfishness, short-sightedness, or still some undiscovered reason for discounting the future (p. 23).

Casual empiricism is hardly an efficient method of determining the social rate of discount which is the centerpiece of his analysis. Presumably, Friedman is referring to Western Europe from the ninth to the eleventh century when he speaks of the stationary state. But this was a period of insecurity and of subsistence economies rather than a stationary point along an optimal and tranquil path. A few quotations from Henri Pirenne (1937, pp. 1–15) will convey these points.

It is true that in the ninth century, the Byzantine's and their outlying ports on the Italian coast, Naples, Amalfi, Bari, and, above all, Venice, traded more or less actively with the Arales of Sicily, Africa, Egypt, and Asia Minor. But it was quite otherwise with Western Europe. Here, the antagonism of the two faiths face to face kept them in a state of war with each other. The Saracen pirates never ceased to infest the littoral of the Gulf of Lyon, the estuary of Genoa, and the shores of Tuscany and Catalonia. They pillaged Pisa in 935 and 1004, and destroyed Barcelona in 985. . . . The insecurity was so great along the coast that the bishopric of Maguelonne had to be transferred to Montpellier. Nor was the mainland itself safe from attack. We know that in the tenth century the Moslems established a military outpost in the Alps. . . . Whence they held to ransom or massacred the pilgrims and travellers passing from France into Italy.

Any expected private rate of return derived from an act of savings would have to be discounted against private risk from the uncertainties of weather, from the attacks of those in short supply, or from marauding bands. Assuming for a moment that Medieval Europe was in a steady state, such a situation was associated with a considerable amount of individual uncertainty. By abstaining from a unit of consumption per capita, utility would decline by u_1, the marginal utility of consumption. The act of saving is expected to produce a return of r units, where r is a stochastic variable. The expected increment of utility from the subsequent consumption of the savings plus interest would be $E[u_1 \cdot (1 + r)]$ when future utilities are not discounted and E is the mathematical expectation. In the steady state the marginal loss of utility is equal to the expected marginal gain:

$$(14) \qquad -u_1 + E[u_1 \cdot (1 + r)] = 0.$$

Insofar as there is risk aversion, equation 14 does not imply that the equilibrium rent per unit of capital is zero. In fact, the steady state rent per unit of capital would be positively related to the subjective estimate of risk. Even though there is no time preference in the utility functional W (that is, $\delta = 0$), the presumed stationary state of the Middle Ages to which Friedman refers is consistent with a positive marginal product of capital. Risk aversion, resulting from the concavity of a utility function, is not the equivalent of δ in a social utility maximization process. Moreover, the subjective measure of risk need not be constant over time.

Students of economic history would be surprised at Friedman's assertion that the Middle Ages could be compared to a steady state. During this period there was a development of trade and towns, the rise of local and distant markets, the growth of a merchant class, and the use of money. It was the period of the emergence of an exchange economy (Heaton, 1936, Ch. VII–XII). How can Friedman draw any inference from this period concerning the optimum steady state rent per unit of capital or the optimum constant rate of monetary expansion per worker?

The discount rate δ serves as a fixed star in the immortal family models: it determines the destination of the growth process. Mathematically it is a useful concept since it guarantees that a maximum social welfare exists when the horizon is infinite. Its social science meaning, however, is unclear. Is it a cultural constant which changes slowly? Or is it a reflection of changing social, political, educational, and economic conditions? If it is the latter, then it is a variable affected by public policy, and there is no reason why it should be treated as the fixed star of optimal growth theory.

What economists call time preference, social psychologists call the "sensitivity to delayed gratification." One of the main tasks of socialization is to teach the child to delay acting for immediate rewards, that is, restrain his impulses, in order to avoid subsequent punishments or to obtain larger rewards later. Social psychologists have examined the determinants of sensitivity to delayed gratification in order to understand impulse control. It is most instructive to survey briefly[11] some of the recent work in this field in order to understand better the social science meaning of the discount rate δ.

Several experiments were performed on school children in Trinidad where they were offered a choice of a small reward now (for example, a five-cent candy bar) or a larger reward later (for example, a twenty-five cent candy bar). In one experiment with seven- to nine-year old school children, it was found that Negro subjects were more likely than East Indian subjects to select the immediate smaller reward. Is time preference a cultural phenomenon as many anthropologists believe?

There is evidence that it may not be a cultural phenomenon. It was found that children from father-absent homes were more likely to select the smaller immediate reward. This factor may explain the difference between the Negro and the East Indian behavior since the Trinidad Negro home is more frequently fatherless. The experimenter (who was a male) hypothesized that the ability to refuse a smaller present-reward in favor of a larger future reward depends upon one's confidence that the future reward will actually be forthcoming. Children whose fathers are absent from home seem to have less of this trust than do children from stable homes in which the father is regularly present. This suggests that what we call time preference δ may reflect the risk that the future rewards from savings may not materialize. If that is the case, then time preference should decrease as the variance of the expected returns diminishes.

The same experimenter found that a sample of juvenile delinquents were more likely to exhibit time preference than normal elementary school children in the same culture. Sixth-grade Boston school children were

[11] I am drawing upon Edward E. Jones and Harold B. Gerard (1967, pp. 95–99).

tested for (a) time preference and (b) their tendency to cheat at a game. The experimenters found a positive relationship between preference for immediate gratification and tendency to cheat. Jones and Gerard (1967, pp. 95–99) conclude (from M. Mischel's work) that "resistance to temptation, or impulse control, seems to require placing the importance of immediate rewards in a broader time perspective. At least, the same subjects who resist the temptation of cheating are able to resist the lure of an immediate but small reward."

These observations are suggestive. The limited sensitivity to delayed gratification that existed in the Middle Ages, when institutions were changing and life was nasty, brutish, and short, is no reflection of the rate of time preference in Friedman's hypothetical model. In the latter, the steady state has been reached, all price changes are fully anticipated, and there is no trade-off between price changes and employment. Moreover, as social, political, and economic forces decrease impulsive behavior, the observable rate of time preference can also be expected to decrease. It would appear that time preference, or the ability to restrain impulses, is an endogenous variable in the social system. If that is the case, should optimal growth revolve so completely around the concept of a fixed δ?

I conclude that, within his own framework, he cannot determine the optimal constant rate of monetary expansion per worker $\mu^* - n = -\delta$. The reason is that the discount rate appropriate for the steady state is unknown. He certainly could not infer it from the history of the Middle Ages.

B. AN INTERGENERATION MODEL IMPLIES THAT THE STEADY STATE
SOLUTION IS UNLIKELY TO BE OPTIMAL

A much more serious problem concerns the model itself. Why interpret economic history as the effects of an immortal family maximizing a utility functional (equation 3) over an infinite horizon? Instead of assuming that all persons are identical and have infinite horizons, consider a variant of the Samuelson (1958)-Diamond (1965) intergeneration model. At any time two generations are alive: a younger generation which works to produce output and an older generation which is retired. Each generation lives for two periods of equal but arbitrary length;[12] and then

[12] The rates discussed below are defined on this period of arbitrary length.

it disappears. No generation has any regard for its heirs. Under these conditions:

1. Friedman would not be able to determine the *optimum* steady state rent per unit of capital r^* simply by observing the steady state rent per unit of capital r_e. Therefore, he would not be able to determine the optimum *constant* rate of monetary expansion per worker.

2. Moreover, an economy characterized by a vicissitude of generations could converge to a dynamically inefficient point, such that the steady state rent per unit of capital r_e is less than the growth rate. Would Friedman set the constant rate of monetary expansion per worker equal to $-r_e$ in such a case? Or should monetary policy be used to drive the rent per unit of capital out of the dynamically inefficient region? These questions are not satisfactorily discussed in his essay.

A brief discussion of these points is the subject of this section. Consider a "real" intergeneration model[13] where equities circulate as money. What are the characteristics of the steady state?

The typical family's utility function is described by equation 15 and 15a, where $c_1(t)$ is its consumption during the first period and $c_2(t + 1)$ is its consumption during the retirement period. In equation 15a, the family's marginal rate of time preference for present relative to next period's consumption is measured by $\beta/(1 - \beta)$. When $\beta = 0.5$, there is no time preference.

(15) $$u = U[c_1(t), c_2(t + 1)]$$
(15a) $$u = \beta \ln c_1(t) + (1 - \beta) \ln c_2(t + 1).$$

Assume that the production function, relating capital per worker k to output per worker y, is described by equation 16a.

(16a) $$y = k^\alpha.$$

It can be shown[14] that the steady state rent per unit of capital, denoted by r_e, will be equal to:

(17a) $$r_e = \frac{\alpha}{1 - \alpha} \frac{(1 + n)}{(1 - \beta)}.$$

[13] See Chapter 7.
[14] Diamond (1965), and Chapter 7.

There is no reason why r_e (in equation 17) cannot be less than the growth rate, although this is a dynamically inefficient situation. Although money and capital both yield r_e, this is not an optimal situation. If there were an outside noninterest-bearing money, should the optimum rate of price deflation be set equal to the dynamically inefficient equilibrium rent per unit of capital? What would be the optimal monetary policy in such a situation? It is difficult to understand why Friedman views optimal monetary policy simply in terms of eliminating the difference between the yield on real balances and the yield on assets (which yield no marginal nonpecuniary services), but neglects to discuss the question of how monetary policy can be used to ensure that the economy will not end up with an inefficient rent per unit of capital.[15]

The optimal steady state rent per unit of capital in such a model depends upon the planner's utility functional. Samuelson (1958 and 1968) and Lerner (1959) have disagreed about the nature of this optimum. Regardless of the correct answer to this question, it is extremely unlikely that the free market steady state solution described by equation 17a will coincide with our concept of an optimum. Therefore, Friedman would not be able to infer the optimum steady state rent per unit of capital $r*$ by observing the equilibrium rent[16] per unit of capital.

If economic history is generated by a vicissitude of generations, in the manner described above, then the steady state rent per unit of capital is neither optimal nor does it imply anything about the discount rate at which future utilities should be discounted. My conclusion is that he cannot infer the optimal constant rate of monetary expansion per worker from an inspection of r_e, the steady state rent per unit of capital.

III

HIS PROPOSAL WOULD LEAD

TO INSTABILITY

According to S. C. Tsiang (1969), Friedman's ostensibly sensible proposal to sate the economy with real balances by producing a rate of deflation equal to the discount rate, would leave the economy vulnerable to shocks.

---

[15] See Chapter 6 and 7.
[16] There is no problem of statistical inference in this example.

If the economy were displaced above Friedman's optimum point as a result of an ephemeral disturbance, there will be no tendency to return to the equilibrium, and hyperinflation would result. The instability argument which I develop here was inspired by Tsiang's paper.

Suppose that (1) the optimal[17] capital intensity k_e were attained such that the marginal product of capital $y'(k_e)$ were equal to the discount factor $\delta > 0$, (2) full employment of all resources prevails, and (3) the constant rate of monetary expansion per worker $\mu - n$ is equal to $-\delta$ such that the steady state rate of price deflation is equal to the discount rate. Since the opportunity cost of holding real balances would be zero, the marginal utility (productivity) of real balances would be zero. Society is at an optimum stationary point. How would such an economy react to shocks arising from unanticipated deviations of the growth rate, or rate of monetary expansion per effective worker, around their respective trend values? Before we can answer that question, we must recall the instability elements that exist in a frictionless Neoclassical model. We know that[18] if: (4a) all markets are always in equilibrium and (4b) all price changes are fully anticipated such that the actual and expected rates of price change are equal, then the Neoclassical model possesses saddle point instability. If the displacements from equilibrium are random, then the model is explosive. Frictions must be introduced to stabilize such a model. Two possibilities exist. (5a) Relax the assumption that all price changes are fully anticipated, and assume that price expectations are formed on the basis of adaptive expectations. Or (5b) relax the assumption that markets are always in equilibrium.[19] Since Friedman explicitly allows for individual uncertainty, he would permit the substitution of (5a) for (4b). Therefore, there is some region in which the Neoclassical model can be stable. On the other hand, there is reason to believe that it will be unstable if his proposal were adopted.

Suppose that the yields on all financial assets, which have no marginal nonpecuniary services, were always equal to the yield on capital.[20] Then,

---

[17] Assume that the relevant model is the immortal family.

[18] Stein (1970, pp. 96–97); Nagatani (1970).

[19] For reasons of space, only the former will be shown here.

[20] As the opportunity cost of holding real balances declines, they will be substituted for financial assets which have no "marginal nonpecuniary services." Either the quantity demanded of these assets will go to zero first, or the marginal nonpecuniary services of real balances will go to zero first. We do not know whether an interior maximum

insofar as portfolio decisions are concerned, the choice will be between real balances and the composite good, which is fully represented by capital. We may therefore consider a two-asset economy, with capital and real balances as the stores of value.

If all markets are always in equilibrium, then the stock of real balances per worker in existence m must be equal to the quantity demanded. The latter depends upon the transactions demand and the opportunity cost. If the transactions demand is positively related to real expenditures, the m would be positively related to output per worker $y(k)$. In a two-asset model, the opportunity cost of holding real balances is equal to the real yield on capital less the real yield expected on money. According to assumption (1), the capital intensity is at the optimum stationary point k_e, where the real yield on capital is equal to the discount rate δ. Full employment of all resources is assumed to prevail. The real yield expected on money is $-\pi^*$, the negative of the expected rate of price change. Equation 18 describes the equilibrium condition in the money market. The interest rate $\delta + \pi^*$ is zero at the equilibrium.

(18) $m = L[y(k_e), \delta + \pi^*] = L(\delta + \pi^*)$,   since $k = k_e$.

$$L'(\delta + \pi^*) < 0 \quad \text{and} \quad y'(k_e) = \delta.$$

Expectations of price changes are assumed to be formed by equation 19, the adaptive expectations equation, where expectations are revised in proportion to the deviation between the actual (π) and expected (π^*) rates of price change. At the equilibrium the expected rate of price change $\pi_e^* = -\delta$.

(19) $$D\pi^* = b(\pi - \pi^*), \qquad b > 0.$$

The proportionate rate of change of real balances per worker is equal to the rate of monetary expansion per worker ($\mu - n$) less the actual rate of price change π as described by equation 20a.

(20a) $$\frac{Dm}{m} = (\mu - n) - \pi.$$

---

exists concerning the quantity demanded of these financial assets. The answer to the question asking if bonds are completely displaced by money when the opportunity cost of holding money is zero, is not required in my analysis of the stability of his system. For simplicity, I make the assumption in the text above.

Following Friedman, suppose that the rate of monetary expansion per worker were fixed at $-\delta$. If m were constant, the rate of deflation would be equal to $\delta = y'(k_e)$, and the interest rate would be zero. Since the monetary authorities are assumed to fix $\mu - n$ at $-\delta$, equation 20b follows.

$$(20b) \qquad \frac{Dm}{m} = -(\delta + \pi).$$

At the equilibrium optimal solution, the opportunity cost of real balances would be zero. This can be seen from (20b) and (19) when $Dm = D\pi^* = 0$. The economy will be sated with real balances, and both stores of value will yield a real return of δ. What would happen if the opportunity cost $\delta + \pi^*$ were displaced from zero? Would the equilibrium (optimal) solution be restored? The answer is no if it were displaced above zero and maybe if it were displaced below zero. This can be seen by solving the above equations.

The proportionate rate of change in the quantity of real balances demanded per worker is derived by differentiating (18). It is equation 21 when k is held constant at its optimal level, and full employment prevails:

$$(21) \qquad \frac{Dm}{m} = \frac{L'}{L} D\pi^*.$$

Since money-market equilibrium always prevails, equation 21 must equal the proportionate rate of growth of the quantity in existence described by equation 20b. Equating the two, we derive:

$$(22) \qquad \frac{L'}{L} D\pi^* = -(\delta + \pi).$$

Using the adaptive expectations equation 19 to express π in terms of π^*, equation 22 is converted into equation 23.

$$(23) \qquad D\pi^* = \frac{-(\delta + \pi^*)}{(1/b) + (L'/L)}.$$

Our model is reduced to a first-order nonlinear differential equation in π^*. Denote the opportunity cost $\delta + \pi^*$ by x. Then (a) $D\pi^* = Dx$. Let (b) $1/b + L'(x)/L(x) = B(x)$, $x = \delta + \pi^*$. Then equation 23 can be written as equation 24.

$$(24) \qquad Dx = \frac{-x}{B(x)}, \quad \text{when} \quad B(x) \neq 0.$$

The question is whether the system is stable when the capital intensity k is constant at the optimal value. Alternatively, we ask whether the short-run equilibrium system is dynamically stable if the capital intensity is relatively constant at the equilibrium level.[21]

An explicit consideration of the demand for real balances function is necessary for a dynamic analysis. An intuitive explanation of this statement can be given before we return to the mathematical analysis. Start from the equilibrium where $x = 0$ and people are holding their desired stocks of real balances. Let the actual rate of price change rise by one unit. What will happen?

The stock of real balances per worker will decline by one per cent as a result of a unit rise in the rate of price change. What will happen to the quantity demanded? A unit rise in the actual rate of price change will raise the expected rate of price change by $b.1$ units, based upon the adaptive expectations equation. The quantity of real balances demanded per worker will change by $bL'(x)/L(x)$.

Therefore, the excess demand will change by:

$$(25a) \qquad \frac{bL'(x)}{L(x)} + 1$$

when the actual rate of price change rises above the equilibrium. Divide (25a) by b, and (a multiple $b > 0$ of) the excess demand for real balances will change by:

$$(25b) \qquad \frac{L'(x)}{L(x)} + \frac{1}{b} \equiv B(x)$$

when the actual rate of price change rises.

If $B(x)$ is negative, then the excess demand for real balances per worker declines when the actual rate of price change rises. Thereby, the price rise

---

[21] The full model would be as follows:
    i) $m = L(k, \pi^*)$
    ii) $Dm/m = -(\delta + \pi)$
    iii) $D\pi^* = b(\pi - \pi^*)$
    iv) $Dk = y(k) - nk - c(k, m)$.
Its stability will depend not only upon the stability of the short-run system (analyzed in the text) but also upon the nature of the consumption function per worker $c(k, m)$. It is not necessary to enter into these matters in this chapter. See Stein (1970), Nagatani (1970), and Chapter 1 above.

is aggravated, and the movement is away from equilibrium. When $B(x)$ is positive, then a rise in the rate of price change raises the excess demand for real balances, and the rate of price change is reduced. When $B(x) = 0$, then there is no change in the excess demand for real balances. Therefore, the stability of the system will depend upon $B(x)$ or the shape of the demand function for real balances per worker.

Tobin (Feb., 1958, p. 79) developed the theory of portfolio selection (liquidity preference) from the assumption that portfolio choices are designed to maximize expected utility. As the opportunity cost of holding real balances declines, the demand for real balances becomes more elastic. Although he used a quadratic utility function, the same result can be derived from a wide set of concave utility functions. Moreover, with sufficient risk aversion, a liquidity trap can be generated. Formally the theories of portfolio selection, based upon expected utility maximization, imply that $-L'(x)/L(x)$ rises as the opportunity cost x declines to zero. We assume sufficient risk aversion (that is, concavity of utility functions) such that $-L'(0)/L(0)$ is infinite.

Friedman is not too explicit concerning his demand for real balances function in an economy with capital as an alternative store of value.[22] He did not derive his demand curve directly from an expected utility maximization procedure when there are alternative stores of value, but he works with basic concepts such as the marginal nonpecuniary services of real balances. The reader does not know if he accepts the portfolio selection result that $-L'(x)/L(x)$ becomes very large as the opportunity cost of holding real balances declines to zero.

The liquidity preference curve (Tobin, 1958) is graphed in Figure 1. The right-hand part is based upon equation 18 and relates the quantity demanded to the anticipated opportunity cost x. At a zero-opportunity cost, the equilibrium level m_e would be held.[23] The left-hand side of Figure 1 relates $-L'(x)/L(x)$ to the opportunity cost x. As the opportunity cost of holding real balances decreases, the degree of substitutability (defined

[22] In a simple economy with no capital, equities, or bonds, Friedman permits real balances to bear positive ($-\pi > 0$) and negative ($-\pi < 0$) returns. As the rate of price change (π) declines, the quantity of real balances rises. However, this was not a problem of portfolio choice among assets. It was the choice between consumption and saving as his equation shows. See Friedman (1969, p. 17, figure 6, and equation 8).

[23] See Samuelson (1947, p. 120, equation 115). We do not know whether or not u_2 has gone to zero before money has replaced all bonds.

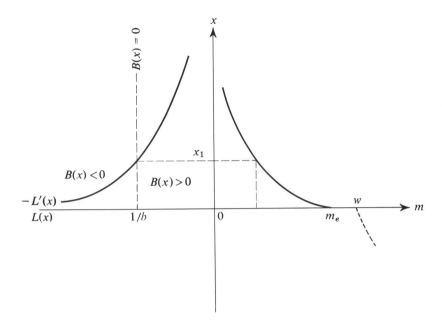

FIGURE 1. The relation between the opportunity cost of holding real balances x, the quantity demanded per worker m, and the degree of substitutability $-L'(x)/L(x)$ between real balances and capital.

as $-L'/L$) increases. The relation is based upon the theory of portfolio selection.

When the opportunity cost x is zero, then real balances will not be less attractive than any other store of value. People will either be indifferent among stores of value or will want to hold all of wealth in this form.[24] Therefore, the value of $-L'(x)/L(x)$ should be infinite as people may wish to shift entirely into real balances up to the full extent of their wealth. Let us defer for a while a discussion of the situation that will prevail if the opportunity cost x is negative.

Given the adaptive expectation coefficient $b > 0$, the degree of substitutability $(-L'/L)$ will exceed $1/b$ when the opportunity cost is below

[24] In Friedman's terms, suppose that the marginal nonpecuniary services (MNPS) of any asset were a constant fraction of those yielded by real balances. Then, when MNPS of real balances are zero, so is the MNPS of any other asset. See Friedman (1969, p. 25).

x_1. Then $B(x)$, in equation 24, will be negative. When x exceeds x_1, then the degree of substitutability $(-L'/L)$ is less than $1/b$; and $B(x)$ is positive. When the opportunity cost is equal to x_1, then $B(x_1) = 0$.

1. Stability Analysis when the Opportunity Cost of Holding Real Balances is Positive. The stability question can be posed as follows. If the economy were displaced above the Friedman optimal (equilibrium) point $x = 0$, would the economy tend to return to that point? Alternatively, if the rate of deflation were displaced below δ, would it tend to return to that value? The answer is definitely not.

A direct global proof[25] can be developed using a Liapunov function. Let:

$$(26a) \qquad\qquad V = \tfrac{1}{2}x^2,$$

be our Liapunov function which is nonnegative and is unbounded from above. When the opportunity cost is zero, then the value of V is zero. Clearly, V measures the deviation of the opportunity cost from its equilibrium (optimum) level. To see how the error changes over time, differentiate V with respect to time.

$$(26b) \qquad\qquad DV = x\, Dx.$$

Using (24), it follows that:

$$(27) \quad DV = -x^2/B(x), \quad \text{when} \quad B(x) \neq 0, \quad \text{that is, when } x \neq x_1.$$

Equation 27 describes the stability of the system. If the economy were at the equilibrium $x = 0$, then it would stay there. The value of V would remain at zero.

Suppose that the opportunity cost of holding real balances were displaced above zero: that is, the rate of deflation decreased. Then $x^2 > 0$. Insofar as $0 < x < x_1$, then $B(x) < 0$ and $DV > 0$. The system will diverge from the equilibrium. On the other hand, if $x > x_1 > 0$, then $x^2 > 0$ and $B(x) > 0$. Hence, $DV < 0$, and x will decline. Therefore, if the system were displaced above the equilibrium, it would never return to it. Instead, it would head toward $x = x_1 > 0$. A strictly positive opportunity cost will exist, and society will hold less than the satiety level of real balances.

The actual rate of price change π will become infinite when the economy

---

[25] An intuitive economic argument was given above.

is displaced above $x = \delta + \pi^* = 0$. This can be seen from equations 22 and 27. According to the former, which describes money-market equilibrium:

$$(28) \qquad \delta + \pi = \frac{-L'(x)}{L(x)} Dx, \quad \text{since} \quad D\pi^* = Dx.$$

We know that $-L'(x)/L(x)$ is positive. Therefore, the actual rate of inflation π will follow Dx. When x rises from zero toward x_1, then $B(x)$ goes to zero and:

$$(29) \qquad\qquad Dx = \frac{-x}{B(x)}$$

will rise to plus infinity. Consequently, π must rise to plus infinity. Deviations of x above Friedman's equilibrium will lead to an infinite rate of inflation and the breakdown of the monetary system.

2. *Stability Analysis when the Opportunity Cost of Holding Real Balances Is Negative.* If x were displaced below zero, it would mean that the rate of deflation exceeded the discount rate. The stability of the system would depend upon the shape of the demand for real balances when the yield on real balances exceeds the yield on capital. As the opportunity cost declines to zero, people may wish to substitute real balances for capital to the full extent of their wealth. The perfectly elastic section of the demand curve, $m_e w$ in figure 1, is generated. When people wish to hold all of their wealth in the form of real balances, then the relevant yield on savings is $\delta - x$, the yield on real balances. Under these conditions the demand for real balances is the demand for wealth. It is reasonable to expect the elasticity of demand for wealth to be smaller than the elasticity of demand for one component of wealth. The value of $-L'(x)/L(x)$ may be less than $1/b$ when $x < 0$. In that region $B(x)$ would be positive, and the system would be stable. If x declined below zero under these conditions, it would return to equilibrium.

This optimism is only justified within the framework of a Neoclassical model which assumes that investment is identically equal to savings and markets are always in equilibrium, regardless of the rate of price change. S. C. Tsiang argues that, if the rate of anticipated deflation exceeds the rate of return on capital, such that $\pi^* + \delta$ is negative, investment in real capital is not profitable. The return on real balances is greater than the return on real capital. If savings continue, with a reward of $-\pi^*$ while investment stops completely, the rate of deflation would increase. If a Keynes-Wicksell approach is taken whereby prices change in response to excess demand or supply, then the instability of Friedman's proposal would be apparent both for positive and negative deviations of x from the equilibrium.

IV

EVALUATION

Friedman has concentrated upon one aspect of optimality: How can the economic agents be induced not to economize on real balances? Or, how can they be induced to operate on the maximal production and utility functions? He does not know the magnitude of the potential gain that can be expected from a policy which would satiate the economy with real balances.

The results are clearly extremely sensitive to the assumption about the internal rate of discount. If the internal rate is as low as 5 per cent, then the potential gain, while not negligible, is minor—$2 billion to $4 billion a year. . . . On the other hand, if the internal rate of discount is as high as 33 per cent, then even though it is cut in half in the process, the potential gain is from $60 to $100 billion *per year* . . ." (p. 44).

Since the discount rate δ is unknown (see section II), the reader has no idea of the potential gain to be derived from the implementation of his proposal. Moreover, the optimal rate of anticipated deflation will tend to destabilize his ideal economy for positive deviations in the rate of price change from the equilibrium. We are left with the conclusions that:

(1) We do not know the optimal constant rate of monetary expansion per worker, for reasons summarized in section II.

(2) Even if we did, the expected utility from following the proposal was not shown to be greater than the expected disutility resulting from its destabilizing qualities (in his ideal world).

On utility grounds it is not a gamble worth taking even in the context of an idealized economy where there is no trade-off between price changes and employment.

A crucial question ignored by Friedman is: How can the economy be induced to accumulate the "optimal" (by any definition) capital intensity?

He just focuses upon the opportunity cost of holding real balances, that is, yield differentials. After all, the optimum rate of anticipated deflation in the steady state should be equal to the yield derived from the optimum steady state capital intensity. If the latter is not optimal, then the welfare functional W (in equation 3) is not maximal; and the optimum quantity of real balances per worker will not be held.

Suppose that we introduce a competitive nonregulated banking system into the immortal family model. Friedman devoted two and one-half out of fifty pages to this institutional arrangement. He wrote:

"The analysis supports also the desirability of minimizing restriction of entry into banking. Free entry would promote competition and thereby bring the interest paid on deposits closer to the nominal yield on real capital." (p. 47)

If the medium of exchange were provided exclusively by such a competitive and unregulated industry operating in Friedman's ideal world, what would happen? Insofar as the loan rate charged by banks for advances to entrepreneurs always equaled the interest rate paid by banks to savers, there would be a zero-opportunity cost involved in holding real balances. Economic agents would hold the satiety level of real balances. It follows that:

(3) There would be no unique optimal rate of monetary expansion from the point of view of society.

Any rate would be optimal. Why? The rate of price change cannot affect the yield on real balances relative to the yield on real capital: when the banking system is competitive, the two are equal. Therefore, the rate of monetary expansion is neutral when price changes are fully anticipated and there is no trade-off between price changes and employment.

Why should the banking industry be regulated any more than the bread industry? Why should there by any restriction on the rate of monetary expansion? Such a competitive economy would produce a zero opportunity cost of holding real balances and the economy would travel along the maximal production and utility functions. Friedman never explained why the extension of competition to all sectors of the economy is not preferable to his policy of fixing the rate of monetary expansion per worker at rate $-\delta$ in his ideal world.

When all is said and done, despite the theory concerning the optimal rate of anticipated deflation, he advocates the 5 per cent rule. The rigor and subtlety of analysis used to justify the optimal rate of anticipated deflation are not used to justify the 5 per cent rule. It may turn out that his intuition is correct. But this was to be an essay in pure theory, not in the art of economic policy.

There is a fundamental difference between Friedman's policy prescriptions and those developed in Chapter 6 concerning stabilization policies. We can control the steady state rate of price change and real rate of interest, without detailed knowledge of the economic system. Moreover, our control laws ensure that the dynamic system is stable. All that we require in this connection is that parameter q_1 exceed unity. Our controls are: (a) the composition of the federal interest plus noninterest-bearing debt, implemented through open-market operations and debt-management policies and (b) the proportionate rate of growth of this debt. The optimal stationary rent per unit of capital r^* will equal the growth rate n, the discount rate δ, or their sum $n + \delta$ depending upon the utility functional chosen. If we wish to state the economy with real balances, then the optimum steady state rate of price change is $-r^*$. Accordingly, we should select control parameters α_0 and ρ_0 such that:

$$r^* = \rho_0 + (1 - q_1)r^*,$$

or

$$r^*q_1 = \rho_0.$$

To achieve the desired rate of price change, select α_0 such that:

$$\frac{\alpha_0 - n}{1 + \alpha_1} = -r^*,$$

or

$$\alpha_0 = n - r^*(1 + \alpha_1).$$

Our control laws enable us to drive the economy to the optimal capital intensity, sate the economy with real balances, and guarantee that the economic system is stable. For these reasons, I prefer the stabilization policies developed in this book to those advocated by Friedman.

> ... and if my words have credit in your ears
> The tale is rendered.

REFERENCES

Borts, G. H., and J. L. Stein, *Economic Growth in a Free Market*, New York: Columbia University Press, 1964.

Cagan, Phillip D., *Determinants and Effects of Changes in the Stock of Money, 1875–1960*, New York: Columbia University Press, 1965.

——, *Changes in the Cyclical Behavior of Interest Rates*, New York: National Bureau of Economic Research, Occasional Paper 100, 1966.

——, "The Non-neutrality of Money in the Long Run," *Journal of Money, Credit and Banking*, I, No. 2 (May, 1969).

——, "The Revenue from Money Creation and its Disposition—A Theoretical Analysis," unpublished, 1969.

Cass, D., and M. Yaari, "Individual Saving, Aggregate Capital Accumulation and Efficient Growth," in K. Shell (ed.), *Essays on the Theory of Optimal Economic Growth*, Cambridge, Mass.: MIT Press, 1967.

Diamond, P., "National Debt in a Neoclassical Growth Model," *American Economic Review*, 55 (1965), pp. 1126–50.

Fisher, Irving, *The Theory of Interest*, New York: Macmillan and Co., 1930.

Foley, D., and M. Sidrauski, "Portfolio Choice, Investment and Growth," *American Economic Review*, 60 (1970), pp. 44–63.

Friedman, Milton, "A Monetary and Fiscal Framework for Economic Stability," *American Economic Review*, 38 (1948).

——, *The Optimum Quantity of Money*, Chicago: Aldine Publishing Company, 1969.

Friedman, Milton, and Anna J. Schwartz, *A Monetary History of the United States, 1867–1960*, Princeton: Princeton University Press, 1963.

——, "The Definition of Money," *Journal of Money, Credit and Banking*, I, No. 1 (February, 1969).

Hahn, F. H., "The Stability of Growth Equilibrium," *Quarterly Journal of Economics*, LXXIV (1960), pp. 206–26.

——, "Money, Dynamic Stability and Growth," *Metroeconomica*, XII (1961), pp. 57–76.

——, "Equilibrium Dynamics with Heterogeneous Capital Goods," *Quarterly Journal of Economics*, LXXX (1966), pp. 633–46.

——, "On Money and Growth," *Journal of Money, Credit and Banking*, I (May, 1969), pp. 172–87.

Heaton, Herbert, *Economic History of Europe*, New York: Harper and Brothers, 1936.

Johnson, H. G., *Essays in Monetary Economics*, Cambridge, Mass.: Harvard University Press, Ch. IV, 1967.

——, "Inside Money, Outside Money, Income, Wealth and Welfare in Monetary Theory," *Journal of Money, Credit and Banking*, I (February, 1969), pp. 30–45.

——, "Is There an Optimal Money Supply?" *Journal of Finance*, XXV, No. 2 (May, 1970).

Jones, Edward E., and Harold B. Gerard, *Foundations of Social Psychology*, New York: John Wiley and Sons, 1967.

Keynes, J. M., *A Treatise on Money*, I & II, London: Macmillan and Co., 1930.

——, *The General Theory of Employment, Interest and Money*, New York: Harcourt, Brace and Company, 1936.

Knight, Frank, *Risk, Uncertainty and Profit*, Boston: Houghton Mifflin Company, Ch. XI, 1921.

Koopmans, T. C., "On the Concept of Optimal Economic Growth," *Pontificiae Academiae Scientiarum Scripta Varia*, 1965.

Lerner, A. P., "Consumption-Loan Interest and Money," (Reply), *Journal of Political Economy*, LXVII (1959).

Levhari, D., and D. Patinkin, "The Role of Money in a Simple Growth Model," *American Economic Review*, LVIII (September, 1968), pp. 713–53.

Liviatan, N., "Competitive Growth under Alternative Expectations Models," unpublished, 1968.

Marty, A., "The Optimal Rate of Growth of Money," *Journal of Political Economy*, 76 (July/August, 1968), pp. 860–73.

——, "Some Notes on Money and Economic Growth," *Journal of Money, Credit and Banking*, I (May, 1969), pp. 252–65.

Meiselman, David, "Bond Yields and the Price Level" in D. Carson (ed.), *Banking and Monetary Studies*, Homewood, Ill.: Richard Irwin, Inc., 1963.

Meltzer, Allan, "Discussion," *Journal of Finance*, XXV, No. 2 (May, 1970).

Mundell, Robert, "Inflation and Real Interest," *Journal of Political Economy*, LXXI, No. 3 (June, 1963).

Nagatani, Keizo, "A Monetary Growth Model with Variable Employment," *Journal of Money, Credit and Banking*, I (May, 1969), pp. 188–206.

——, "A Note on Professor Tobin's 'Money and Economic Growth,' " *Econometrica*, 38 (January, 1970), pp. 171–75.

Niehans, J., "Efficient Monetary and Fiscal Policies in Balanced Growth," *Journal of Money, Credit and Banking*, I (May, 1969), pp. 228–51.

Patinkin, Don, *Money, Interest and Prices*, 2nd ed., New York: Harper and Row, 1965.

——, "Money and Wealth: A Review Article," *Journal of Economic Literature*, VII, No. 4 (December, 1969).

Pesek, B., and T. Saving, *Money, Wealth and Economic Theory*, New York: Macmillan and Company, 1967.

Pirenne, Henri, *Economic and Social History of Medieval Europe*, New York: Harcourt, Brace and Company, 1937.

Rose, H., "Unemployment in a Theory of Growth," *International Economic Review*, 7 (September, 1966), pp. 260–82.

——, "Real and Monetary Factors in the Business Cycle," *Journal of Money, Credit and Banking*, I (May, 1969), pp. 138–52.

Samuelson, Paul A., *Foundations of Economic Analysis*, Cambridge, Mass.: Harvard University Press, 1947.

——, "An Exact Consumption-Loan Model of Interest with or without the Social Contrivance of Money," *Journal of Political Economy*, 66 (December, 1958).

——, "Reply," *Journal of Political Economy*, LXVII (1959).

———, *Collected Papers*, I, Cambridge, Mass.: MIT Press, 1967.

———, "The Two-Part Golden Rule Deduced as the Asymptotic Turnpike of Catenary Motions," *Western Economic Journal*, VI, No. 2 (March, 1968).

Sargent, Thomas, "Commodity Price Expectations and the Interest Rate," *Quarterly Journal of Economics*, LXXXIII (1969).

Sidrauski, M., "Rational Choice and Patterns of Growth in a Monetary Economy," *American Economic Review*, LVII (May, 1967), pp. 534–44.

Solow, R., "A Contribution to the Theory of Economic Growth," *Quarterly Journal of Economics*, 1956, pp. 65–94.

Stein, J. L., "Money and Capacity Growth," *Journal of Political Economy*, LXXIV (1966), pp. 451–65.

———, "The Optimality of Competitive Growth," unpublished, 1967.

———, "Rational Choice and the Patterns of Growth in a Monetary Economy: Comment," *American Economic Review*, LVIII (1968), pp. 944–50.

———, "A Minimal Role of Government in Achieving Optimal Growth," *Economica*, 36 (May, 1969), pp. 139–50.

———, "Neoclassical and Keynes-Wicksell Monetary Growth Models," *Journal of Money, Credit and Banking*, I, No. 2 (May, 1969), pp. 153–71.

———, "Monetary Growth Theory in Perspective," *American Economic Review*, LX (March, 1970).

Stein, J. L., and Keizo Nagatani, "Stabilization Policies in a Growing Economy," *Review of Economic Studies*, XXXVI, No. 2 (April, 1969), pp. 165–83.

Swan, T., "Economic Growth and Capital Accumulation," *Economic Record*, 1956, pp. 344–61.

Tobin, James, "A Dynamic Aggregative Model," *Journal of Political Economy*, LXIII (1955), pp. 103–15.

———, "Liquidity Preference as Behavior Toward Risk," *Review of Economic Studies*, 67 (February, 1958), pp. 65–86.

———, "Money and Economic Growth," *Econometrica*, 33 (1965), pp. 671–84.

———, "Notes on Optimal Monetary Growth," *Journal of Political Economy*, 76 (July/August, 1968), pp. 833–59.

———, "A General Equilibrium Approach to Monetary Theory," *Journal of Money, Credit and Banking*, I, No. 1 (February, 1969).

Tsiang, S. C., "A Critical Note on the Optimum Supply of Money," *Journal of Money, Credit and Banking*, I (May, 1969), pp. 266–80.

[United States] Economic Report of the President, Together with the Annual Report of the Council of Economic Advisers, Transmitted to the Congress, January, 1969, U.S. Government Printing Office, Washington, D.C., 1969.

[United States] Studies by the Staff of the Cabinet Committee on Price Stability, January, 1969, U.S. Government Printing Office, Washington, D.C.

Uzawa, Hirofumi, "On a Neoclassical Model of Economic Growth," *Economic Studies Quarterly*, 1966, pp. 1–14.

INDEX

Accumulation process, 203–204
Adaptive expectations equation, 65, 97, 123; *see also* Price change
Aggregate demand, 62, 87
Allocation of output, 62
Anticipated price deflation, 238–64

Banking system, 9, 12, 69–73, 209–13, 263–64
Barter economy, 10
Bond market, 53, 54, 67–68, 88, 91
Borts, G. H., 10, 265
Budget restraint, *see* Utility maximizing process, Walras' Law

Cagan, Phillip D., 26, 51, 68, 71–72, 121, 138–39, 144, 265
Capacity output, 57, 79
Capacity utilization, rate of, 57, 79–83
Capital, share of, 14; rent per unit of, 37, 39, 57–58, 110–11, 195, 199, 225–26, 243–45, 252; formation, 62, 98, 122, 125; social, 229–36
Capital intensity, 4, 9, 16, 17, 18; in infinite horizon model, 29, 31–33, 213–14, 217–19, 244; in intergeneration model 37–50, 224, 226, 232–36; in Keynes-Wicksell model, 76, 78–79, 82, 86, 109–14; in Synthesis model, 122, 125–31, 168–70; when stabilization policies used, 188, 193–98
Capital-labor ratio, *see* Capital intensity
Capital value of an asset, 59–60
Capitalized output, *see* Wealth
Cass, D., 29, 34, 47, 265
Consumption function, 7, 9, 14–21, 61; in intergeneration model, 43, 223, 226, 229; in immortal family model, 206–209, 213, 218

Control laws, 170–72, 175–81, 185, 198
Costs of control, 165; *see also* Performance criterion
Currency, 68

Debt, federal, 7, 169, 170, 172, 174, 178–81, 184, 188, 196; internal, 230–36; *see also* Wealth
Debt-management policies, 198–99
Deposits, 68–71; *see also* Banking system
Development and inflation, 9, 17
Diamond, P., 29, 33, 221, 223, 230, 251–52, 265
Discount rate, 31–32, 204, 208, 213–15, 218–20, 240–46, 247–51
Disposable income, 6–7, 18–21, 43

Entrepreneurs, 203–204
Euler-Lagrange equation, 208, 217–18
Excess aggregate demand, 62–63

Feedback control, *see* Control laws
Fisher, Irving, 144, 146–47, 265
FM curve: in Keynes-Wicksell model, 99; in Synthesis model, 121
Forced savings, 63, 74–77, 192
Franchise owners, 72; *see also* Banking system
Free market solution: in immortal family model, 220–21; in intergeneration model, 223–26
Friedman, Milton, 12, 68, 143, 181, 238–64

Generation, *see* Intergeneration model
Gerard, Harold B., 250–51
Gibson paradox, 144–54
Golden Rule, 47, 50, 166–67, 213–14, 219, 226, 228, 232–36

Price change, expected rate of, 8, 22, 42, 64–66, 107, 255; rate of, 53–57, 87, 121, 124, 132, 172, 180, 194, 260–61
Price deflation, anticipated, 238–64
Production function, 4, 15, 215–17, 220, 227, 239, 244; conditions, 57–58

Rate of price change, see Price change
Rational behavior: in intergeneration model, 33–45, 222–24; in infinite horizon model, 29–33, 205–209
Real balances: argument in consumption function, 7, 12, 14–15; demand for, 8, 11, 12, 19, 21, 255–62; as a producer's good, 9–18, 210, 239; part of wealth, 12–13, 18; as a consumer's good, 18–21, 239; utility yield of, 19, 30, 38–39, 41, 239, 243–44; real balance effect, 20–21, 92–94, 101–102, 104–105, 133, 135–38, 174–75,185; demand for, in intergeneration model, 43; demand for, in Keynes-Wicksell model, 63–64, 103; effect of a change in the rate of monetary expansion upon, 78, 95–98, 131–38; demand for, in Synthesis model, 121–22
Real public debt, see debt
Real rate of interest, see Interest rate, real rate
Rose, H., 51–52, 266

Samuelson, Paul A., 29, 33, 221, 223, 227, 229, 251, 253, 258, 266
Sargent, Thomas, 144, 267
Saving, T., 12, 266
Savings function: in intergeneration model, 43, 223; in Keynes-Wicksell model, 60–62, 77, 81, 173; forced, 63, 74–77
School children, 250; Trinidad, 250; East Indian, 250; Boston, 250–51
Schwartz, Anna J., 12, 68, 265
Sensitivity to delayed gratification, 250–51
SFM curve, 91

Short-run equilibrium, in Keynes-Wicksell model, 88, 89–98
Sidrauski, M., 6, 26, 29, 31, 267
SIS curve, 89
Social capital, see Capital, social
Solow, R., 6, 267
Specialists, 56, 121, 124, 175
Speed of market adjustment, 54, 55, 59, 78
Stabilization policy, 163–201
Substitution effect: in demand for real balances, 103–104, 127, 129
Swan, T., 6, 267
Synthesis model, 120–62; steady state solution, 123–31; short-run dynamics, 131–38

Tax policy, 179, 231
Technological change, 4, 92–93
Time preference, see Discount rate
Tobin, James, 6, 7, 30, 60, 63, 110, 239, 258, 267
Transactions demand, for real balances, 63–64, 103–104, 127
Transfer payments, 7, 31, 34–35, 44, 227–28
Tsiang, S. C., 51, 64, 253, 254, 261, 267

Unfilled orders, 87, 114–15
Utility function, 29, 38, 204; maximal, 239
Utility maximizing process: in infinite horizon model, 31–33, 204–209, 240–44; in intergeneration model, 38–45
Utilization rate, 57, 79–83

VV' curve, 136

Wage, real, 37, 57, 224
Walras' Law, 66–68, 77, 91, 174
Walrasian assumption of price change, 55
Wealth, 12, 13, 14, 18, 61; financial, net private, 61, 64, 169

Yaari, M., 29, 34, 47